Ed Davis

Latin America, the United States, and the Inter-American System

Other Titles in This Series

Westview Special Studies on Latin America and the Caribbean

*Latin America, the United States,
and the Inter-American System*
edited by John D. Martz and Lars Schoultz

This collection of original essays focuses on the dynamics of the contemporary system of inter-American relations, with emphasis on changes in the hemispheric political economy, the control exercised by the United States over the behavior of Latin American governments, and the issue of human rights. The authors discuss varying facets of the complex relationships that are the result of the differing, yet inextricably intertwined, legacies, values, and interests that have characterized the mutual history of the Americas.

John D. Martz, professor and head of the Department of Political Science at Pennsylvania State University, was editor of the *Latin American Research Review*, 1974–1979. Lars Schoultz is associate professor of political science at the University of North Carolina at Chapel Hill.

BACHRACH

Federico Guillermo Gil

Latin America, the United States, and the Inter-American System

edited by John D. Martz
and Lars Schoultz

Westview Press / Boulder, Colorado

Westview Special Studies on Latin America and the Caribbean

Copyright © 1980 by Westview Press, Inc.

Published in 1980 in the United States of America by
    Westview Press, Inc.
    5500 Central Avenue
    Boulder, Colorado 80301
    Frederick A. Praeger, Publisher

Library of Congress Cataloging in Publication Data
Main entry under title:
Latin America, the United States, and the inter-American system.
    (Westview special studies on Latin America and the Caribbean)
    Includes index.
    1. Latin America—Foreign relations—United States—Addresses, essays, lectures.
2. United States—Foreign relations—Latin America—Addresses, essays, lectures.
I. Martz, John D. II. Schoultz, Lars.
F1418.L356 1980   327.8073   79-26931
ISBN 0-89158-874-4

Printed and bound in the United States of America

Contents

Preface

A unique mixture of love and hate between Latin America and the United States has been a basic reality of the Western Hemisphere for well over a century. Disparate cultural legacies, distinctive value systems, dissimilar patterns of socioeconomic development, and conflicting national interests have characterized the history of the Americas. At the same time, both geopolitical and humanistic dimensions of the relationship have contributed to an intimate fusion of political and personal ties. Thus the frequently conflictual quality of hemispheric affairs has been accompanied by the recognition of mutual needs and desires. The result has been a fabric of richly variegated hues and shades, the fibers inextricably intertwined.

In the United States, a numerically miniscule generation of political scientists emerged during the 1940s to undertake the formidable task of attempting to analyze and understand the dynamics of interrelationships in the Americas. Among this pioneering group was one scholar uniquely endowed, through birth, education, experience, and talent, to unravel the complexities and illuminate the substance of inter-American affairs. In order to follow in his tradition and to honor that scholar— Federico G. Gil—this collection of original essays has been written.

The contributors, both Latin and North American, constitute a small but representative cross section of those privileged to study and work with Federico Gil through the years. We come from a wide variety of backgrounds and have sought through different paths to encourage and advance the objectives of scholarly discourse and hemispheric communication to which he has dedicated his life. We share the ineradicable imprint of his personal and professional example—a scholar of impeccable rigor and insight, a friend of uncommon warmth and humanity—the epitome of a gentle man in the best of senses. Our lives and careers have all been profoundly touched by coming to know and working with him. Some of us know him simply as "Fred"; to others he is "Don Federico," "Maestro," or, with tongue in cheek, "Jefe"—the latter unfailingly producing a characteristically modest if bemused demurral. We can but offer these essays as an inadequate measure of appreciation to this scholar, friend, and warm human being.

Born in Havana, Federico Gil was destined from his early childhood to become a person of international experience and outlook. Raised and educated in Cuba and in the Spain of his forebears, he received his graduate degrees from the University of Havana: Doctor of Laws in 1940, Doctor of Political and Social Sciences in 1941, and Licentiate of Diplomatic and Consular Law in 1942. He came to the United States as an instructor at Louisiana State University in 1942, moving a year later to the University of North Carolina at Chapel Hill. Beginning as a teacher of Spanish in the Department of Romance Languages, he soon found his proper home in the Department of Political Science. Progressing through the customary professorial ranks, he attained a full professorship in 1955 and in 1966 was appointed Kenan Professor of Political Science, the highest distinction his university could confer upon an active member of its faculty. Seven years earlier he had been named director of the Institute of Latin American Studies, and from that position he ably built and developed one of the nation's major centers for training and investigation in this field.

His intellectual trajectory soon placed him in the forefront of what was essentially the founding generation of North American political scientists specializing in Latin American affairs. Bringing to the task his multicultural background and insight, he helped to introduce the principles and tenets of disciplinary inquiry, the intellectual rigor and systematic approach that had been largely unknown in this field of scholarship. His sensitivity and receptivity to new ideas and new procedures, and to the growing emphasis upon empirically based research, eased the incorporation of the best of behavioral methodology into Latin American studies. His unfailing catholicity of taste and understanding is reflected in the widely differing orientations of his former graduate students, whose interests range from predominantly historically inclined studies to the most advanced and sophisticated exercises in quantification. Another measure of this man's stature as a scholar is his record of success in gaining research support over the years from such organizations as the Rockefeller and Ford foundations, the Social Science Research Council, and the National Science Foundation.

Federico Gil's contributions to the literature have been broad and varied. *The Governments of Latin America,* coauthored with his colleague the late William Whatley Pierson, became upon its 1957 publication the first widely adopted text in the field. After years of study and travel that established him as the dean of Chilean studies in the United States, he published his second book, *The Political System of Chile,* in 1966. This work, later translated into Spanish, still remains basic reading for all those seriously engaged in analyses of Chilean political and socioeconomic life. Drawing upon years of classroom teaching, he published *Latin American–United States Relations* in 1971, which in turn stands today as a widely used introduction to the subject for students throughout the country. It, too, was published in Spanish. He further enhanced the literature on Chile by organizing a conference that led to the multiauthored *Chile 1970–1973: Lecciones de una experiencia.* In cooperation with two other contributors (Ricardo Lagos and Henry Landsberger), Federico Gil brought together in one volume the collective experience and wisdom of many of Chile's major contemporary political actors. This work also appeared in English in 1979.

Space precludes an exhaustive enumeration of his publications. Articles have appeared in Argentina, Chile, Spain, and Venezuela. In his adopted country, they have been printed in *The Journal of Politics, Inter-American Economic Affairs, The Journal of Inter-American Studies,* and *Nation.* It is striking that of more than thirty book reviews, both the first and the most recent (as of this writing) were published in the major journal of his academic discipline, *The American Political Science Review.* In 1950 he reviewed René de Visme Williamson's *Culture and Policy: The United States and the Hispanic World;* twenty-nine years later he reported on Davis and Wilson's edited volume, *Latin American Foreign Policies: An Analysis.* There have also been numerous chapters in collaborative volumes, monographs, and encyclopedia entries, with more yet to come.

Although such citations bespeak unusual academic credentials, they are but a partial measure of the man and his work. Truly a son of the Americas, he has played a significant role in the world of public affairs. In 1960 he joined a group of scholars at Cambridge and helped develop the framework for the Alliance for Progress. He served as consultant and adviser to FLACSO (the UNESCO-sponsored Facultad Latinoamericana de Ciencias Sociales in Chile), the Inter-American Development Bank, and the Peace Corps and also directed Peace Corps projects at his university especially designed to strengthen higher education in Venezuela. In 1965 he helped to found the Instituto de Integración Latinoamericana in Buenos Aires, and his lectures from its first year of existence were soon published as *Instituciones y desarrollo político de América Latina.* As recently as 1978 he conceived, organized, and directed a program to bring selected leaders in the professions from Mexico to the University of North Carolina for a semester of specialized study.

His career as an institution builder has also benefited the study of Latin America. He was a member of the founding Executive Council of the Latin American Studies Association from 1966 to 1969 and served as national president in 1971. For years he has been an active member of the Consortium of Latin American Studies Programs. At the same time his long succession of speeches and conferences throughout the hemisphere has also brought uncommon international recognition. Over two decades ago he became one of the first two North Americans ever admitted to the Academia Nacional de Derecho y Ciencias Sociales of Argentina. He was the first foreigner in fifteen years to be admitted as an honorary member of the Facultad de Derecho y Ciencias Sociales at the University of Chile in Santiago. He later received honorary membership in both the Chilean and Latin American Associations of Sociology, and in 1974 he was named honorary chairman of the Argentine Conference of Professors of Constitutional Law at the University of Belgrano in Buenos Aires.

His standing with political as well as intellectual leaders is also a matter of record. He was an official guest of the Venezuelan government for the respective inaugurations of Presidents Rómulo Betancourt, Raúl Leoni, and Carlos Andrés Pérez. A singular honor came in 1970 when he was named Commander of the Order of Merit Bernardo O'Higgins, the highest award given by the government of Chile. No less important to Federico Gil than his international involvement in the world of scholars and political leaders, however, has been his participation in the life of his university.

He has served throughout his professional career as a member of the University of North Carolina faculty in the Department of Political Science. Those of us privileged to know him as a departmental colleague can readily attest that he has few peers in working consistently and effectively for the common good, instinctively finding the sure way to mediate conflict and promote consensus. Always ready to offer a word of encouragement or constructive appraisal and to lend a helping hand, he has set a high standard of colleagueship for all around him. Whomever he has found in need of support, whether a confused graduate student, a struggling junior colleague, a former student seeking a new position, or a senior faculty scholar of long association, he has approached with the same genuine compassion, the same profound respect for the individual without regard to status, and a deep concern for his problem. All of us who have known Federico as a teacher or faculty colleague have found comfort and sustaining strength from his personal loyalty and understanding.

In the training of graduate students, Federico Gil belongs to that small class of master teachers. Over more than three decades he has helped to guide several dozen doctoral students through their degree programs, preparing them for careers as teacher-scholars in political science. These successful professionals now dot the faculties of major universities in the United States and a growing number of institutions in Latin America and Europe. Despite this heavy and continuing involvement in training professional scholars, however, he has always found special satisfaction in teaching undergraduate students. Since he first joined the political science faculty at UNC, he has carried a heavy instructional load in basic introductory teaching. When a freshman honors program was initiated in the late 1960s, he promptly volunteered and has continued to teach these seminars regularly. His frequent facetious comments to the contrary notwithstanding, Federico remains young in heart and in spirit. He enjoys nothing more than working with undergraduates and does so with a quiet vigor and zest to which his students respond with respect and affection. Their high regard for him was clearly evidenced when they selected him a decade ago for membership in the undergraduate honor society, the Order of the Golden Fleece. And of all the honors Federico Gil has received through the years, perhaps there is none he has more highly valued, nor more richly deserved, than the coveted Salgo Award for Excellence in Undergraduate Teaching.

If this biographical litany of distinguished professional accomplishment is easily recorded, it is far more difficult to describe him adequately in human terms. The love and admiration he has elicited from all who have known him go far beyond the usual boundaries of interaction among professionals. Indefatigable world traveler, lover of music and the arts, connoisseur of gourmet cooking and fine Chilean wines, confidant of Latin American statesmen, master teacher and exemplary faculty colleague, loyal son of the Americas, and adopted Tar Heel— he is all this and much more. We cherish his friendship, prize his scholarship, and eagerly await yet further important contributions that lie ahead. In following his example as scholar and humanitarian, we are far better as a consequence. Such is the legacy of and our enduring obligation to Federico G. Gil.

John D. Martz
Frederic N. Cleaveland

The Contributors

Enrique A. Baloyra is associate professor of political science at the University of North Carolina at Chapel Hill. A student of the politics of Venezuela, Cuba, and Mexico, his research has concentrated upon public opinion and political economy.

Frederic N. Cleaveland is professor of political science at Duke University, a position to which he recently returned after nearly a decade of service as university provost. An authority on public administration, he has contributed extensively to institution building in Latin America.

Richard L. Clinton is associate professor of political science and associate dean of the College of Liberal Arts at Oregon State University. His writings focus upon the policy implications of population, resource, and environmental problems.

Kenneth M. Coleman is associate professor of political science at the University of Kentucky. He is currently collaborating with Venezuelan and Mexican scholars on a study of labor unions.

John S. Gitlitz is assistant professor of political science at the State University of New York at Purchase. He is a long-time student of peasant movements, with a particular interest in Peruvian politics.

R. Kenneth Godwin is associate professor of political science at Oregon State University, where he teaches political participation and public policy. His most recent book, coauthored with Warren Miller, is *Psyche and Demos*.

Steven W. Hughes is associate professor of political science at California State College, Stanislaus. Although he is presently engaged in a study of city planners in California, his previous research has focused upon legislative-executive relations in Chile and Costa Rica.

Gustavo Lagos is professor of international relations at the Instituto de Estudios Internacionales, Universidad de Chile. His publications in both English and Spanish include the recent *Revolution in Being: A Latin American View of the Future.* Among his many awards is an honorary doctorate from the University of North Carolina at Chapel Hill.

Henry A. Landsberger is professor of sociology at the University of North Carolina at Chapel Hill. A noted authority on the Latin American peasantry and industrial labor, his particular focus on Chile and on Mexico has also been utilized in cross-national studies including the United States.

John D. Martz is head and professor of political science at Pennsylvania State University.

Kenneth J. Mijeski is associate professor of political science at East Tennessee State University. His teaching and research interests are in the areas of Latin American politics and the psychological dimensions of political life.

Lars Schoultz is associate professor of political science at the University of North Carolina at Chapel Hill. His current research focuses upon U.S. policy toward political repression in Latin America.

Joseph S. Tulchin is professor of history at the University of North Carolina at Chapel Hill. He is the author of *The Aftermath of War: World War I and U.S. Policy Toward Latin America,* as well as a number of articles on U.S. relations with Latin America. His present research concerns the social and economic transformation of Argentina from 1880 to 1930. After serving an apprenticeship under John Martz, he was named editor of the *Latin American Research Review* for the three-year period beginning in July 1979.

Alberto Van Klaveren is associate professor of international relations at the Instituto de Estudios Internacionales, Universidad de Chile. He has studied law, international relations, and political science in Chile, the United States, and Holland, with a particular focus upon the inter-American system.

Latin America, the United States, and the Inter-American System

between Argentina and Chile over the Beagle Channel is a notable example. But even when considering only bilateral actions, one is hard pressed to find many such examples in recent decades, especially if the possibilities are limited to events or activities of major significance. Even the case of Cuban-Soviet relations is best understood as a reaction by Cuba's leaders to the policies of the U.S. government. As Enrique Baloyra's chapter demonstrates, it is difficult to conceive of Cuban foreign relations in general or Soviet-Cuban relations in particular being conducted without an active concern for the U.S. reaction. The United States may not determine the nature of Cuban foreign policy, but the U.S. position must be included in the policy calculus of the Castro government's decision makers.

The dominance of the United States is most clearly evidenced in multilateral relations among the hemisphere's nations. Few observers now disagree with Fidel Castro's early observation that, unlike the British, the United States does not need a Colonial Office because it has instead the Organization of American States (OAS). Acting as the institutional focus of multilateral hemispheric relations, the OAS has traditionally responded vigorously to those issues, and only those issues, that concern the United States. Other Latin American nations may also be interested in a particular issue—as was Venezuela with the behavior of the Trujillo government and, later, with the Castro government's support for Venezuelan guerrillas—but the concern of the OAS over any particular issue varies directly and unfailingly with the level of U.S. interest. If there is one axiom of inter-American relations, surely it is stated in the preceding sentence.

Nowhere has this been more clearly demonstrated than in the OAS approach to the issue of human rights. Although its human rights mechanism has existed since the signing of the Act of Bogotá in 1960—and before then in more rudimentary, less specific form—until the mid-1970s human rights was but a minor interest of the OAS. The Inter-American Commission on Human Rights only emerged from obscurity when called upon by the United States; indeed, the commission's most prominent activity in the 1960s was to mediate among the various factions in the wake of the U.S. incursion in the Dominican Republic. Generally the commission worked quietly on a handful of individual cases each year, launched an occasional broadside at the Cuban government, and filed its annual report with the secretary-general. He in turn asked the OAS foreign ministers to accept the report at their annual meeting, which they did without discussion. The report was then placed in the hands of the OAS Secretariat, thus insuring its continued obscurity, and the commission began to produce the next year's document.

But then Henry Kissinger went to Santiago, Chile, in mid-1976 to attend the Sixth General Assembly of the OAS. In his speech he concentrated exclusively upon the issue of human rights. The motivation behind Secretary Kissinger's newfound interest in this issue is unclear. But whatever its impetus, the new U.S. policy of using the OAS as a forum for human rights continued into the Carter administration. Reflecting this interest, the OAS suddenly became a center of human rights activity. Human rights reports, which previously had taken years to be published, were now in print within a few months—sometimes weeks—of their completion. By the time Secretary of State Cyrus Vance attended his first OAS General Assembly in 1977 in Grenada as the spokesperson for the Carter administration, human rights issues dominated the agenda.

In addition to the OAS, other multilateral activities are heavily influenced if not controlled by the United States. For example, several efforts to create common markets among groups of Latin American nations were encouraged by the Johnson administration's formal shift in this direction at both the Eleventh Meeting of Consultation of Foreign Ministers in April 1967 and the meeting of hemispheric presidents at Punta del Este later that year. Even the multilateral initiatives that specifically exclude the United States often if not invariably relate directly to the United States. The Consensus of Viña del Mar and the Latin American Economic System (SELA) exemplify this tendency. The purpose of the 1969 consensus was to express the policy of the Special Latin American Coordinating Committee (CECLA) of the Group of 77 toward North-South relations, particularly those related to development issues. Significantly, the document CECLA produced was presented by Chilean Foreign Minister Gabriel Valdés in June 1969 to the new U.S. president, Richard Nixon. This action was appropriate, for the 6,000-word document is primarily a catalog of obstacles to Latin America's development created by the United States. SELA, which was characterized by Venezuelan President Carlos Andrés Pérez as Latin America's "own permanent forum for the defense of common interests," was from the beginning oriented toward relations with the United States. At the first SELA ministerial meeting in early 1976, the delegates concentrated much of their attention upon the threat to Latin America posed by the punitive aspects of the U.S. Trade Reform Act of 1974, which inter alia denied GSP (General System of Preferences) tariff advantages to certain oil-exporting countries, including Venezuela and Ecuador.

Although most of the contributors to this volume support the perception that the United States dominates inter-American relations, only one actively attempts to explain *why* U.S. hegemony is such a persistent feature of the international relations of the region. Many variables undoubtedly combine to produce the power differential that permits the United States to hold potential hegemony. Kenneth Coleman suggests, however, that the translation of this potential power into the active exercise of authority is promoted at least in part by a value held by the U.S. public, one that forms, in Coleman's words, a "social psychology of hegemony." Given the norms of nonintervention and self-determination that shape U.S. public policy toward Latin America, Coleman searches for the reason why the policy can be so frequently overruled by direct interference in the internal affairs of Latin American republics. The answer is a political myth, a belief that systematically denies the existence of U.S. self-interest. Using the Monroe Doctrine as a specific point of reference, Coleman concludes that the fact of hegemony is made palatable to the U.S. public in general and foreign policy officials in particular by the popular assumption that the United States acts to benefit all of humanity, exercising in the Western Hemisphere a special moral responsibility to do for others what they presumably cannot do for themselves. If they could, Latin Americans too would choose freedom, stability, and progress. Because they often cannot make such a choice, the United States must help. In the process, hegemony persists.

The Role of Humanitarian Values

Coleman's analysis serves to introduce a second major and pervasive theme of this volume: the utility of humanitarian values in interpreting events in Latin America and in inter-American relations. Since the mid-1970s, the most obvious and omnibus issue of humanitarian concern has been human rights. As Baloyra indicates, in recent years human rights considerations have become an integral, if not central, component of U.S. policy toward Cuba. In the Cuban case, human rights is defined as the right to be free from imprisonment for political reasons. In the broader context of U.S.–Latin American relations, however, human rights is defined as the more inclusive right to be free from torture and other forms of cruel and unusual treatment, including prolonged detention without trial. This definition conforms to the reality of Latin America during the 1970s, a period in which torture became an increasingly frequent instrument of public policy.

The Carter administration's human rights policy has often been attacked as naive. Any government that feels so threatened as to be forced to rule by torture, it is argued, would certainly be immune to pleas from the United States or other external powers that it halt its barbarous behavior. The United States can withhold economic and military aid, engage in vigorous diplomatic activity at both the bilateral and multilateral level, and threaten to employ even harsher methods to force a reduction in the level of physical abuse; but only when the perceived threat has been exterminated, critics argue, will the repression cease. Outside forces, including the United States, can have little impact upon the extent of human rights violations.

Viewed from this perspective, human rights may indeed be the product of naive humanitarianism. But Richard Clinton and Kenneth Godwin argue persuasively from another perspective that the promotion of human rights is the most realistic policy the United States can adopt in its relations with Latin America.

For late-modernizing countries such as those of Latin America, one major problem that accompanies the breakdown of traditional economic systems is a breakdown in social control and social cohesion. As the West industrialized and destroyed its own traditional normative structure, it was able to develop new forms of control and cohesion. Collectively, these forms are referred to today as "human rights," a code of conduct that guarantees in most (but not all) cases a measure of civilized behavior. This code is the constructive contribution of the industrialized nations that has served to ameliorate the destructive but apparently inexorable "detraditionalization" of social life accompanying industrialization. Would not the United States be acting both realistically and honorably, then, to disseminate the Western concepts of human rights as rapidly as possible? A foreign policy reflects the values of a government and, ultimately, of the people who create it. Clinton and Godwin suggest that to add the values we call human rights to the values associated with the export of riot shields and tear gas, frisbees and Peace Corps volunteers would not diminish our stature in the world.

On the other hand, the pursuit of any policy, including the export of humanitarian values, is never free of costs. As Joseph Tulchin argues in his analysis of U.S. policy toward Argentina, the Videla government and, perhaps, other Argentines as well have interpreted U.S. policy as an unacceptable intervention in the internal affairs of the nation—specifically, an intervention in a civil war with leftist terrorists. Tulchin notes that the history of Argentine foreign policy can be written as a two-century struggle for independence from foreign control and that Argentines are uncommonly sensitive to infringements upon their nation's sovereignty. Thus any hint of outside interference is destined to be rejected regardless of the intent or the substance of the intervention. Indeed, external pressure on behalf of human rights may be more than ineffective; it may be counterproductive. A leader of a repressive government may feel obliged to continue repressive measures in order to demonstrate his or her ability to withstand foreign pressure.

There can be no doubt that the pursuit of humanitarian values has strained U.S. relations with several extremely repressive Latin American governments, including that of Argentina since 1976. The costs in terms of effectiveness on other foreign policy issues are probably, but not conclusively, real. The question is whether the costs are too high. Here there are no clear answers. To the suggestion that the Videla government may be replaced by a more repressive regime if the United States persists in applying pressure, it could be argued in response that a more repressive regime is difficult to imagine. Perhaps the world's next Hitler is a conspiracy-oriented general in the Argentine army, but it would take a Hitler to make the Videla government seem moderate. And if the legitimacy of the Videla government is so low that it needs to employ severe militaristic tactics to maintain the existing structure of privilege in Argentina, is it not logical to contend that the United States is creating enormous goodwill among significant numbers of Argentines? Perhaps when adding up the costs of alienating the Videlas and Pinochets, U.S. policymakers are consciously attempting to purchase the friendship of more progressive forces in Latin American politics. Finally, it can be argued that the alternative to a policy of promoting human rights in countries like contemporary Argentina is to turn our backs on human suffering. For better or worse, the United States does maintain a measure of power over Argentina. Not to use that power in the face of consistent and gross violations of human rights is to condone and even to encourage the repression. Given the nature of U.S. hegemony, not to intervene is to act on behalf of the status quo.

In the perspective of many U.S. foreign policy decision makers, the human rights issue is inextricably linked to a second humanitarian concern—the promotion of democratic values. This is indeed a very old theme of U.S.–Latin American relations, and in recent years it has been resurrected as an initial step away from the extreme repressiveness that characterized much of Latin American politics in the 1970s. From its inception in 1977, the Carter administration was clear in its preferences, especially with smaller countries such as Bolivia where U.S. influence was strongest. For example, when the army and the incumbent administration of the Dominican Republic threatened to overturn the electoral victory of opposition candidate Antonio Guzmán in the May 1978 elections, the United States exerted an abnormal amount of pressure to ensure that the threat was not carried out. In this instance, the Carter administration went so far as to order the commander in chief of the U.S. Southern Command to persuade the Dominican general staff that tampering with the democratic process would involve grave consequences for U.S.–Dominican relations. In general, the administration was eager to applaud even the slightest move by a repressive government toward the establishment of an electoral timetable. After viewing the beginning of a civil war, the State Department even suggested that Anastasio Somoza, the long-lived client of the United States, test his popularity among Nicaraguans in a plebiscite. The withdrawal of U.S. support probably contributed to Somoza's downfall in mid-1979.

But as John Martz observes, the United States has been extraordinarily ambivalent in its promotion of democracy in Latin America. In different times, under different circumstances, different administrations have shown little interest in support-ing democracy. Not a few U.S. administrations have demon-strated a willingness to undermine a democratic regime when U.S. national security has been at stake. Other things being equal, the United States has regularly professed a preference for democratic over authoritarian governments. Other things are rarely equal, however, and the vacillating U.S. policy toward the support of democracy suggests that other variables, particu-larly national security, are often perceived as threatened by democracy. When confronted with this conflict of concerns, U.S. policymakers are quick to abandon the ethical issue of democracy for the realpolitik of hegemonic control.

The Critical Importance of Economic Variables

Just as U.S. policymakers respond to their perceptions of the most critical problems posed by Latin America to U.S. interests—from Communist insurgency to human rights violations—so Latin Americans interpret inter-American relations in terms of their own perceptions of the region's major policy issue, the lack of development (or the misdevelopment) of Latin America's economic systems. As a result, spokespersons for the national security concerns of the North have always had to contend with economic considerations in the battle for the attention of both policymakers and policy analysts. Indeed, one of the most fascinating aspects of U.S.–Latin American relations is the ease with which U.S. officials can convert an economic issue raised by Latin Americans into a question of U.S. national security.

There is no better example of this phenomenon than the Alliance for Progress, an inter-American program first proposed in 1958 by President Juscelino Kubitschek of Brazil to attack the generalized poverty among Latin American peoples. This idea, which had its roots in a variety of studies by the Economic Commission for Latin America, reached the ears of North Americans only after it had been translated into palatable national security language. When President Kennedy announced the formation of the Alliance for Progress to the assembled representatives of Latin American governments on March 13, 1961, he employed the language of economic development: "Our unfulfilled task is to demonstrate to the entire world that man's unsatisfied aspiration for economic progress and social justice can best be achieved by free men working within a framework of democratic institutions."[1]

But the next day, in his message to Congress requesting appropriations for the Inter-American Fund for Social Progress (later the Social Progress Trust Fund), Kennedy assured budget-minded legislators that economic development was not the purpose of U.S. economic aid; rather aid was the means to achieve the ultimate purpose, U.S. national security: "If we are unwilling to commit our resources and energy to the task of social progress and economic development—then we face a grave and imminent danger that desperate peoples will turn to communism or other forms of tyranny as their only hope for change. Well-organized, skillful, and strongly financed forces are constantly urging them to take this course."[2] As Federico Gil has demonstrated, from the beginning the Alliance for Progress was "the response of the United States to the Soviet challenge in Latin America."[3] In the Foreign Assistance Act of 1961, Congress expressed its perceptions of the implications of underdevelopment:

> The Congress declares that the freedom, security, and prosperity of
> the United States are best sustained in a community of free, secure,
> and prospering nations. In particular, the Congress recognizes the
> threat to world peace posed by aggression and subversion wherever
> they occur, and that ignorance, want, and despair breed the extremism
> and violence which lead to aggression and subversion. The Congress
> declares therefore that it is not only expressive of our sense of
> freedom, justice, and compassion but also important to our national
> security that the United States, through private as well as public
> efforts, assist the people of less developed countries.[4]

This sentence remains to this day the initial policy guideline for
U.S. economic assistance programs.

In the meantime, economic concerns have remained paramount in the minds of Latin American policymakers of all
political stripes. Issues of trade, technology transfer, and foreign
debts remain extremely prominent regardless of the ideological
outlook of Latin American governments. This is so because the
industrialized West, while clearly differentiating among Latin
American governments, continues to relate to Latin America
principally through the market mechanism. Adjustments are
regularly made in this mechanism to reflect the friendliness or
the hostility of the industrialized nations to various Latin
American governments, but the essential constraints of the
market remain unchanged. Loans may be increased and debts
rescheduled, but borrowed money must be serviced. Import
quotas may be liberalized, but the basic structure of demand
for Latin American products is determined by the market. Thus
when any Latin American government addresses the issue of
relations with the United States or its industrialized allies,
economic considerations inevitably play a key role in creating
the agenda for discussion.

Clearly the most salient aspect of the economic relationship
between Latin America and the United States has become the
sociopolitical implications of delayed dependent development.
The *dependentistas* have been so enormously successful in establishing the legitimacy of their arguments that the dependency
explanation for Latin American underdevelopment is now clearly
part of contemporary academic orthodoxy. John Gitlitz and
Henry Landsberger suggest that dependency theory may have

achieved part of its prominence because of the weakness of the
only other contender, the liberal-developmentalism of the 1950s
and 1960s. Facing this void, dependency analysis has made
quick and enthusiastic converts. Perhaps because of the lack of
substantial intellectual opposition, dependency theory has been
spared certain tests normally demanded of a new intellectual
current. Gitlitz and Landsberger note in particular that dependency analysts have never been forced to specify the scope of
their approach or to establish the validity of their prescription.

The More Things Change, . . .

Most of the readers of these pages will have lived through (or
been taught by someone who has lived through) a number of
allegedly substantial changes in U.S.–Latin American relations.
Knowledge of the Big Stick and Wilsonian democracy is no
longer available in the oral form, but there are many who can
talk about the advent of the Good Neighbor Policy, the neglect
of the war years, and the rising interest in "development" during the 1950s. We witnessed the explosion of interest in the
1960s, with the twin policies of an Alliance for Progress and
support for counterinsurgency. These policies in turn gradually
merged before our eyes into the Nixon-Kissinger realpolitik
and, ostensibly, politics of a low profile. Most recently we have
seen a return to what might be termed "benign hegemony,"
a policy toward Latin America that stresses humanitarian
variables. As the decades flow by, the inter-American relationship appears to focus upon the most pressing issue of the
moment. If there is none, the region is ignored. This is the cyclical nature of U.S.–Latin American relations noted by Federico
Gil: "Periods of rising interest in and concern with Latin
America have invariably been followed by periods of declining
interest, increasing conflict, and almost total disregard for the
fate of these nations."[5]

The dynamic of U.S.–Latin American relations has never
been as clearly expressed as in the mid-1970s, when U.S. policy
appeared to change from supporting the repression of human
rights to actively seeking to improve the human rights practices

of Latin America's most egregious violators. To accommodate this change, the United States went so far as to redefine its traditional concept of the term "human rights." Throughout U.S. history, the emphasis has been upon civil and political rights. In recent decades, this tended to alienate the United States from the Third World, which typically is more concerned with economic, social, and cultural rights. The United States emphasized the freedom of the press; the Third World concentrated upon the freedom not to starve. Little meaningful dialogue was possible. In an attempt to find a common ground upon which to build a workable human rights policy, the Carter administration decided to emphasize the one basic right upon which there appears to be universal agreement: the right to the physical integrity of the person. "Of all human rights," asserted the president, "the most basic is to be free of arbitrary violence."[6] By concentrating upon the right to be free from torture and other forms of governmental violence, the United States recognized the reality that progressive elements in Latin Americ were working to change.

Despite these shifts in U.S. policy, definitional and otherwi the reader of this volume will be struck by the evidence one constant governs the inter-American system: U.S. hegem Whenever U.S. policymakers perceive a threat to U.S. sec as in the cases of Cuba, the Dominican Republic, and the policy of dominating the hemisphere is placed in its relief. In the absence of a threat, the evidence of heg more difficult to isolate, but it is no less real by vir obscurity. In the mid-1970s, no threat was appare reflecting its principles, the United States turned port of a humanitarian concern: human rights. Th point, however, is that the policy of hegemony rer differing little if at all from that of earlier era example, the perspective of Representative Tr father of much of the human rights legislatio "We have to start being more adamant and mc relationships with those countries. We always we don't want to interfere in those countrie go in there and mess in their internal affair

not. We have been doing it for over a hundred years anyway."[7]
How little different this sounds from the words of Theodore
Roosevelt or Henry Kissinger. U.S. hegemony is a political reality
because it is a positive value to U.S. foreign policy officials.
Regardless of the differences in policies among U.S. administrations, no one has been willing to abdicate the position of
dominance held by the United States.

The nine chapters that follow are divided into three sections.
The first of these concentrates upon inter-American relations,
and the second and third upon U.S.–Latin American relations.
Following Steven Hughes and Kenneth Mijeski's discussion of
contemporary approaches to the study of inter-American relations, John Gitlitz and Henry Landsberger examine the inter-
American political economy, criticizing dependency theory but
emphasizing its proponents' role as generally sympathetic social
scientists. The first section then concludes with Gustavo Lagos
and Alberto Van Klaveren's analysis of the future of inter-
American relations, concentrating upon the global changes
that could lead to changes in hemispheric interaction.

The second section consists of three chapters on the hegemonic characteristics of U.S.–Latin American relations. Kenneth
Coleman first analyzes the mechanism by which the U.S. public
supports a hegemonic policy in the hemisphere. This leads to
Enrique Baloyra's specific study of the major opponent to continued U.S. hegemony, the Cuban government of Fidel Castro,
and its relations with the United States. This study in turn is
followed by John Martz's discussion of another mechanism of
hegemony, the imposition of values, particularly of democracy.

The third section contains three chapters on the subject of
human rights and U.S. policy toward Latin America. Lars
Schoultz chronicles the history of U.S. diplomacy and human
rights during the 1960s and 1970s, Joseph Tulchin assesses the
impact of the Carter administration's human rights policy in the
specific case of Argentina, and Richard Clinton and Kenneth
Godwin optimistically suggest how the United States can
contribute to a reorientation of Latin America's conceptualization of development and, by so doing, reduce the level of U.S.
influence over Latin American affairs.

Notes

1. *Public Papers of the Presidents of the United States: John F. Kennedy, 1961* (Washington, D.C.: Government Printing Office, 1962), p. 171.

2. Ibid., p. 178.

3. Federico G. Gil, *Latin American–United States Relations* (New York: Harcourt Brace Jovanovich, 1971), p. 238.

4. Public Law 87-195, Sec. 102(a).

5. Gil, *Latin American–United States Relations,* p. 284.

6. *Department of State Bulletin* 79 (January 1979):1.

7. Tom Quigley et al., *U.S. Policy on Human Rights in Latin America (Southern Cone): A Congressional Conference on Capitol Hill* (New York: Fund for New Priorities in America, 1978), pp. 75–76.

Part 1

Perspectives on Inter-American Relations

Contemporary Paradigms in the Study of Inter-American Relations

Steven W. Hughes
Kenneth J. Mijeski

Once the virtual preserve of the historian and diplomat, the study of inter-American relations has come to be discovered, colonized, and dominated by the social sciences. One sign of this shift has been the growth in concept formation and theory construction to investigate hemispheric relations. To follow the literature of the past two decades, it has been necessary to grapple with such concepts as linkages, dependency, import substitution, foreign policy distance, satisficing, and the like. The amount and sophistication of theorizing have steadily increased. This development has led to new concerns in the field. In recent years, scholars have become interested in determining the numbers and types of concepts and theories available. Is there still too little theorizing? Is there too much? Do the existing theories and concepts offer differing perspectives on inter-American relations or is the field of study actually dominated by a very limited perspective? Do we need more approaches or fewer approaches? [1]

The purpose of this chapter is to address some of these questions. In framing our arguments, we have been influenced by the recent essays of Paul Feyerabend. [2] In his book *Against Method*, Feyerabend writes: "Science is an essentially anarchistic enterprise: Theoretical anarchism is more humanitarian and more likely to encourage progress than its law-and-order alternatives." [3] Later he argues that

it is . . . *possible* to create a tradition that is held together by strict
rules, and that is also successful to some extent. But is it *desirable*
to support such a tradition to the exclusion of everything else?
Should we transfer to it the sole rights of dealing in knowledge, so
that any result that has been obtained by other methods is at once
ruled out of court? This is the question I intend to ask in the present
essay. And to this question my answer will be a firm and resounding
NO.[4]

Feyerabend's plea is not for the abolition of scientific
method or theory but for the acceptance of differing perspectives, approaches, and epistemologies. Feyerabend is concerned
that science is governed by an authoritarian set of rules characterized by rigidity, intellectual hegemony, and the inability to
meet change effectively.

We share similar concerns with regard to the study of inter-
American relations. In spite of the variety of "approaches" currently in use, the field is dominated by two fundamental perspectives that we will call paradigms. Although it is obvious that
paradigms, in the strictest sense of the term,[5] do not exist in
the social sciences, a compelling argument can be advanced that
virtual paradigms, or paradigm-surrogates, do exist. In the
second section of this chapter, we review some of the recent
literature on the study of inter-American relations in order to
demonstrate the extent to which these two paradigms currently
dominate analyses in the field.

In the third section we turn to the central points of our argument. First, we clarify certain differences between the dominant paradigms. Our primary purpose is to illustrate some of the
ways in which each model provides us with differing methodologies and perspectives on critical issues. One potential advantage
of allowing for pluralism is a kind of Hegelian dialectic; that is,
out of differing and opposing approaches we might be able to
reach a higher synthesis. We demonstrate the possibility of this
by a brief look at the work of Guillermo O'Donnell—work we
believe constitutes a new and unique paradigm.

Although the possibilities of synthesis and the dialectical
payoff are quite real, our fundamental concern is with the
current tendencies toward scientific authoritarianism, and
the remainder of the third section returns to this point. We seek

to describe some of the common problems of both paradigms in order to advance our plea for greater pluralism.

In order to avoid misunderstandings, we should like to state clearly that we are not particularly interested here in the greater merits of any one paradigm over another. Nor do we seek to argue that the current paradigms are useless. Ultimately, our point is a simple one: we object to any single framework designed to define reality for all. Our assumption is that reality cannot so easily be bound and tied. Instead, we are better served when we accept the *need* for differing approaches. If, as some have contended, the study of inter-American relations is besieged by a bewildering array of approaches—a claim we cannot support—then so much the better.

Paradigms in the Study of Inter-American Relations

It is apparent that the number of approaches one can identify in the study of intrahemispheric relations is partly dependent upon the definitional scope of the term "approach." In a recent essay, Jorge I. Domínguez[6] describes eight different approaches to, or what he called "perspectives" on, inter-American relations. In another effort, Susanne Bodenheimer[7] identifies only two approaches, or what she calls "paradigms" or "paradigm-surrogates." Although Domínguez is sensitive to the inherent arbitrariness of any classificatory scheme and the resulting fuzziness along category boundaries, he opts for a "narrower" notion of the term "perspective" for several reasons, one of which is particularly relevant here. One should differentiate among these perspectives, he argues, even though they are not mutually exclusive, because "there is often confusion when scholars are lumped together at a very high level of aggregation as if they all agreed."[8]

Conversely, Bodenheimer's central point is that although there are obvious differences in hypotheses, competing theories, and alternative perspectives, these differences mask a "consensus at a more fundamental level."[9] Until the recent emergence of an alternative paradigm, this consensus upon one major "paradigm-surrogate" controlled most empirical research in Latin American studies.

Although we do not agree with Bodenheimer's position in

toto, we do agree with her observation that fundamental and often unarticulated consensus governs the study of inter-American relations. Domínguez bemoans the pluralistic, non-paradigmatic state of inter-American studies; Bodenheimer claims that social scientists' blindness to the existence of an all-encompassing approach prevents them from realizing that although they may be using different oars, they are all rowing in the same boat.

Our purpose here, like Bodenheimer's, is primarily to point out not the differences but the overarching similarities in analytical styles and assumptions in the field. First, however, we shall attempt to demonstrate the existence of two primary paradigms and the emergence of a third paradigm that, in part, synthesizes the former two. These paradigms we shall loosely label liberal-developmental, dependency, and organizational ideology. Table 1.1 presents our categories and illustrates how they incorporate the approaches identified by Domínguez, Bodenheimer, and others.

TABLE 1.1
Paradigms in the Study of Inter-American Relations

Paradigms described in this essay	Liberal-developmental	Dependency	Organizational ideology
Other approaches:			
Bodenheimer	Developmental or paradigm-surrogate	Dependency	
Chalmers	Development, developmentalism	Dependency	
Lowenthal	Liberal, bureaucratic	Radical	
Domínguez	Liberal, bureaucratic, strategic, presidency, political systems	Orthodox dependency, Unorthodox dependency	Organizational ideology

The Liberal-Developmental Paradigm

The liberal-developmental paradigm is chronologically the first of the three, and although it is dealt with somewhat differently by various writers, there appears to be a consensus as to its core. The basic assumptions of this model are that the interests of the United States and Latin American countries are compatible;[10] that revolution, particularly of a Communist sort, is a "bad" solution to hemispheric problems;[11] and that U.S. aid can encourage orderly change in Latin American nations as well as the growth of stable, pluralistic, and increasingly modernized societies—in short, carbon copies of the United States.[12] Additional key liberal assumptions are that the United States has a national interest in Latin America "different from and superior to the private interests of any sector of American enterprise or of business enterprise as a whole and that the U.S. government is capable of defining and pursuing that interest."[13] In general, this paradigm has been associated with such scholars as Samuel Huntington, Merle Kling, Martin Needler, Alfred Stepan, Raúl Prebisch, Gino Germani, and Adolph Berle and with such programs and institutions as the Alliance for Progress and the Economic Commission for Latin America.

As Douglas Chalmers cogently points out, the liberal-developmental paradigm has gone beyond approach and become an ideology. By the 1950s, the descriptive and interpretative sociological concept of development became an ideology; it "came to be thought of as *the* historical process which shaped all else."[14] Bodenheimer states that "the paradigm-surrogate may be seen as an ideology—a body of ideas whose substantive content reflects concrete interests of particular social classes."[15]

The recent essays of Bodenheimer, Chalmers, Lowenthal, and others clearly demonstrate the existence and predominance of a particular body of assumptions and a particular framework for viewing and analyzing inter-American relations. Although it is apparent from Domínguez's essay that there are variants within this paradigm, a fundamental consensus is pervasive. This consensus, outlined above, we call the liberal-developmental paradigm.

The Dependency Paradigm

The second, and more recent, dominant paradigm is the dependency model. As an essentially neo-Marxist approach to the study of inter-American relations, dependency apparently stands in stark contrast to the liberal-developmental paradigm. However, as Domínguez suggests, the dependency approach, or aspects of it, is not as terribly different as some think.[16] Nevertheless, there are a significant number of competing assumptions and viewpoints between the two dominant paradigms. Fernando Cardoso states the case as follows:

> Studies of dependency continue a live tradition in Latin American thought, reinvigorated in the 1960's by the proposition of themes and problems defined in a theoretical-methodological field not only distinct from what inspired Keynesian and structural-functionalist analyses . . . but radically distinct with respect to its inherent critical component.[17]

A full treatment of the differences between the paradigms is not possible here. However, it is possible to outline some of the more cogent contrasts. Where liberal-developmentalists see a compatibility of U.S.–Latin American interests, *dependentistas* see a basic conflict between U.S. aims to dominate the region and Latin America's struggle for independence and development. Where the liberal-developmentalists believe assistance from the United States is carried out in the interests of further Latin American development, *dependentistas* argue that U.S. "aid" is no more than an imperialist tool designed to increase rather than decrease the dependency of Latin America upon dominant capitalist interests. Where liberal-developmentalists treat problems in U.S.–Latin American relations as unintended mistakes and misunderstandings, the *dependentistas* view these "problems" as logical outcomes of a rational, continuous pattern of intentional domination on the part of the United States. Moreover, where the liberal-developmental approach emphasizes the primacy of politics in inter-American relations, *dependentistas* are preoccupied with the economic stakes of these relationships.[18]

There are, of course, variants within the dependency paradigm just as there are in the liberal-developmental paradigm. Domínguez, for example, speaks of orthodox and unorthodox schools of dependency.[19] The latter, among others, tends to deemphasize U.S. intentions to subjugate Latin America. Ronald Chilcote distinguishes between a bourgeois version and a Marxist version of dependency, the former being comparable to Domínguez's unorthodox dependency and the latter to the orthodox school. Nevertheless, the basic positions are similar and do not represent significantly different epistemological assumptions and approaches to understanding inter-American relations.

The Organizational-Ideology Paradigm

The organizational-ideology paradigm, best represented by the preliminary efforts of Guillermo O'Donnell,[20] comes closest to being a new approach, while also representing a serious effort at synthesizing and bridging other paradigms. In the latter sense, O'Donnell's model is truly a hybrid that borrows from the theories of some strange intellectual bedfellows, including Huntington, Marx, Cardoso, Falleto, Apter, Dahl, and Frank. It is a paradigm that owes much to at least four separate areas of study: conventional analyses of modernization and nation building, studies of bureaucratic values and structure, Marxist and dependency investigations of modern capitalism and imperialism, and analyses of populism and labor movement repression in Latin America.

However, this approach is distinct from the two dominant paradigms in several ways. It differs from liberal-developmentalism by its emphasis on conflict rather than compatibility of interests; its deemphasis of the role of the monolithic rational actor; its heavier stress on the economic stakes involved in inter-American relations; and its greater sympathy with Marxist and dependency critiques of Latin America's inexorable progression toward modernization as a result of U.S. "aid." It may be argued then that O'Donnell's approach has more in common with the dependency paradigm than with the liberal-developmental paradigm, but there are a number of significant contrasts with the dependency model.

Unlike the *dependentistas*, O'Donnell allows for some degree of institutional autonomy and for the possibility of intra- and interorganizational conflict. Although O'Donnell pays more attention to problems of economic dependency than do the liberal-developmentalists, he gives greater weight to noneconomic factors than the *dependentistas*. Moreover, O'Donnell emphasizes the diffusion of certain values as the critical link between the United States and Latin America; yet, he relates these to political conflict in a manner different from the traditional diffusionist model. Clearly O'Donnell's model represents a major effort to synthesize apparently opposing approaches.

As noted in Table 1.1 we have included in the larger category of liberal-developmentalism what both Lowenthal and Domínguez identify as yet another approach, the so-called bureaucratic perspective. Whereas both Domínguez and Lowenthal suggest that the bureaucratic approach, represented by scholars such as Graham Allison and Ernest May, is distinct from the liberal perspective, the bureaucratic politics perspective contains core assumptions that do not differ significantly from the assumptions of the liberal-developmental approach. Adherents of both approaches accept the notion of the essentially pluralistic nature of politics in the United States, tend to make gradualist and incrementalist assumptions about change, and view formal political actors in general as independent—or potentially independent—of basic social and economic forces.[21]

Finally, we include Domínguez's remaining perspectives (strategic, presidency, and political systems) within the liberal-developmental paradigm, since scholars adopting these alternative perspectives make the same basic assumptions, usually unarticulated, that we find in the liberal-developmental school. Concepts like strategic and presidency usefully refer to approaches at a concrete and specific level, not at the level of fundamental epistemological assumptions. Rather, they are subcategories or subfields of a more generic model. Their utility lies in their identification of critical variables, particularly of critical actors in the policy process. Although there are differences here, they are differences among species within a larger class: liberal-developmentalism.

In summary, we have identified, at a general level of consensus, two dominant and competing paradigms for the study of inter-American relations and one emerging synthetic and unique third approach. The following section contains a discussion of the contrasts between the liberal-developmental and dependency paradigms, followed by a discussion of O'Donnell's organizational-ideology approach as a useful step in combining the strengths and avoiding the pitfalls of liberal-developmentalist and dependency thinking. Our goal is to indicate the potential dangers that arise with any ascendant paradigm, regardless of its apparent strengths. These various dangers or problems generally originate in the quest for an ordered structure, for a rigid theoretical imperative, for intellectual and scientific hegemony.

Critique of the Paradigms: Contrasts, Similarities, and the Common Problem of the Theoretical Imperative

The two dominant paradigms, as briefly described in the previous section, differ significantly in methodologies and styles of analysis. Table 1.2 summarizes the contrasts we shall discuss. Conventional science, and its contemporary off-shoots such as the liberal-developmental paradigm, emphasize a methodology based on maximizing quantitative data. In turn, the quantitative data are then subjected to various forms of correlational analyses to test hypotheses concerning potential relationships between and among various events. O'Donnell provides a number of examples of research based on these tech-

TABLE 1.2
Contrasts in the Dominant Paradigms

	Liberal-Developmental	*Dependency*
Methodology	Quantitative-correlational	Historical, philosophical
Central analytical assumption	Institutional autonomy	Institutional dependence
Process of change	Evolutionary, continuous	Revolutionary, discontinuous
Role of the U.S.	Primary assistant in development	Primary hindrance in development

niques.[22] More current examples include articles by George
Meek[23] and Thomas Volgy and Henry Kenski.[24] Quantitative
data and correlational techniques are useful means by which to
ground our theories in empirical, testable terms. It makes little
sense to ignore such techniques; to do so leads to the temptation to base all arguments on rhetorical disputation. Correlational analyses have their limits however. They give us part of
the picture, part of a view of "reality"; but only a part. "A correlation is like a snapshot. It tells us where the actors portrayed
stand, but it does not give us any information about how they
came to occupy their present positions or in which directions
they are likely to move in the future."[25]

The dependency model, by contrast, primarily utilizes a
historical, philosophical approach. To the extent that dependency owes its origins to a Marxist sociology, the dependency
model necessarily is historical and philosophical in its analytical
style.

> Marx emphasizes that man should be viewed historically; what he
> makes of himself depends on the interaction of his forces with the
> environment—including the man-made institutions of society. None-
> theless it will not do to make a positivist out of Marx. . . . However
> scientific and empirical in intention and in its methodical treatment
> of problems, his sociology rests ultimately upon a view of human
> nature which is philosophical.[26]

Referring specifically to the dependency approach, Cardoso
argues for greater analytical attention to historical developments and less concern with formal, quantitative-based theory
testing. He concludes a review of recent works on dependency
with the following suggestions:

> I do not agree with the idea that to improve the quality of analysis,
> the theory of dependency should be formalized so that, after hy-
> potheses derived from this formalization, one could venture out into
> the world waving the banner of the percentage of variance explained
> by each factor within the situation of dependence. Instead of asking
> for analyses within the mold of empiricist structural-functionalism,
> it would be better to ask for an improvement in the quality of
> historical-structural analyses.[27]

The two paradigms also differ on a critical analytical assumption, namely the relative autonomy of various institutions and social forces. In the literature on inter-American relations, the issue of autonomy arises twice. First, this issue concerns the degree to which governmental institutions function independently of other institutions or forces. Virtually all analyses within the liberal-developmental paradigm assume a significant degree of independence. For instance, studies of the Alliance for Progress that raise issues concerning U.S. government commitment, bureaucratic jealousy, and so on have no relevance unless one assumes the government can develop and pursue policies independently of private, economic powers. Similarly, debates over the relative merits of bilateral, multilateral, and private economic aid make little sense unless one ascribes different actions, goals and/or values to the various institutions. Studies such as May's[28] and Allison's [29] also have little meaning without an autonomy assumption.

Second, the issue of autonomy concerns the extent to which less powerful nations (those of Latin America) are free to set policies independent of the desires of more powerful nations (the United States, for example). Once more, liberal-developmentalists assume a rather broad scope of freedom. George Meek, for instance, seeks to demonstrate in his study of voting in the OAS that U.S. influence is less than what many believe. "The data show that the overall batting average for the United States is .604, a remarkably poor showing for a country that is alleged to dominate decision-making in the OAS."[30] In fact, the autonomy assumption makes it possible for some to discuss Latin American development programs and foreign policies with barely a nod to U.S. influence.

Obviously, the *dependentistas* assume a very high degree of dependency. In the case of external relations, they speak of such phenomena as "dependent development" or of Latin America as a satellite of the capitalist metropolis. Internal dependence is slightly more problematic, however, for it is an assumption more obviously held by the "purer" Marxist *dependentistas.*[31] Nevertheless, the tendency within this paradigmatic approach is to assume that governments essentially reflect the values and goals of the economic forces within society. Dale

Johnson, for instance, argues that the various policies of the U.S. government are under the control of the dominant business community and serve the purpose of extending international capitalism.[32]

A third glaring difference between the paradigms concerns the views of the nature and process of social change. Liberal-developmentalists assume that change normally occurs in a continuous, evolutionary fashion. Their model of development is based on the presumed histories of change in England and the United States. Accordingly, the United States should support peaceful reforms in the context of a democratic and stable system.[33]

Within the framework of dependency, the essence of meaningful change (empirically and normatively) is interpreted in revolutionary and discontinuous terms. The liberal-developmentalist can speak of reforms and orderly progress; the *dependentista* speaks of radical breaks with the past. The former measures change by such indicators as GNP per capita, industrial output, the number of peaceful elections, and the balance of payments. The latter measures change in terms of control of product distribution and so forth.

Finally, the two paradigms differ in the view taken of the present and potential roles assigned to the United States. Proponents of both paradigms typically tend to be critical of the United States. Nevertheless, most liberal-developmentalists believe the United States can be a positive force for change in Latin America. For instance, it is common for liberal critics to chide the Alliance for Progress for its failure to make and meet stronger commitments. The concept of the Alliance, however, is seen as positive.[34]

In contrast, the dependency paradigm points to the United States as the primary hindrance to Latin American development. Moreover, this is not due simply to a failure of U.S. will, but results from the very structure of the U.S. economic system. The constant need of U.S. capital to expand inevitably leads it to control those societies incapable of resisting such economic power. Hence, until the United States itself is radically restructured, its role in Latin America will on balance be negative.

Additional contrasts between the two approaches might become evident in the future. Nevertheless the discussion above at least suggests some of the fundamental differences the two models currently exhibit. In principle, the emphasis of one approach can in most cases supplement or correct the emphasis of the other. However, it has become apparent that this, unfortunately, has usually not occurred.

The organizational-ideology approach of Guillermo O'Donnell indicates means by which to synthesize or combine some of the polarities of the two dominant approaches, despite the fact that O'Donnell's analyses have somewhat greater affinity to the dependency paradigm. In an article published in 1978, for instance, O'Donnell addresses in some detail the "deepening of dependent capitalism."[35] Nevertheless, the framework he proposes is more than another variant of dependency. It is, instead, a unique contribution.

In the first place, O'Donnell attempts to wed a quantitative-correlational analysis to historical-structural analysis. In *Modernization and Bureaucratic-Authoritarianism,* he writes quite critically of the former analytic style.[36] He does not do this, however, as part of an argument to reject that style; he simply seeks to illustrate its shortcomings. Recognizing these shortcomings, O'Donnell then proceeds to engage in some quantitative hypothesis testing of his own. But he carefully supplements this testing with a more descriptive and structural historical analysis. Indeed, in a more recent article, he explicitly states the need to utilize a variety of methodological approaches. "As a consequence, the boundary between the historian and the social scientist, as well as the limits between the social science disciplines . . . is obscured."[37]

On questions of both internal and external autonomy, O'Donnell adopts a view that combines the perspectives of the two dominant paradigms. At the same time, he simply refuses to make a priori assumptions about the exact degree of autonomy and leaves this as an empirical question. With regard to internal, institutional autonomy, O'Donnell clearly rejects the assumption of any "omniscient and unitary actor."[38] Discussing the early stage of the bureaucratic-authoritarian state, O'Donnell writes, "This state . . . is highly autonomous with respect to that society."[39] In his formulation of the recent history of

Argentina and Brazil, political actors are not simply reflections
of economic forces; instead, conflict arises from a constellation
of factors, including economic power and goals, political and
technocratic values, and so on.

On the other hand, O'Donnell believes that governmental institutions tend to be dominated by certain widely shared values
and goals. This restricts the range of meaningful opposition and
suggests that there is intrinsic conflict between institutional
autonomy and dependence. "We share with Allison and May
the criticisms of the unitary actor. . . . But this does not prevent
us from recognizing dominant goals that are shared by the actors
who constitute the government and for which each one seeks—
according to his biases—'satisfactory' solutions."[40]

At the external level, O'Donnell attempts a similar type of
synthesis. The development and direction of Latin American
societies, he argues, are circumscribed by North American
influence. This influence is felt through the diffusion of technocratic values.[41] Thus foreign, especially U.S., influences set
limits on the behavior of governments in Latin America. Within
these limits the state's freedom of action may increase or
decrease. "For example, the state renationalizes itself in the
case of a crumbling BA [bureaucratic-authoritarianism] . . .
putting some distance from international capital."[42]

This brief view of O'Donnell's approach illustrates the types
of new approaches available to the analyst willing to consider
insights from competing and apparently contradictory paradigms.
Similar comments could be made about O'Donnell's attempts
to synthesize the other opposing perspectives of the paradigms,
e.g., those concerning the process and nature of change. But
O'Donnell has not provided us with a panacea. Panaceas simply
do not exist. In fact, much of the potential danger inherent in
all three approaches comes not from their differences but from
their common grounding within the peculiarly narrow, conventional epistemological framework of contemporary social science.

Panaceas, Intellectual Hegemony,
and Theoretical Imperative

In the conclusion to her useful monograph on the nature of
the paradigm-surrogate of developmentalism, Susanne J. Boden-

heimer notes that it is likely that some characteristics of the developmental approach will be absorbed within the new dependency framework. Nonetheless, she argues, the bulk of developmentalism must be put aside "once the basic assumptions of the paradigm-surrogate are discarded."[43] It is precisely this push to intellectual hegemony, this either-or perspective, that helps create the core epistemological problem of much contemporary thinking about inter-American relations. This quest for a new (presumably nonsurrogate) paradigm is the quest for an intellectual monolith. The paradigm, as Thomas Kuhn notes in his seminal work, is designed to provide an entire array of rules, research topics, methodologies, and perspectives for the practitioner.[44] It necessarily "outlaws," at least for the time being, alternative rules, research topics, and so on. It is to this *authoritarian* science that we level our criticisms. Bodenheimer implies that one monolithic structure is to be exchanged for another. Our perspective, by contrast, is reflected in a recent statement by Robert Packenham:

> The oscillations [of approaches] from one extreme to another may reflect, among other things, a desire for comprehensiveness, for intellectual simplicity and coherence, for a total picture, for something to believe in. . . . But [these desires] probably cannot be met. The world is simply too complex and variegated to be satisfactorily ordered in terms of any of the extant total pictures.[45]

Moreover, the complexity of reality is even less satisfactorily ordered when many of the proponents of the existing "competing" approaches themselves share a similar narrow-gauged perspective on the nature of social scientific understanding. In short, existing approaches and emerging approaches that are ensconced in the tunnel vision of a rigid science all share the following problems: they tend to intellectual hegemony; their quest for "theory" often darkens more of reality than it enlightens; they are overly deterministic and mechanistic and unable to deal with the unique and the novel; they have an inordinately materialistic view of the human condition.

While critically describing the scholarship of political develop-

ment in the late 1950s and much of the 1960s, Robert Packenham makes a relevant observation:

> It seems safe to say that botanists, geologists, or (closer to home)
> economists would not dream of explaining a phenomenon until
> they had relatively good descriptions of what they wanted to explain.
> . . . The idea scarcely seems to have occurred to political develop-
> ment theorists; if it did, it was a much lower priority for them than
> *explanatory* studies. . . . They felt a theory was needed in order to
> approach the data.[46]

Although Packenham is directly addressing a historical "stage"
of political science and political development theory, it is interesting to note the persistence of such assumptions concerning
the need for theory as a prerequisite to "meaningful" research
among scholars with an interest in understanding U.S.–Latin
American relations, regardless of the approach to which they
may adhere.

In a recent collection of papers on Latin America and the
United States, the editors view this very same theoretical imperative as one way out of scholarly squabblings over the nature
of reality.[47] Although Julio Cotler and Richard Fagen take
pains to point out the significantly different emphases found
between adherents of the dependency and liberal-developmental
approaches, they suggest that both sides nevertheless appear to
embrace "[the] conventional wisdom of the social sciences
[that] pays homage to the unbreakable bond between theory
and research. Without constant testing against reality, theory
stagnates and eventually turns to dogma. Without the guidance
of theory, research founders, ultimately degenerating into a
mindless empiricism that confuses data with reality."[48] Having
said this and having implicitly accepted this position as their
general orientation toward understanding inter-American relations, Cotler and Fagen go on to discuss the various analyses
of the Alliance for Progress in a curious way. It is apparent,
they say, that liberal-developmentalists can find in the history
of the Alliance support for their "theory" that the U.S. government has been committed to Latin American development.
At the same time, the *dependentistas* use the same data to
underscore their contention that the continued subjugation of

Latin America has always been the ultimate purpose of U.S. policy. Why is this the case?

First, Cotler and Fagen point out, there is an objective basis for alternative interpretations. The Alliance was complex and variegated, so much so that the whole is not necessarily equal to the sum of its parts. More importantly, they argue,

> Investigators approaching the Alliance from different perspectives will *necessarily* use it in different ways to discover different "truths."
> . . . The meanings of the Alliance, which is to say its reality as reconstructed, are not and cannot be independent of the theoretical perspectives brought to bear on it, whether the latter are consciously or unconsciously held. . . . More research—further information about the Alliance, no matter how detailed or exhausted—will not adjudicate or reconcile all the differences.[49]

Whereas Cotler and Fagen explicitly choose not to explore the epistemological assumptions of this quandary, those assumptions are the very focus of this chapter. On the one hand, conventional social science urges that theory be constantly tested against reality to avoid ideological stagnation. On the other hand, theory must guide research to avoid a "mindless empiricism that confuses data with reality." But as Cotler and Fagen accurately point out, in the case of apparently irreconcilable differences in interpretation among liberal-developmentalists and *dependentistas,* theory virtually determines reality.

This dilemma is cogently described by Paul Feyerabend.[50] He points out that in the experimental sciences the decision between alternative theories is based upon crucial experiments that generally work well with theories of a low degree of generality. However, these theories are usually ultimately encompassed by more general "background theories," which, like any other theory, are in need of criticism. If the alternative background theories, he goes on to say, differ quite radically from one another,

> it is bound to happen, then, that the alternatives do not share a single statement with the [competing] theories they criticize. Clearly, a crucial experiment is now impossible. It is impossible . . . because there is no statement capable of expressing what emerges from the observation.[51]

In this sense, we might loosely characterize liberal-developmentalism and the dependency approach as general background theories, each of which classified all observations made within its own respective framework, thereby eliminating the possibility of alternative explanations and ultimately stultifying the process of understanding. If, as Cotler and Fagen point out, the theory defines its own reality and the adherents to each theory claim the "truth," then the basic epistemology shared by *both* approaches is a classic demonstration of "how empirical 'evidence' may be *created* by a procedure which quotes as its justification the very same evidence it has produced in the first place."[52] The irony here turns the "conventional wisdom" of social science on its head. Rather than theories helping us to find reality and truth, the major competing theories of U.S.– Latin American relations create their own realities and therefore prevent us from seeing alternative visions.

The continual preoccupation of scholars with understanding the Alliance for Progress within the framework of one or another of the competing approaches has created an additional, related, though more subtle, problem: a rigidity and insensitivity to change. Ultimately, relationships between nation-states are derived from individual human efforts to achieve some purpose or goal. If we assume that those very purposes and goals are static, if having once made a choice human beings are essentially determined by it in the future, and if they are unable to reason with one another and effect any significant change in what has either become "institutionalized" or "coopted by dominant-class interests"; then theory based on the reconstruction of historical occurrences can adequately explain and predict future occurrences.

If, on the other hand, we see human beings as capable of growing, of developing, and of changing not only their circumstances but their purposes and goals through autonomous and *novel* processes and actions, then a significant part of the theoretical "insights" *dependentistas* and liberal-developmentalists alike provide is ultimately locked in the past. Assuming the latter perspective on human capacity, Charles Hampden-Turner levels the following charge against all of the contemporary epistemology of social science:

What social science has done is banish human *purpose* from its universe of discourse. *Purpose and process are destroyed in analysis.* . . . Hence, while life processes face forwards toward greater complexity, variety and higher synthesis, the vast majority of social scientists face backwards, searching for the cause of present behavior in a myriad of separate incidents, group affiliations, economic conditions, and occupational roles.[53]

Variations on this perspective have recently been explored in the works of scholars with an interest in U.S.–Latin American relations. Albert O. Hirschman notes that there are problems related to what he calls paradigmatic thinking in social and political analysis.[54] First, when approaching reality with the construction of a paradigm (theory) in mind, it often happens that what one sees as "reality" appears more solidly entrenched than it really is. This results in what Hirschman sees as the essential conservatism of social analysis, which has the immediate effect of converting "the real into the rational or the contingent into the necessary."[55]

Perhaps more importantly, Hirschman addresses the problem of the social sciences "looking backwards." Ironically, both liberal-developmentalists and the *dependentistas* purport to offer a model of change, be it continuous or discontinuous. Moreover, both approaches offer evidence according to the canons of science. But as anthropologist Max Gluckman so concisely and lucidly states: "Scientific method cannot deal with unique complexes of many events. The accounts of the actual course of events which produce change therefore necessarily remain historical narratives."[56] Similarly, Hirschman notes the "despair of the paradigm-obsessed social scientist" when confronting "that peculiar open-endedness of history."[57]

In the constant search for various laws of behavior, the dominant paradigms reveal another shortcoming; they are deterministic and mechanistic. Of course, the actual nature of their determinism varies from one paradigm to the next. The developmentalists emphasize autonomous, evolutionary growth from the primitive, rural, and undeveloped society to the modern, urban, and developed society. The *dependentistas* emphasize revolutionary change moving from dependent capitalism to independent socialism. The fact is, however, that both paradigms are based on a particular conception of progress with a particular beginning and end point. Furthermore, this type of analytic or theoretical determinism inevitably leads to predetermined strategies and policies for individual or governmental actions. Yet Lenin, among others, recognized the need to be as opportunistic and flexible as possible in achieving revolutionary success.[58] This flexibility at the action level, however, is not possible (unless one chooses to be completely amoral) without some flexibility at the level of theory.

> Why should all of Latin America find itself constantly impaled on the horns of some fateful and unescapable dilemma? Even if one is prepared to accept Goldenweiser's "principle of limited possibilities in a given environment," any theory or model or paradigm propounding that there are only two possibilities—disaster or one particular road to salvation—should be *prima facie* suspect. After all, there *is*, at least temporarily, such a place as purgatory![59]

Fortunately, some proponents of each paradigm recognize the tendency toward determinism and have cautioned their colleagues accordingly. Hirschman, for instance, is not completely dissociated with the liberal-developmental paradigm. In the case of the dependency paradigm, F. H. Cardoso, often "accused" of being one of the founders of the dependency approach, has recently criticized much of the deterministic, let's-find-the-ultimate-explanation thinking that seems to have pervaded this and any other paradigm:

> It is necessary to have a sense . . . of the ridiculous, and to avoid the simplistic reductionism so common among the present-day butterfly collectors who abound in the social sciences and who stroll through history classifying types of dependency, modes of production, and laws of development, with the blissful illusion that their findings can remove from history all its ambiguities, conjectures, and surprises.[60]

The final criticism we would like to make is the emphasis on materialism that pervades the paradigms. The paradigms are materialistic in that they concentrate heavily on economic factors. This is most obviously the case with the dependency paradigm and is inevitable given its Marxist roots. In fact, dependency is first and foremost an economic phenomenon. However, the liberal-developmental paradigm also stresses economics, although to a lesser degree.

This is seen most clearly in the Alliance for Progress program and in the subsequent developmental critiques of the program.[61] The Alliance sought to engender social and political changes by manipulating such economic factors as increases in per capita GNP, increases in direct taxes as a percentage of government revenue, large infusions of U.S. government aid, and so on. Criticisms often focus on the failure of Latin American governments to achieve "their" economic goals and the failure of the United States to provide sufficient economic aid.

Obviously, economic factors are important; in fact, the rediscovery of economics by political scientists in the 1950s and 1960s was a healthy intellectual development. Yet perhaps the pendulum has swung so far in the economic direction that it is now necessary to rediscover fundamental political and, especially, cultural factors.

Conclusion

Although alternative and conflicting approaches to the understanding of relations between Latin America and the United States might well inform one another, ameliorating respective shortcomings while accentuating achievements, this has infrequently been the case. On the contrary, the quest for a rigid "scientism" and intellectual dominance has generally resulted in an equally rigid, noncompromising, deterministic, and often dehumanizing perspective on U.S.–Latin American relations.

Moreover, although O'Donnell's systematization is a useful and enlightening synthesis of the currently dominant paradigms in the field, any single approach, particularly to the extent to which it purports to encompass much of reality, may carry with it the potential to become equally as rigid, as authoritarian, and as insensitive to the process of growth and change as Bodenheimer's paradigm-surrogate. And we have laid much of the blame for this potential on the pernicious practice of social science engaging in theorizing as a justification for an a priori vision of an overly ordered existence.

Thus far, our critique of the theoretical imperative and its intimate connection with the conventional wisdom of the social sciences might be interpreted as leading inexorably to two conclusions/prescriptions: (1) give up theory as a guide and, instead, let the facts "speak for themselves"; and (2) throw out scientific method lock, stock, and barrel since, rather than enabling social scientists to understand reality, it has desensitized if not totally blinded them to reality. However, this very logical deduction, if made, would be part of the same kind of thinking we have identified as a core problem and epistemological cornerstone for most of the contemporary scholarship in social science generally and in U.S.–Latin American relations specifically. This thinking is rigid, Aristotelian, categorical, and it ultimately forces us into dichotomous, arbitrary, and potentially dehumanizing choices. We reject that logical imperative as well as the theoretical imperative. The study of inter-American relations is in trouble *not* because "the degree of scholarly consensus is grossly insufficient,"[62] but precisely *because* of an adherence to a dogmatic, rigid, and mechanistic science.

Theory should, in its best sense, serve as a humble guide to understanding, not as a turnkey to a jail cell. Likewise, science should, in its best sense, help us to widen our perspectives and to accept alternatives, particularly alternatives that share no common language of understanding with one another. In short, there is a great need not for consensus but for the tolerance and encouragement of theoretical and scientific pluralism—for what Feyerabend calls methodological anarchism.

Notes

1. A rather sizable body of literature has emerged in the last several years dealing with these questions. Among some of the more recent and notable works, see Susanne J. Bodenheimer, *The Ideology of Developmentalism: The American Paradigm-Surrogate for Latin American Studies* (Beverly Hills, Calif.: Sage, 1971); Douglas A. Chalmers, "The Demystification of Development," in D. Chalmers (ed.), *Changing Latin America* (New York: Academy of Political Science, 1972), pp. 109–122; Ronald H.

Chilcote, "A Question of Dependency," *Latin American Research Review* 13, no. 2 (1978):55–68; R. H. Chilcote and Joel Edelstein (eds.), *Latin America: The Struggle with Dependency and Beyond* (Cambridge, Mass.: Schenkman, 1974), pp. 1–87; Jorge I. Domínguez, "Consensus and Divergence: The State of the Literature on Inter-American Relations in the 1970's" *Latin American Research Review* 13, no. 1 (1978):87–126; Richard R. Fagen, "Studying Latin American Politics: Some Implications of a Dependencia Approach," *Latin American Research Review* 12, no. 2 (1977):3–26; Abraham F. Lowenthal, " 'Liberal,' 'Radical,' and 'Bureaucratic' Perspectives of U.S. Latin American Policy: The Alliance for Progress in Retrospect," in Julio Cotler and Richard R. Fagen, *Latin America and the United States: The Changing Political Realities* (Stanford: Stanford University Press, 1974), pp. 212–235.

2. See especially Paul Feyerabend, *Against Method* (London: Verso, 1978); and "How to be a Good Empiricist—A Plea for Tolerance in Matters Epistemological," in Baruch Brody (ed.), *Readings in the Philosophy of Science* (Englewood Cliffs, N.J.: Prentice-Hall, 1970).

3. Feyerabend, *Against Method,* p. 17.

4. Ibid., pp. 19–20.

5. The standard definition of a paradigm is to be found in Thomas S. Kuhn, *The Structure of Scientific Revolutions* (Chicago: University of Chicago Press, 1962). According to Kuhn, paradigms provide models of law, theory application, and instrumentation that arise from "particular coherent traditions of scientific research," p. 10.

6. Domínguez, "Consensus and Divergence."

7. Bodenheimer, *Ideology of Developmentalism.*

8. Domínguez, "Consensus and Divergence," p. 89.

9. Bodenheimer, *Ideology of Developmentalism,* p. 5.

10. Lowenthal, "Perspectives on U.S. Latin American Policy,"; Chalmers, "Demystification of Development"; Domínguez, "Consensus and Divergence."

11. Bodenheimer, *Ideology of Developmentalism*; Robert Packenham, *Liberal America and the Third World* (Princeton: Princeton University Press, 1973).

12. Bodenheimer, *Ideology of Developmentalism*; Lowenthal, "Perspectives on U.S. Latin American Policy"; Packenham, *Liberal America.*

13. Lowenthal, "Perspectives on U.S. Latin American Policy," p. 215.

14. Chalmers, "Demystification of Development," p. 111.

15. Bodenheimer, *Ideology of Developmentalism,* p. 9.

16. Domínguez, "Consensus and Divergence," p. 17.

17. Fernando Henrique Cardoso, "The Consumption of Dependency Theory in the United States," *Latin American Research Review* 12, no. 3 (1977):17.

18. An extensive body of critical and explanatory literature now exists with regards to dependency. See, for instance, Bodenheimer, Chilcote, Cardoso, Lowenthal, Domínguez.

19. Domínguez, "Consensus and Divergence," especially pp. 106–108.

20. See Guillermo O'Donnell, *Modernization and Bureaucratic-Authoritarianism* (Berkeley, Calif.: Institute of International Studies, 1973); idem, "Reflections on the Patterns of Change in the Bureaucratic-Authoritarian State," *Latin American Research Review* 13, no. 1 (1978):3–38; and idem, "Commentary on May," in Cotler and Fagen, *Latin America and the United States,* pp. 164–175.

21. See, for example, O'Donnell, "Commentary on May."

22. See O'Donnell, *Modernization,* Chapter 1.

23. George Meek, "U.S. Influence in the Organization of American States," *Journal of Interamerican Studies and World Affairs* 17, no. 3 (August 1975).

24. Thomas Volgy and Henry Kenski, "Toward an Exploration of Comparative Foreign Policy Distance Between the United States and Latin America: A Research Note," *International Studies Quarterly* 20, no. 1 (March 1976).

25. O'Donnell, *Modernization,* p. 2.

26. George Lichtheim, *Marxism: An Historical and Critical Study* (New York: Praeger, 1961), pp. 42–43.

27. Cardoso, "Consumption of Dependency Theory," p. 21.

28. Ernest R. May, "The Bureaucratic Politics Approach: U.S.-Argentine Relations, 1942–47," in Cotler and Fagen, *Latin America and the United States.*

29. Graham Allison, "Conceptual Models and the Cuban Missile Crisis," *American Political Science Review* 43, no. 3 (1969):689–718.

30. Meek, "U.S. Influence," p. 319.

31. For a discussion of some differences between Marxist and bourgeois theories of dependency, compare Ronald Chilcote, "A Question of Dependency."

32. Dale Johnson, "Dependence and the International System," in James D. Cockcroft, Andre Gunder Frank, and Dale L. Johnson, *Dependence and Underdevelopment: Latin America's Political Economy* (Garden City, N.Y.: Doubleday, 1972), pp. 91–102.

33. See, for example, the recommendations of Yale Ferguson, in "The United States and Political Development in Latin America: A Retrospect and a Prescription," in Yale Ferguson (ed.), *Contemporary Inter-American Relations* (Englewood Cliffs, N.J.: Prentice-Hall, 1972), pp. 348–391.

34. See, inter alia, Ferguson, "United States and Political Development."

35. O'Donnell, "Reflections," pp. 9–16.

36. O'Donnell, *Modernization*, see Chapter 1.

37. O'Donnell, "Reflections," p. 4.

38. O'Donnell, "Commentary on May," p. 174.

39. O'Donnell, "Reflections," p. 4.

40. O'Donnell, "Commentary on May," p. 172.

41. This point is one of the clearest demonstrations of O'Donnell's attempt to fuse a diffusionist and dependency perspective. See his *Modernization*, pp. 55–70, 79–89; and "Reflections," pp. 16–27.

42. O'Donnell, "Reflections," p. 25.

43. Bodenheimer, *Ideology of Developmentalism*, p. 40.

44. Kuhn, *Structure of Scientific Revolutions*.

45. Packenham, *Liberal America*, p. 356.

46. Ibid., p. 223, emphasis added.

47. Cotler and Fagen, *Latin America and the United States*.

48. Ibid., p. 9.

49. Ibid., p. 11.

50. Feyerabend, "How to be a Good Empiricist."

51. Ibid., p. 322.

52. Ibid., pp. 332–333.

53. Charles Hampden-Turner, *Radical Man* (Cambridge, Mass.: Schenkman, 1970), p. 10.

54. Albert O. Hirschman, "The Search for Paradigms as a Hindrance to Understanding," *World Politics* 22, no. 3 (April 1970).

55. Ibid., p. 338.

56. Quoted in ibid., p. 342.

57. Ibid., p. 339.

58. In addition to the works of Lenin, see quotes and comments by Hirschman, ibid., pp. 323-343; and Feyerabend, *Against Method,* pp. 17–19.

59. Hirschman, "Search for Paradigms," pp. 336–337.

60. Cardoso, "Consumption of Dependency Theory," p. 21.

61. See, for instance, the discussion in Martin Needler, *The United States and the Latin American Revolution* (Boston: Allyn and Bacon, 1972), especially Chapter 5.

62. Domínguez, "Consensus and Divergence," p. 113.

2

The Inter-American Political Economy: How Dependable Is Dependency Theory?

John S. Gitlitz
Henry A. Landsberger

In this chapter we will discuss "dependency" and "world system" theory from the point of view of two very intrigued but somewhat skeptical consumers. Although our current position is at least as favorable toward, as it is critical of, these neo-Marxist approaches, let us nevertheless emphasize our role here as raisers of awkward questions rather than as missionaries. We suspect that as a whole our readers, especially those who have entered the field recently, are more often than not supportive rather than critical of these theories. They represent a new kind of theoretical posture that makes quick and enthusiastic converts. What can be more attractive than a reasoned attack upon the evils of the present and an implicit hope for a better future?

There is a further justification for dialogue from the position of a judicious skeptic: it is our impression that reasoned discourse between the two contending schools of thought has been rare. There have been few attempts on the part of "orthodox" developmentalists (who, as a matter of fact, speak even less from a single theoretical position than do the neo-Marxists) to rebut in a measured and item-by-item fashion the various forms of dependency theory.[1] In their turn, protagonists of the new approach tend to isolate themselves in almost sectlike fashion. And like sects, they tend to fight each other even more bitterly than they fight their supposed adversaries. The exchange, some years ago, between Andre Gunder Frank and the editors of *Latin American Perspectives*[2] and the tone of some of the contributions to that journal in general raise questions as to how much light, as distinct from heat, one can really expect if one is a mere bystander.

Thus, in the absence of dialogue, let us attempt to begin one. The majority of the points we discuss are addressed as much to issues in the logic of the social sciences, i.e., to epistemological issues, as to the truth of the facts and theories themselves, though the latter is by no means ignored. This is, of course, highly appropriate whenever one examines basically Marxist (and in that sense variants of Hegelian) theory. For it is to the credit of these theories and of others pitched at similar levels of seriousness and profundity that they explicitly raise not only customary questions about their empirical truth or falseness but also second-level questions in the social philosophy of knowledge, such as: Whence do these concepts come? Are they as novel as they appear or are they semantic substitutes for earlier concepts? What is the ideological function of a theory at a given moment in time? Why is it finding acceptance today when it did not yesterday, even though, after all, it had already been formulated? To what extent is a theory a redefinition, perhaps a tautology, rather than an assertion about facts? How does it compare as theory with other theories? It is these kinds of questions that we shall discuss briefly in this chapter.

The Positive Characteristics of
Dependency Theory: A Brief Summary

Let us begin by summarizing what appear to be the basic propositions of dependency theory.[3] (Without attempting to be exhaustive, we shall briefly note at the end of our summary some of the major differences that exist among the protagonists of dependency theory.) The *dependencia* "approach," as Richard Fagen prefers to call it,[4] has in fact grown in opposition to "modernization," another preexisting approach popular in the optimistic 1950s. To understand the fundamental ideas of dependency theory, we have chosen to highlight what dependency theory rejects. These propositions are therefore presented here in a negative form. We believe many of the criticisms dependency theorists have made of the modernization approach are valid. Nevertheless—no doubt to the chagrin of the committed on both sides—we accept substantial parts of both approaches while maintaining important reservations about each.

The essence of the dependency approach can be summarized in the following propositions.

1. *The so-called development of the Third World countries today can be understood only if the process is analyzed as forming part of a much larger dynamic: change in the worldwide capitalist system.* It is absurd to treat the Third World countries as more or less autonomous entities. It is likewise futile to investigate the extent to which they must repeat, or must differ, in their development processes from the historical development of others.

2. *Indeed, the image conjured up by the very term "development" is misleading. Third World countries change in response to changes in the larger system.* Sometimes, for some groups, these changes are for the better. Sometimes, for all or for some groups, they are for the worse. Sometimes they are simply changes. In any case there is no necessary unilinear evolution toward an ever-higher plane.

3. *It is the reactive nature of all, or most, changes in Third World countries and the inability of these countries to exert much control over their own destinies, let alone over the larger system, that justify the term "dependent," both in fact and in theory.*

4. *Economic change is not an isolated, mechanistic process mainly within the purview of the field of economics. Economic change is, rather, the consequence of classes pursuing their interests and exerting power to do so, admittedly within the context of some (very imperfect) market.* The real object of study, as well as the name of our discipline and its theory, should be "political economy." To study either economics purely through economic science or politics through political science, each in isolation from the other, is unfruitful. All social institutions—the family and the role of women, culture and the media, religion and the church—are linked to the political (world) economy and the (world) class structures underlying it. They must be studied with this in mind.

5. *The influence of the worldwide capitalist system may be*

and has in the past been exerted through an impersonal market. However, today there is an increasingly important actor or set of actors that behaves with visible and deliberate purpose: multinational corporations (MNCs). It is through MNCs that, today, dependence is largely structured. Whether or not the activities of MNCs are a response to some implacable and ultimately unmeetable need of the underlying capitalist system, their daily, yearly, and even decade-long activities are certainly not shaped by any invisible hand. Moreover, since MNCs do not have the interests of the Third World at heart, their impact on the Third World—even if they do produce "change" of some kind—is generally harmful. For example, the industrialization they sponsor often requires sophisticated technology, which must be imported. This in turn requires foreign currency (of which there is little), but little locally unemployed labor (of which there is much). The products of this process are usually aimed at a high-income market—a small portion of local populations—and not at the needy. Moreover, in this process of industrialization MNCs absorb local capital and drive out locally owned businesses. We need hardly mention other effects often cited in the literature: that MNCs export scarce capital through profit remittances, transfer payments, patent royalties, and the like; that they pay limited taxes; or that they corrupt local politics, and so on.[5]

6. *Examination of class structure—essential for an understanding of Third World maldevelopment—is likely to show that many groups, consciously or otherwise, are dependent on the existing system and hence unlikely to challenge it. On the other hand, there are many who do not benefit.* Revolution is prevented either by keeping the latter so weak that they cannot rebel, or by outright repression if and when they do rebel. Weakness is often caused by division (deliberately fostered or otherwise) within the exploited sectors. Thus, the work force may be split into a small labor aristocracy, steadily employed in modern establishments and allowed to unionize or to receive higher wages and social-security benefits without unionization, and a larger urban work force, unemployed or employed in menial tasks in small shops, without benefits or protection. If not coerced into quiescence, the peasantry, in particular, may be bought off with small

parcels of land and little else in an essentially meaningless agrarian reform (as is often argued to be the case in Mexico).

Among those classes who do clearly benefit from the existing system, we find some not directly associated with the multinational corporations. (In most countries they would surely be a very small group, although the wording when this point is made is often rather open-ended.) In addition, there are all those who generally do well under the existing system: the landowners, the growing state bureaucracies, the national entrepreneurial bourgeoisie (who, it is disputed, may or may not be permitted sufficient economic territory to prosper in a limited way), the military, and perhaps some labor and even peasant sectors.

7. *The road to change is therefore a difficult one, to say the least. Some sort of dissociation of the dependent periphery from the capitalist core is probably necessary.* However, what form this dissociation may take and how it is to be pursued are not easy to specify in advance. Can dissociation be peaceful, or must it be violently revolutionary? What groups can lead the effort? Who will support them? Against what targets should their attacks be aimed? What policies should they adopt? On the answers to these questions there is little agreement. Those countries that have tried have shown only that the structure of dependency is very resilient indeed.

Throughout the above discussion we have referred to dependency as a "neo-Marxist" approach. Nevertheless, we recognize that not all advocates of dependency theory are Marxists. After all, at least one of the early sources of dependency thinking was the ECLA (Economic Commission of Latin America)[6] team of the 1950s. Under the leadership of Raúl Prebisch, this group developed the argument that the terms of trade were permanently moving against late-modernizing countries, making their development difficult. This countered the optimism of the neoclassical economists, who argued that each side of the North-South partnership benefited as it produced and sold what was most to its comparative advantage. Even the non-Marxists, however, would probably accept the general propositions we have enumerated, particularly the first three. We also realize that among those *dependencia* devotees who do, in one way or another, acknowledge a debt to Marx—certainly a majority today—there is much disagreement. We have already referred to the bitter debates in *Latin American Perspectives*. For example, some argue—as Andre Gunder Frank is perhaps unfairly accused of doing to excess—that concentration on the core-versus-periphery distinction is most central to any analysis. Others, often in attacking Frank, insist that local class structures, though clearly conditioned by the center-periphery relationship, are still more fundamental. There is no need to enumerate the various schools of dependency thought here; for those who are interested there are numerous summaries.[7] We believe and hope, however, that in spite of their differences most adherents of dependency theory would express at least minimum agreement with the propositions we have outlined.

Let us now highlight, however briefly, what we regard as the positive characteristics of the dependency approach and other approaches like it. First and foremost, they emphasize the prevalence of institutions, not of individual behavior. This is all to the good. No one, of course, denies that institutions—slavery, the plantation, the so-called free market, sophisticated technology, authoritarianism both Left and Right—are also necessarily patterns of individual behavior. Consequently, no one denies that at some point a convincing account must be given of why individuals decide to behave in a new way in the first place and then why they continue to behave in that way: why in the past they pressed for the abolition of guild restrictions and tariffs or for the abolition of elections when they began to produce inconvenient results. But regarding the explanation of individual behavior as one necessary part of a complete theory of institutional development, as most people do, is very different from focusing primarily on individual behavior, even when it is aggregated, as in the case of birthrates, voting behavior, migration, and crime rates. Marxism, dependency theory, and world-system theory focus not on individual behavior but on the evolution of institutions, and they are to be acclaimed for it.

Second, these approaches are particularly receptive to social change. Indeed, their adherents see societies as always in motion, especially through forces generated methodically if unwittingly by the system itself: by its "contradictions," as neo-Marxists of all schools would put it. What politically moderate theorists consider "a problem" is for their more radical colleagues a "systemic crisis due to inherent contradictions." Yet both may be talking about the same phenomenon and may even agree on its causes. That is *one* difficulty with both kinds of thinking: inflated *or* understated rhetoric.

Third, the manner in which this theoretical trend has pushed aside all those overly rigid disciplinary boundaries (especially among economics, political science, history, and sociology) that academicians have developed in the last half-century is to be thoroughly applauded. If these recent incarnations of Marxism had nothing further to their credit than a focus on institutions and institutional change, on internal contradictions producing that change, and on the breach of disciplinary boundaries to explain it all, they would be worthy of praise as antidotes to much of today's social science.

At another level, proponents of the dependency school and of similar approaches are to be commended for their insistence that we cannot study internal national development in the Third World in isolation from external factors. However obvious this may seem today, one need but glance at most of the textbooks on Latin America in use less than a decade ago to be struck by the conspicuous absence of any serious reference to the United States or to multinational corporations as permanently significant actors in internal Latin American politics. Whether dependency writers will be able to prove their contention that international capitalist evolution more fully explains the poverty and exploitation of Latin American peasants than does the feudal nature of hacienda work relations, we do not know. At least the dependency writers have forced us to face the question. At the same time they have called into question the facile assumption so often made in the 1960s that there is a basic compatibility of interests between developed countries and the Third World. Again, we do not know whether they are correct in their assertion of a basic contradiction between core and periphery or of the need for the periphery to dissociate itself from the core to develop. But again we have been forced to ask, and this is good.

We must be a little careful, however, not to give the impression that these merits are exclusive to dependency theory. Nevertheless, we think it is true that no other orientation is so strongly characterized by their combination. Psychologists like David McClelland undoubtedly emphasize the individual's role in development, and sociologists like Joseph Kahl and Alex Inkeles emphasize values. But most political scientists and economists always focus their analyses at the level of institutions (and Inkeles, though this is rarely acknowledged, seeks primarily to explain values with reference to institutions rather than to posit them as causes). Whatever other deficiencies the various orthodox theories might have, a myopic concentration on the individual and his motives and values characterizes only a very few of them. Moreover, most orthodox social scientists are also interested in change and even in the resistance to change by economically and politically privileged groups, including those created by earlier changes, i.e., by contradictions in the system itself. There is little need to pursue this point further. We merely want to caution against exaggerating the difference in approaches between neo-Marxists and others. Others, too, are interested in institutions and have little time for psychological theories of development. Others, too, are aware of the resistance of economically motivated interest groups. Others, too, are aware that the pattern of development of one society cannot be repeated by others precisely because the first is already developed. Some non-Marxist economists (like Albert Hirschman) are also very sensitive to social and political factors, while others defend with some plausibility the desirability of specialization over a collective quest for expertise in every discipline.

It is, of course, unfair to attack dependency simply by claiming that it says nothing new. At least in its emphasis on combining these perspectives it is new. Let us turn instead to examining what it does say and the logic of its arguments.

What Exactly Is Explained?

One of the major problems with latter-day dependency theory and with world-system theory is that their advocates do not specify very clearly what they claim to explain. The same point can be put in reverse: the advocates of dependency and world-system theories never explicitly or implicitly delineate what they do not claim to be in a position to explain. This is, of course, also a problem with the broader genus to which these species of theory belong, namely Marxism. We all know that Marx allowed for historical peculiarities to determine specifics. He did so when explaining the rise to power of Louis Bonaparte and the policies the emperor pursued. This kind of modest disclaimer does impose some restraint on those who would accuse Marx and the school in general of theoretical imperialism. And yet the nonbeliever, even the sympathetic nonbeliever, or the half-believer who still retains some other links is left with an uneasy feeling that when all is said and done total explanation is still claimed—at least, explanation of all the "essential" features of societal structure and development. What is to be regarded as an "essential," however, is undefined. Theory advocates can always find excuses for failure by asserting that the contradictory or the difficult-to-explain phenomenon is, after all, simply the result of locally specific circumstances or more a matter of detail; that is, of secondary importance, rather than an essential.

Because dependency and world-system theorists fail to delimit exactly what and how much they are explaining (while seeming to claim that it is everything essential) and because they allow for variations caused by historically specific circumstances, they built into their arguments a large degree of flexibility. Varying—even contradictory—institutional structures can all be said to result from basically similar processes. But if this is the case, if similar processes can have different outcomes, what is it that has been explained?

Let us examine one example: dependent development in agriculture. What happens in Third World countries when demand for their agricultural products increases, particularly when multinational corporations are present? It is often suggested that among the usual results are further concentration of land, a proletarianization of at least a significant part of the peasant labor force, and capital-intensive development that increases rural unemployment. Clearly there are cases where these have been the results. Peter Klaren's fascinating study of the development of the sugar industry in northern Peru, for example, documents the reduction of forty Chicama valley haciendas in 1880 to one controlled by German capital in 1920. In the same process a large wage-labor force was also created.[8]

The results, however, are not always so clear-cut. In the 1950s in the northern Peruvian valley of Cajamarca, the Nestle Corporation built a small milk-condensing plant. The effect was not a concentration of landholdings, but the opposite, a dispersion. As landowners focused their attention on those portions of their land where improved pastures could easily be developed, they increasingly lost interest in their remaining lands, which they began to sell. The result was a very significant growth in the small and minifundia property sector. At the same time, landlord needs for labor decreased; cattle demanded less attention than grains. But a rural proletariat (except for a small labor force used primarily for milking) was not created, dependency predictions not withstanding. Because land was available for purchase by displaced peasants, open unemployment did not rise significantly either. Admittedly, the peasants who purchased the land benefited very little if at all. They were left in debt and never gained control over marketing their produce.[9] But this is not the point. The point is that dependent agricultural development in the two cases resulted in *very different* arrangements.

In the Mantaro valley of central Peru—one of the main suppliers of food for Lima—the outcome was different still. The expansion through highland enclosures of the Cerro de Pasco Mining Corporation is well known. Less well known is the impact that the corporation and the growth of Lima had in the fertile Mantaro valley itself. What seems to have occurred was a gradual breakup of estates and some *comunidades* ("Indian communities") into small truck farms. Unlike the Cajamarca peasants, who were pushed onto ever less-useful land and further impoverished by the process, the Mantaro peasantry did rather well. With a source of investment capital (from the wages earned by family members working in the mines), peasants were often able to buy land without going deeply into debt and to maintain control of marketing.[10]

Our point is not that development was uniformly good, that exploitation ceased, that a surplus was no longer extracted, or that some were not hurt while others benefited. Our point is only that in each case different institutional structures—different modes of production—emerged from the process of dependent development, that is development instigated by external factors in which international capital and multinational corporations were deeply involved. It is true that these differences can largely and perhaps adequately be explained by reference to specific local circumstances. Perhaps also there are still essential underlying similarities. But we are left with the uncomfortable feeling that reference to their dependence has explained very little.

Indeed, Marxism, and the various forms of neo-Marxism we are considering, have often been accused with some justice of presenting an interpretation of everything in general and of nothing in particular, except on a catch-as-catch-can basis. Of course, the claim that everything "really important" is explained is not confined to Marxism. It is, by definition, a characteristic of all monistic theories. It is true, for example, of Freudianism (at least in its earlier and more orthodox phases), where everything was to be explained in terms of sex or the broadened concept of "libido." And it is true also of idealism, whether the broad, somewhat mystical form it took with Hegel (who postulated that history was best interpreted as consciousness' growing consciousness of itself) or the later, more concrete and specific forms, as typified by the early and rather sadly overlooked British sociologist L. T. Hobhouse, who had his own general theory of intellectual and moral evolution.[11] We repeat: all monistic, single-factor approaches to events have imperialist claims built into them. That is their nature!

The failure to identify what precisely are the essential characteristics of society that monistic theories explain lays their advocates open to charges of making themselves invulnerable by definition. On the other hand, if they stake out clearly what the "dependent" variable is (to make a dreadful and confusing pun), they lay themselves open to refutation. Thus Immanuel Wallerstein, in his *World System,* does stake out, at least once, what he regards as the essence of the system. And not surprisingly for a Marxist, it is the relationship of labor to the means of production. "Free labor is the form of control used for skilled work in the core countries, whereas coerced labor is used for less skilled labor in peripheral ones. The combination thereof is the essence of capitalism."[12] Note the ambiguity, a critical ambiguity, in that statement: it contrasts the control of skilled labor in metropolitan countries with that of unskilled in peripheral ones. It is therefore a double contrast that leaves the reader confused as to what precisely is being contrasted. For if skilled labor in peripheral countries were to be likewise controlled by free markets as in core countries and if unskilled labor in core countries were also coerced as in peripheral countries, then there would be no contrast at all and the distinction between core and periphery would disappear.

This obviously cannot be what Wallerstein intends. We guess that he intends to emphasize that the international division of labor (a key idea) is such that core countries specialize in work requiring skilled labor, leaving less-skilled work to the peripheral countries. The fact that unskilled labor is coerced would then become secondary. Even though there may be more unskilled labor, and therefore more coercion, in the peripheral countries, it is not a distinguishing characteristic of these countries alone. As in so many instances, when writings are based on a single, highly dramatic, and flexible image (as is the case of Wallerstein's use of the concept "labor"), the key ideas are often indirectly conjured up and evoked, rather than stated with requisite precision.

Once the two ideas (pertaining to the international division of labor on the one hand and to the different institutions used to control different types of labor on the other) are clearly separated from each other, the second, at least, becomes more challengeable. No one would argue with the assertion that unskilled labor is often obtained, and often controlled, through coercion. It is indeed often so controlled, but not only in latter-day peripheral societies within the capitalist system. In the past whenever large masses of unskilled labor were needed for unpleasant work (and most unskilled work is not pleasant), coercion was needed to get people to do it, unless a labor surplus in a free market forced people to work without the direct intervention of those who wanted the labor done. Egyptian pyramids were built that way, as was the White Sea Canal in the Soviet Union. Caribbean plantations supplying a world capitalist system were indeed based upon coercion, but then so were Roman ones. The powerful have always tended to use coercion to get done whatever dirty work they wanted done, and what they have wanted has always included a good deal of economically relevant work as well as religious and political work.

In sum, by not stating very clearly exactly what the theory is supposed to explain and what it cannot explain, evaluation becomes very difficult. The situation becomes even more acute when additional concepts are invented, ex post facto, to explain inconvenient facts: for example, when "false consciousness" is used to explain the absence of working-class revolutionary consciousness or when "semiperiphery" accounts for the development of countries that theoretically should not have been able to develop.

Statistical Association Versus Causality: *Post Hoc, Ergo Propter Hoc*, and Other Possible Problems with Dependency Theory

Another epistemological trap that dependency theory risks falling into is the old one of *post hoc, ergo propter hoc.* Merely because some event A occurs after some event B or in the context of event B, can we say that A occurred as a result of B? It should be obvious to almost anyone that a great deal of "maldevelopment" exists in the Third World and that much of this maldevelopment is directly or indirectly associated with capitalism—after all, for the last few centuries the world has been largely capitalist. But can we conclude logically that capitalism is the necessary cause of these evils and, especially, that they would not be present in some other institutional arrangement? Dependency theorists have done a fascinating job of documenting both Third World maldevelopment and the practices of multinational corporations that seem linked to it. But this is not sufficient. It shows association but not necessarily a unique type of causality. At some point they must at least attempt to deal with the latter. Note that we are not rejecting their contentions. We are only arguing that they have not yet proven their case.

Since it is frequently argued that dependency today takes

form primarily through the activities of multinational corporations (MNCs), we will illustrate our argument by focusing on
these corporations. One of the most serious charges brought
against MNCs is that they have brought to development an inappropriate level of technology, i.e., technology with high
capital content—especially capital based on foreign purchases—
and low labor usage. Mobil's refineries in Venezuela or Toyota's
assembly plants in Peru are but two examples of high-technology
investments, costing millions yet employing relatively few.
Barnet and Müller cite a study of high-technology industry in
Colombia in which it was found that the cost of investment per
job created more than doubled between 1957 and 1966.[13]
Certainly technology is being diffused by MNCs in countries
that have all too little foreign exchange and too much labor,
and in this sense it is unquestionably inappropriate. But is such
a development pattern spread *only* by MNCs and *only* because
of them? Or are there good reasons—as well as some bad ones—
for technological proliferation in any case? Capital-intensive
development does avoid labor problems. But avoiding labor
problems may be attractive to many people in many systems,
not only to MNCs. And after all, capital-intensive technology
is what exists and it is readily available. Investors, whether
MNCs, local businessmen, or governments, may find it easier
and in the short run cheaper to purchase existing technology,
whether from ITT or from the USSR. Has the Soviet Union,
whose motives should theoretically be somewhat dissimilar
from those of MNCs, brought to its aid projects in Africa or
to its joint enterprises in Eastern Europe a more appropriate
level of technology? The Soviets did help Egypt build the Aswan
Dam, widely considered to be inappropriate. For reasons of
status, if nothing else, local leaders in any institutional order
may still prefer atomic energy plants to smaller, perhaps
cheaper, but much less "modern" hydroelectric stations. One
of the authors has heard even a self-styled Maoist in Peru argue
vehemently for purchasing large tractors for peasant cooperatives, although it is clear that this would put peasants out of
work. In other words, although there is no question that MNCs
do bring to development an inappropriate technology, the problem might well continue to exist without the actions of the MNCs.

It is often noted that capital-intensive investment not only creates a limited number of new jobs but also actually increases unemployment in the process by displacing local traditional producers. Thus, when the Cerro de Pasco Mining Corporation enclosed pastures to begin developing purebred cattle, peasants were driven from their lands. Even though meat production rose, employment was lowered. Textile industries everywhere have put local weavers out of work. Plastic dishes have made traditional potters obsolete. We agree that MNCs probably do drive local artisans out of work, but so do local private and government investments. The industrialization process seems to displace people, and it most likely would do so under any system, whether capitalist or socialist, unless the decision was made not to industrialize. We do not think that is what the dependency theorists are advocating.

Another of the charges frequently brought against MNCs is that they do not invest in new areas but expand primarily by buying up local small enterprises, thus discouraging national entrepreneurs who cannot compete. The Peruvian fish-meal industry was initially developed largely by Peruvian nationals, but when many of the local entrepreneurs overextended themselves and could not pay their debts, foreign capital, with greater access to credit, moved in. We are all aware that ITT expanded its operations in Chile chiefly by buying up other local firms or, perhaps just as important, other MNCs.[14] This process undoubtedly does account for much (but not all) multinational expansion, and it strikes us as a shame. But is this a function of MNCs qua MNCs, or simply of power? Would eliminating MNCs change the situation drastically? We suspect not. Assuming that some semblance of a private market were maintained, would not local investors with access to adequate financing buy out those without? That seems to be what is occurring in Chile today. Indeed, it is what Marx predicted 120 years ago. And if the private sector were curtailed in favor of the state, would not the state engage in similar kinds of activities? After all, in Peru the Velasco government took over the fishing industry—both national and foreign—when the latter found itself in even graver financial difficulties.

Let us examine one last charge against MNCs: they are a

corrupting influence. They cheat on taxes, bribe local officials, illegally transfer money out of host countries, and engage in many other petty and major crimes. Thus in 1968 the International Petroleum Company (IPC)—a symbol of evil if ever there was one—was accused of bribing officials in the Belaunde government to obtain a favorable contract (the famous *pagina once*). Whether the IPC was guilty of this particular crime—which served to justify a coup—we do not know, but we are convinced that it was guilty of many others. However, the critical issue is not whether the IPC cheated; it is whether eliminating MNCs, or for that matter capitalism, would eliminate corruption. Would some other form of oil industry—a national private firm, a state corporation, or even an organization run by the workers—be any less corrupt?

We are reminded of an anecdote a banker in Peru related to us concerning an American with a small business who was determined to pay every penny of his taxes and observe Peruvian law to the letter. Every year he was pestered by the tax collector, who somehow managed to find any number of minor evasions. Only after the businessman finally began to keep two sets of books, cheat on his taxes, and agree to pay a portion to the tax auditor did his problems cease. Corruption is, after all, a two-way street. Peruvian businessmen also cheat on taxes, and they also struggle illegally to transfer money abroad. And not just businessmen engage in such activities, but also workers, housewives, bureaucrats, and, we would venture to state, even labor unions.

Clearly MNCs are among the primary participants in corruption—even among the instigators of numerous individual cases—but because of their power they are among the primary participants in everything. Can we conclude that corruption exists because of the MNCs, or that it would not, or would be significantly reduced, in some other institutional arrangement?

The same argument can be extended to capitalism in general. The other great accusation levied against the capitalist world system is that it maneuvered the underdeveloped countries into a worldwide division of labor, compelling them to rely heavily on one or a very few raw-material exports, thus imperiling their stability and growth. It is true that world capitalism did do precisely that. There was no other system around to do it! However, in the latter part of the 1960s, there was. At this time, Fidel Castro enthusiastically accepted the policy of relying on the monoexport of raw materials, although he had rejected it earlier.

> We began purchasing a great number of items that were necessary for our economy from the socialist camp—and especially from the Soviet Union.
>
> As a result of this and the needs of a developing country—we might even say of a disorganized country, as every country in the first stage of revolutionary process is disorganized—our trade deficit with the Soviet Union grew larger with every passing year. . . .
>
> There was only one item whose exports to the Soviet Union could be increased: sugar. As a result of this, we proposed a long-term sugar export agreement to the Soviet Union, an agreement which would help meet the growing needs presented by our economy—and especially our underdevelopment.[15]

With this logic he justified integrating Cuba not into the world capitalist but into the world socialist system with the production of sugar. It simply appeared a rather sensible policy to follow for an island of Cuba's location, soil, and climate, even though Castro carried it to a disastrous extreme. He also carried to an extreme yet another evil supposedly linked to capitalism alone: indebtedness to, and hence dependence on, a metropolitan power, in this instance, the USSR. That the Soviet Union may or may not exploit its advantage as much as did the United States is not germane. From the point of view of the less-developed country, the degree of dependence is the same.

There are probably many evils associated with all systems. At the same time, it is possible and even likely that every system may have some evils that are unique to it. We feel we know those of late capitalism better than those of the later stages of some other system simply because no other system has been around as long. But certainly the early stages of various socialist systems seem to have had their share of problems, just as the early stages of capitalism had theirs, especially once allowances are made for differences in time and place. Socialist developing societies, for example, have gone through long periods of economic stagnation (as did Cuba in the 1960s and East Germany in the 1950s and early 1960s), which have sometimes been followed by bursts of growth, as in capitalist societies such as Brazil. The evils of bureaucracy and the inefficiencies of extreme swings in policy that have marked socialist countries may be less costly. But then again, they may not be less costly than the enormous loss due to underutilized and misapplied resources that so blatantly characterized the capitalist countries on their road to development.

We do not wish to belabor our point, nor do we wish to sound overly reactionary. We are not rejecting the dependency assertions. We are only trying to show that they have not proven their case and that the nature of their argument is such that it may be impossible to do so.

There are three assertions that dependency theorists must at least attempt to formulate with some degree of clarity and precision. Only by doing so can their indictment of capitalism be credible. First, they need to state clearly which evils are only *temporally* associated with capitalism (all of them are) and which are, for good and stated reasons, exclusively and *causally* associated with capitalism. In other words, they must identify those evils that simply could not or would not occur under any other system and specifically under any socialist system as *it would run in practice.* For it is obviously unfair to contrast the evils of an actual system, with all its known warts, with the ideal model of another system. The ideal model of capitalism functions fairly well too.

To accomplish this, dependency theorists must not only present clear and logical arguments, but also show that their own explanations are better or more adequate than those offered by others. Probably everyone except the most recalcitrant supporters of the Pinochet regime will admit that brutal repression goes on in Chile today. It is often asserted that capitalism (at least in the form it has taken in Chile) is what has made this repression necessary. It may well be. But there are alternative explanations, and they ought to be at least considered. Samuel Huntington might argue that it is not capitalism but rather a politically overmobilized system—too many organized groups demanding too much of a government rather weak in resources—

that makes repression a must.[16] Or perhaps we are simply dealing with a group of evil men who find repression and vengeance an easy and somewhat satisfying way to operate.

Second, if critics take the more cautious road of admitting that certain evils are equally likely to occur in another system while claiming that monopoly capitalism exaggerates them, they are unfortunately under an obligation, however difficult to fulfill, of specifying how and by how much capitalism exaggerates these evils. By how much is current repression of dissent worse in Chile, five years after the coup, than it is in Cuba today, or more fairly, than it was five years after the 1959 revolution?

Finally, dependency theorists need to specify what evils they believe to be unique to alternative systems of development and what common evils they believe might in turn be exaggerated by these alternative systems. The extreme swings of policy we have witnessed in the two decades following the Soviet, Chinese, and Cuban revolutions, with the dislocation and "surplus repression" that have accompanied them (to partly misuse Marcuse's term), may be costs the capitalist system does not exact to the same degree.

We really have no intention of prejudging the bottom line on a grand balance sheet weighing all these costs and benefits, even though by challenging dependency theory to greater precision we may unfortunately appear to be unsympathetic toward it. Let us emphasize that we hold no absolute and unconditional brief for capitalism in any shape, manner, or form. We have a nagging belief that it is not possible, either in practice or in logic, to engage in such a quantitative balancing operation. But something of a good-faith attempt has to be made if critiques of either socialism or capitalism are to withstand logical analysis. And if the outcome is indeed uncertain and ambiguous, as we believe it is bound to be, then those who proclaim the absolute merits of one system over another need to do so with appropriate caution.

Dependency and the Dangers of Functionalism

Another problem with dependency and world-system theories is that they are based to a certain extent on a functionalist proposition. Like other functionalists, the advocates of these approaches examine any part of a system, any one institution or event, in view of the support it gives to the survival of the system as a whole. In addition, they are biased toward believing that every event that happens and every institution that exists supports the system and was probably generated or created for that reason. And should some institution, or some trend, be inimical to the system, the approach has a perfect explanation: it shows the contradictions inherent in the system. Note that this, again, is somewhat similar to the Freudian style of reasoning. If a sexual motivation is not apparent, it simply shows that repression is at work. Both theories have postulated mechanisms that make it very difficult for them to be disproven, since logically any element in a system must have either a positive or a negative effect on another element, however slight that effect may be. Rain is either welcome or not; it is rarely neutral.

But this criticism, which is seriously and not flippantly intended, is merely one way of phrasing the general epistemological reservations we have vis-à-vis any and all functional approaches. They are always in some almost indefinable way thoroughly refreshing and stimulating. At least we find them so. But they are logically flawed and cannot by themselves satisfactorily account for specific historical events.

There is one other epistemological trap faced by functionalism in general that lies in wait for dependency theory. We refer to the trap of teleology, which posits that a cause exists because of the effect it has. If a human agent, conscious of the effect, is posited as the creator of the cause, there is no problem. But when supraindividual entities—such as metropolitan countries as a whole or the "system"—are posited as creators of institutions or trends, then there are problems. To postulate that landlords dissolve communal village landholdings in part to create a destitute labor force in dire need of work, however poorly paid each laborer may be, is methodologically acceptable. We know it to be true, so it had better be acceptable! But to postulate that the population is growing *because* the basic system benefits from the existence of a reserve army of unemployed begins to sound uncomfortably anthropomorphic. The gnomes of London and Washington probably did not have the foresight, the energy, or the implementing capacity to do all the things of which they stand accused, often by ambiguous phrasing and innuendo rather than explicit statement. Reasoning of this kind has led to criticism that there is a vaguely paranoid element in some strands of Marxist and dependency theory: advocates allude to hidden but deliberately guiding hands where innocuous but reasonable explanations are possible and therefore preferable.

Summary and Conclusions

In this chapter we have criticized the dependency and world-system approaches at two levels, the first theoretical or epistemological, the second more empirical. At the first level, we have maintained that, because of a certain vagueness and circularity in the arguments presented, the advocates of dependency have not yet proven their case, and that it may, in fact, be impossible to prove. We pointed to their failure to define exactly what the approach is meant to explain, the fact that they often confuse association with causality, and that from effect they frequently infer intent. We do not wish to imply by these criticisms that we necessarily believe these approaches to be wrong; they may very well not be. Nor do we think their advocates cannot in some instances make a better case. Stronger arguments can probably be made. We believe it is incumbent upon dependency theorists to at least try to make them.

However, we have also been advancing criticism on another level. Those who adopt a dependency perspective are to a very large extent advocates of a particular political stance—they are committed to showing that capitalism is bad. It seems to us that they intend to imply by such a position that there were or are "better" alternatives. If not, what do they intend? This implication, however, is practically never explicitly spelled out. It could and should be, and it raises a question that is to some extent empirical. Was there in the 1500s some alternative to capitalist development that might feasibly have led with less pain to a better world today? Is there presently an alternative, whether revolutionary or reformist, that is both feasible and better? The implication is that one does exist and that it is probably some form of socialism. That may well be. And we certainly do not want to defend the present order. But, again, we believe it is incumbent upon dependency theorists to confront the question directly.

Andre Gunder Frank's idea of the historical "development of underdevelopment" further clarifies this dilemma. After 400 years of capitalist evolution, Latin America is unquestionably still poor and exploited, and—understating the problem somewhat—there is still much going on that is not very nice. (Whether this is because of, in spite of, or simply in association with capitalism is another matter. We have tried to show that the argument has not dealt sufficiently with this issue either.) But is the dependency school trying to say that if capitalism had not entered in the past, the state of things in Latin America today would be much better? If this is not what they mean to imply, what *do* they mean? If it is what they intend to say, then we find ourselves feeling a bit uncomfortable. For if capitalism had not entered, what would have? Was there really any feasible alternative to capitalist development in 1536 and would it really have been much better? Where was it to be found? In Latin America? Do they mean to say that if the Incas had not been conquered, Peru might be far ahead of where it is today and have avoided many of the problems it currently faces? Was there some alternative available elsewhere in Europe? We are not being facetious. To posit some abstract socialism 400 years after the fact is not sufficient. We think serious scholars have an obligation to explicitly spell out what that alternative might have been and to show that it was both possible in 1536 and, in terms of those elements that they value, better.

The same difficulty is present if we focus on the contemporary world. These approaches seem to indicate that since dependent capitalist development is clearly bad, what is necessary is a break with the capitalist world system, whether by revolutionary or reformist means. The implication is that such a dissociation would be both feasible and beneficial, i.e., that it would produce effects that, when measured against the present, would be on the whole positive. Unfortunately, to show, however well, that today's world is both dependent and miserable is not a sufficient demonstration for all that follows. Dependency advocates must at some point confront the dilemma directly. Is there any real and practical alternative that avoids the pitfalls of development in today's capitalist world without exacerbating new ones?

Certainly such dissociation is no easy task. There are at least three fascinating examples of nations in the contemporary era that have tried to withdraw, and in each case the results are ambiguous. The first is the People's Republic of China. We are not China scholars and are thus hesitant to advance opinions about the successes or failures of Mao's revolution. But we are intrigued and even a little disturbed by what is occurring in China today. Why, after thirty years of revolutionary development, have experienced Chinese leaders suddenly seen fit to begin to speak of dividing rural cooperatives and of returning to a more capitalist form of agriculture? What has made them decide to come courting the MNCs, seeking foreign investments as a source of Western technology?

The second case is Cuba. Castro's accomplishments, whether in education, health care, or distribution of wealth, have been impressive. But has he succeeded in breaking dependency? As we noted above, financially Cuba seems only to have shifted dependence from the United States to the USSR. After a brief but intense effort to diversify its economy, the country has returned to—and Fidel has endorsed—continued reliance on a single agricultural export. Most recently he too has begun to court the MNCs, though with controls, of course.

The final case is Peru, which between 1968 and 1975 sought— we believe sincerely—to lessen its dependence on the world capitalist system in general and on MNCs in particular. To do so Peru undertook widespread nationalizations, dictated stiff industrial codes governing foreign investments, fought to promote a common international front to outside investors by strengthening the Andean Market, attempted to rally and unify the Third World, and sought to diversify its trade by increasing its ties with the socialist bloc. Moreover, in many of these measures Peru was rather successful. The weight of MNCs in the domestic economy was reduced, better conditions were obtained from firms like Bayer, the Andean Market for a time appeared much stronger, and the country developed considerable trade with the East. However, as Alfred Stepan so brilliantly argues, none of these policies obviated Peru's need for investment capital, which it was unable to raise internally. What in effect occurred was that Peru traded its direct dependence on MNCs for an equally insidious financial dependence on multinational banks, the World Bank, and the International Monetary Fund (IMF).[17] Today the IMF dictates Peru's development policies with at least as much force as did the multinationals ten years ago. To argue that the Generals did not go far enough or that they were not sincere is to beg the question. It is too easy a way to dismiss their lack of success.

In other words, in each of these cases dissociation has proven neither entirely feasible nor entirely good. In each some of the evils associated with international capitalism may have been lessened, but others have clearly remained and new difficulties have arisen. Indeed, it is possible that when all is said and done the root of dependence lies less in capitalism than in under-development per se. Dependence and some of the ills associated with it may be unavoidable, whether under capitalism, socialism, or any other system. Our point here, however, is not to assert this grim conclusion, which in any case we have not really proven. It is only to argue that dependency advocates must respond to this possibility, not just assume it out of existence. Along with analyzing the ills of capitalism, they must consider the difficulties that those who have tried other paths have in fact confronted. By and large they have not done so.

When interpreting the most important world events of the day we ought not to abandon our common sense. The fall of the Shah in early 1979 certainly can be interpreted substantially in terms of world capitalism—but only substantially. Monarchies as general institutions predate capitalism, and they would fall every now and then even if capitalism were not declining. Are the miniwar between China and Vietnam and the strains between the USSR and China also merely ultimate consequences of world capitalism? Or do they represent what are practically eternal struggles? When Libya helped Idi Amin or China helped Cambodia, were these in principle merely the result of capitalist distortions? Or have nations always had unsavory friends—much like the United States in Nicaragua? Is evil perhaps not a good deal more widespread than capitalism?

Finally, and to conclude, we wish to reemphasize that our intention in this chapter has not been to make a case for capitalism or the "modernization" road to development. Nor has it been to reject the dependency approach. We are in many ways sympathetic with key points raised in dependency arguments. We think, however, that the advocates of these approaches fall into a number of errors, both theoretical and empirical. Unfortunately, by not confronting these problems directly, they do themselves a great disservice.

Notes

1. One very enlightening attempt to begin a debate is made in a paper presented at Duke University by Joseph V. Remenyi, an economist seeking to set the record straight on the important, if narrow and specific, issue: did orthodox development economists in the 1950s and 1960s really deny that the fate of the less-developed countries (LDCs) was negatively affected by living in the shadow of the highly industrialized countries ("Toward a reconciliation of dependency theory and neo-classical economics?"). Did the neoclassicists, as they have been accused of doing, in fact conceptualize the LDCs as autonomous economies that would have to, and that could, recapitulate the developmental stages of the industrialized countries? Or does this represent a caricature of the state of economics in the 1960s: a straw man using Walt Rostow as evidence when, in fact, Rostow was never accepted by any large or influential segment of economists.

Another very thorough attempt at reasonable discourse is represented by Alejandro Portes's "The Sociology of National Development," *American Journal of Sociology* 28 (July 1976):55–85.

2. *Latin American Perspectives* 1 (1974).

3. One of the clearest neo-Marxist statements in a limited space is in our opinion Susanne Bodenheimer, "Dependency and Imperialism: The Root of Latin American Underdevelopment," in K. T. Fann and Donald C. Hodges, eds., *Readings in U.S. Imperialism* (Boston: Porter Sargent, 1971), pp. 155–81.

4. Richard R. Fagen, "Studying Latin American Politics: Some Implications of a Dependencia Approach," *Latin American Research Review* 12 (1977):3–26.

5. For a list of charges against MNCs, see Richard Barnet and Ronald

Müller, *Global Reach* (New York: Touchstone, 1974), particularly Chapters 6, 7, and 8.

6. The Economic Commission for Latin America (in Spanish, CEPAL) is a regional research and policy formulating unit of the United Nation's Economic and Social Council.

7. Ronald Chilcote, "Dependency: A Critical Synthesis of the Literature," *Latin American Perspectives* 1 (1974):4-29. See, also, Fagen, "Studying Latin American Politics"; and Arturo and Samuel Valenzuela, "Modernization and Dependency, Alternative Perspectives in the Study of Latin American Underdevelopment," *Comparative Politics* 10 (July 1978):535-57.

8. Peter Klaren, *Modernization, Dislocation and Aprismo* (Austin: University of Texas Press, 1973).

9. We know of no in-depth studies of this process. The conclusions are gleaned from data gathered by one of the authors during dissertation research. Some aspects are considered by Efraín Franco and Francois Gorget, "Evaluación del proyecto Cajamarca–La Libertad," mimeographed (Cajamarca: Proyecto Cajamarca–La Libertad, Programa de Estudios Socio-económicos, 1976).

10. Again, our conclusions emerge from a variety of sources. See, for example, Giorgio Alberti, *Poder y conflicto social an el Valle del Mantaro* (Lima: Instituto de Estudios Peruanos, 1974).

11. See Robert A. Nisbet, *Social Change and History: Aspects of the Western Theory of Development* (New York: Oxford University Press, 1969). See, also, the rebuttal by Gerhard Lenski, "History and Social Change," *American Journal of Sociology* 82 (November 1976):576-84.

12. Immanuel Wallerstein, *The Modern World-System: Capitalist Agriculture and the Origins of the European World-Economy in the Sixteenth Century* (New York: Academic Press, 1974), p. 127.

13. Barnet and Müller, *Global Reach*, p. 169.

14. Thus ITT's properties in Chile included Standard Electric, All America Cables and Radio, two Sheraton Hotels, ITT World Directories, and ITT World Communications. See Dale Johnson, *The Chilean Road to Socialism* (Garden City, N.Y.: Doubleday, 1973), p. 6.

15. Fidel Castro, "Report on the Sugar Harvest," cited in Rolando E. Bonachea and Nelson P. Valdés, eds., *Cuba in Revolution* (Garden City, N.Y.: Doubleday, 1972), p. 262.

16. Samuel Huntington, *Political Order in Changing Societies* (New Haven: Yale University Press, 1968), pp. 1-92.

17. Alfred Stepan, *The State and Society: Peru in Comparative Perspective* (Princeton: Princeton University Press, 1978), Chapter 7.

3

Inter-American Relations in Global Perspective

Gustavo Lagos
Alberto Van Klaveren

Exhaustion of the Traditional Analytic Model

The study of relations between the United States and Latin America, sometimes termed inter-American relations,[1] constitutes one of the most traditional and respected areas of academic specialization in both the United States and Latin America. It could not be otherwise: to us it seems logical to assume that a very close relationship exists between the evolution of the interests of the foreign policy of a country and the development of area studies in its institutions of higher education. In the United States, studies of inter-American relations have reflected the priority assigned to the region by private and official U.S. interests. In the case of Latin America, this relationship is less evident, because there the development of the social sciences has been somewhat accidental and irregular as a result of exogenous factors (political instability, lack of resources, hostility of governing groups, and so on) and of the relative backwardness of some branches of the social sciences. These factors particularly affect the policy-oriented disciplines of political science, international relations, and interpretive history—disciplines within which the study of inter-American relations is normally situated. Despite the differences between regions, however, there exists in Latin America a lengthy, distinguished tradition in the study of inter-American relations which is comparable to that found in the United States.

The first studies of inter-American relations were produced

in the initial decades of this century, during a period in which
the United States, as a consequence of the extraordinary post–
Civil War growth of its economy, became the new imperial
power in the region.[2] This was the period of unbraked competition with the European countries for the not-inappreciable markets of the region, of armed interventions in the countries of
Central America and the Caribbean with the objective of protecting the private-sector investments and ostensibly the national
security of the United States and of various customs union
projects destined to assure the free and perhaps exclusive flow
of U.S. products to Latin America. This was the period of the
displacement of all extrahemispheric influences that could
threaten North American hegemony in the formally independent
countries of the hemisphere. Only the countries of the Río de la
Plata, dominated by the British until the second half of this century, were exceptions to this general pattern.

Two factors seem to have exercised decisive influence on the
evolution of inter-American studies during that epoch: the
general level of development of the social sciences and the demands and repercussions of North American policy in the
region. The first factor explains the abundance of juridical and
historicodescriptive studies in the field of inter-American relations. Numerous large volumes appeared concerning the diplomatic history of these relations, based on correspondence,
personal diaries of protagonists, acts of hemispheric conferences,
and diverse compilations and treaties of universal and especially
of regional international law. During this period few economic
and political works were produced, and, with few exceptions,
those that did appear emphasized descriptive rather than
analytic approaches to understanding hemispheric relations.
This is not surprising if one remembers that both political
science and the discipline of international relations were then in
their infancy. It also partially explains the markedly uncritical,
apologetic perspective from which North American scholars
inspected the official policies of Washington in Latin America.
In Latin America, the evolution of inter-American studies was
no different. Works of descriptive, historical, and juridical
exegesis predominated, a tendency that unfortunately has been
maintained until this day in the academically less-developed

countries of the region. There were also the denunciatory writings of the brilliant and loquacious *pensadores* ("thinkers") and politicians who protested the regional political hegemony of the United States.

The enunciation of the Good Neighbor Policy and the Pan-American enthusiasm that characterized the years preceding World War II introduced some modifications into this picture. Historical studies improved in quality, especially in the United States, and historians tried—not always with success—to maintain in their work a relative autonomy with respect to official Department of State interpretations. Juridical works continued to appear, but attention began to focus on the reality that underlay the formal norms of the inter-American system. This was the period of the classic studies of intervention, of the general Latin American policy of the United States, and of the evolution of Latin American thought with special emphasis on hemispheric relations.

The quantitative and qualitative development of studies on hemispheric relations was not interrupted by World War II, despite the postwar triumph of globalistic tendencies in North American foreign policy. These tendencies encouraged Washington to give preferential treatment to Europe and Asia and to relegate inter-American relations to a secondary level. From the point of view of national security and of North American economic interests, Latin America appeared to be a secure region in which no important threat was likely to emerge. Despite these changes in the priorities of U.S. foreign policy, the end of the conflict inaugurated a great growth in inter-American studies. This was most clearly demonstrated by the surge of economic analyses of relations between the United States and Latin America, empirical analyses employing data that only a few years before were striking by their absence. The Latin American contributions used methodologies developed principally by regional organizations, especially the Economic Commission for Latin America (ECLA). In the area of political analysis, numerous works of rather uneven quality appeared. Although in the majority of these works the dominant focus was upon historicodescriptive analysis, a number of authors interpreted inter-American interactions in the light of theoretical foci that were emerging from the discipline of international relations. Nevertheless, this linking of an area study with theoretical currents fashionable in the fields of political science and international relations was more implicit than explicit; and, in general terms, a separation grew between the theoretical development of these disciplines and that of inter-American studies. With exceptions, the same separate development phenomenon occurred in Latin America. It can be explained in part by the general underdevelopment of social science in the region, where descriptive, impressionistic, and prescriptive studies remained the rule during the 1950s.

These tendencies continued until the launching of the Alliance for Progress, an event that precipitated a veritable boom in inter-American studies. The field of economic relations continued developing on the bases set forth in the decade of the fifties, and the Latin American foci began to be disseminated and followed in the United States in the same fashion that the Alliance for Progress, at least in its formal presentation, produced an echo of aspirations in Latin America. Without denying the merit of various individual works published during this period, the mainstream of political and general studies on inter-American relations continued to be characterized by their historicodescriptive nature and by their lack of theoretical sophistication. This was true despite developments in the discipline of international relations, not only in theoretical postulates but also in practical application to areas such as U.S.–Soviet relations.

The failure of the Alliance for Progress marked the end of an era in the analysis of inter-American relations. The crisis in North American policy toward the region was clearly reflected in the academic world. Traditional models began to lose effectiveness and were ignored by young scholars who were being initiated into the study of inter-American relations. The classics were replaced in bibliographies by foci that a short time before were considered anathema in any established program on inter-American relations. Some authors began the revision with their own foci, adopting paradigms totally different from and even opposed to those that inspired their first works. In summary, an academic and intellectual tradition that had developed in the first decades of this century and had become the established perspective during the apogee of the inter-American system began to be discarded. This tradition had been intimately tied to what Abraham Lowenthal calls the "hegemonic presumption" of the United States in Latin America, the concept that in the rhetoric of the inter-American system was termed the "community of interests" or the "special relationship."[3]

Just as successive U.S. policies toward Latin America were based upon the principle that the diverse peoples of the hemisphere maintained a special relationship different from the rest of the world,[4] studies of inter-American relations also stressed the supposed idiosyncratic features of regional relations. This resulted in the complete isolation of inter-American studies from global phenomena that were altering the economic and political physiognomy of the international system as a whole. In this chapter we stress three basic consequences of this focus. First, the visible divorce of the evolution of the international relations discipline in general from the evolution of inter-American studies created an absence of theoretical models that described, explained, and predicted possible tendencies in relations between the United States and Latin America. Second, the markedly state-centered character of the majority of the works within this tradition was translated into a nonconsideration of important transnational and global actors such as multinational corporations and labor, political, and religious movements. Finally, the focus excluded analyses of the relations of hemispheric members with other actors situated outside this narrow regional ambit (countries of Western Europe, Japan, socialist countries, countries and movements of Asia and Africa, and so on) and of the impact that these relations have had on the hemispheric system. The influence that the hegemonic presumption exercised in these developments cannot be underestimated.

Reactions to the exhaustion of the traditional analytic model for the inter-American system were not long in coming. The discovery of dependency theory is certainly one such reaction, a strangely delayed reaction to the basic postulates of the traditional focus that were expressed in the 1950s in Latin America.[5] Another reaction by various authors has been to analyze inter-American relations by the application of general theoretical categories developed in behavioral political science and the discipline of international relations. In his excellent review of recent inter-American literature, Jorge Domínguez reaches the conclusion that those foci that hold the most promise of success in the field of inter-American relations are the "unorthodox dependence perspectives" and the "political systems perspectives,"[6] whose validity, it seems to us, ranges far beyond the inter-American system. Other recent works on inter-American relations also exhibit the tendency to situate hemispheric reality within a more global context.[7]

But the exhaustion of the traditional model does not merely necessitate seeking theoretical perspectives on those same themes that constituted the object of traditional analysis. It is also necessary to reformulate these themes in the light of significant changes that have occurred throughout the hemisphere in recent decades. For Latin American social sciences the challenge is clear. It involves transcending the limits of the inter-American system and looking for *relevant* themes from the point of view of the ties and interests of the region. Such an approach makes it possible to *maximize* the presence of Latin America, not simply in the narrow and obsolete hemispheric model, but in the broader international system, with a view to construction of a new world order.

In the following pages an agenda is proposed that contains three areas of investigation of the international reality of the Latin American countries, i.e., of Latin America viewed in its global perspective. This perspective seems to be the only appropriate one for dealing with the external ties of the region in an increasingly interdependent and complex world.

A Research Agenda

Latin America in Triangular Relations

The present North American administration seems to perceive the configuration of power at the world level as a combination of a bipolar structure within a broader structure of two superimposed triangles in which various states interact. The structure is bipolar because the power of the Soviet Union and the United States is greatly disproportional with respect to the other countries from the political, military, and economic point of view.

Nevertheless, this power is in large part unusable and therefore conducive to paralysis (which the Chinese have taken advantage of to affect the Soviet–North American relationship). It creates imbalances that increase uncertainty, complicate the adoption of policies, and stimulate the development of additional options.

The two triangles are formed by the interactions among the United States, the Soviet Union, and China on the one hand and by the interactions among the United States, Japan, and the European Economic Community (EEC) on the other. The first is by nature competitive, whereas the second is of a cooperative character. These are the central foci of a multiple-power game that will be maintained as long as there is no major alternative in the bipolar United States–Soviet Union structure. Possible triangular relationships of secondary importance are also emerging—such as the efforts to form a China–Japan–U.S. triangle—but it is yet premature to assign a central character to these new triangles.

The grand design of the Carter administration is inscribed within this vision. It consists of making the U.S.–Soviet Union–China triangle less competitive and the U.S.–Japan–EEC triangle more cooperative. The second triangle is to be transformed into a community of developed nations supported not only by inter-mingled power but also by a common ideology: the human and political values shared by the industrial democracies of which it is formed. This policy has impelled the Trilateral Commission, an organism created by North American initiative, to support such objectives at the private level. The forging of this community is of central importance to Washington; it carries far more importance than the triangular relationships with the two Communist powers. By means of this alliance, the United States believes that world economic recovery can be stimulated while the economic expansion of the capitalist powers is promoted. In addition, this community would promote the cooperation of the countries of the Third World, a crucial consideration after the OPEC–Third World alliance in the North-South dialogue. This explains the desire of the United States to abandon the policy of confrontation or semiconfrontation regarding the developing nations that characterized the Nixon-Ford-Kissinger design. What is essential is that this Washington-based triangular vision of the world rests not on the balance of power but on a policy of maneuvering that these multiple relations make possible.

Whatever the validity of this vision, the objective fact is that the present policy of the Carter administration is based on it. How does Latin America fit into this vision? In our judgment, the transformation of Latin America in recent decades necessitates a reformulation of the interpretation of its relations with the United States and with the rest of the world. The triangular scheme provides this opportunity.

Concretely, we propose that instead of studying U.S.–Latin American relations in the traditional manner, an area of research should be developed that places such ties within the context of multiple political, economic, and military interactions between the region and the capitalist triangle on the one hand and the non–Latin American Third World on the other. Our central hypothesis is that the evolving relations of the most important Latin American countries with Europe and Japan on the one hand and with the Third World on the other are acquiring particular relevance with respect to U.S.–Latin American relations. In other words, Latin America is diversifying its international relationships in various fields, altering the traditional pattern of its ties with the old Colossus of the North. This is encouraged by the multipolar fluidity of the international system and by détente, which permits a greater margin of maneuvers for the international policy of Latin American states.

The extent to which the traditional pattern of U.S.–Latin American relations is altered will vary from country to country and will depend upon the international status of the different Latin American nations. This consideration obliges us to study different cases that will reveal the validity of the general hypothesis. To do this we propose to select cases from three categories of countries: the most powerful (Argentina, Brazil, Mexico, and Venezuela); the "intermediates" (Colombia, Chile, and Peru); and the least powerful (the countries of the Caribbean, Ecuador, and so on). This comparative analysis will permit us to study the global nature of international relations, the structures of power that characterize them, and the evolution of these structures from the bipolar system of the Cold War to the present multipolar system. We can identify the policies followed by the different actors (China, the United States, the Soviet Union, and so forth) with respect to Latin America and the reactions of the different countries studied.

The Transformation of the System of Intra–Latin American International Stratification

The new configuration of international stratification in Latin America is perceptible even though a methodology is not yet available for a precise measurement of each country's status. Whatever the variables employed to measure international stratification at the intra–Latin American level (and its extraregional projections), diverse levels of stratification are the result both of an uneven historical development of the nations of the area and of situations derived from the distinctive endowment and development of these nations' human and natural resources.[8] Utilizing two variables (the degree of national viability and the degree of power and influence), we have created the following scheme of inter–Latin American international stratification and of its extraregional projections.[9]

The first variable—the degree of national viability—refers to the capacity of a country to develop itself with a certain measure of autonomy without the need for economic integration (in a broad sense). This capacity depends on multiple factors: the existing level of economic development, the rate of growth, the endowment of natural and human resources, and the like. The second variable—the degree of power and influence—refers to the capacity of a country to determine the actions of another nation or of its leadership groups (power) or to induce certain actions by acts of leadership, prestige, ideological influence, and so on (influence).

Using these two variables it is possible to identify the effects of intra–Latin American stratification at the subregional, regional, and extraregional level. First, all of the countries with relative individual viability (Brazil, Venezuela, Argentina, Mexico) have a more-or-less generalized area of regional subinfluence, which in some cases reaffirms well-known historical tendencies and in others represents emerging zones of influence. Second, in addition to its traditional power and influence over

Bolivia, Paraguay, and Uruguay, Brazil has used the demonstration effect of its economic model to broaden its sphere of influence to include Chile. Third, Brazil's leaders aspire to convert
the country into a second-level world power. While on the subregional level Brazil strives to create a zone of influence by
means of its Amazonian policy and by contributing to the
development of the Plate River basin, at the regional level Brazil
has not attempted to demonstrate international acts of leadership, despite the fact that its emerging international status
appears to give it potential regional primacy.[10] Its influence on
the Third World bloc is more tactical than strategic; this means
that in the short and middle run Brazil keeps alive its presence
in the bloc while maintaining its long-run objective of acting
individually. Its present attempts to penetrate Africa economically and diplomatically form a part of this tendency. Fourth,
historically, the United States has considered Brazil as a "key
country" in Latin America, that is, as its preferential ally; and
the international policy of Brazil has tended to maintain a
special relationship with the United States. Recent frictions
between the two countries concerning human rights and North
American opposition to the contract between West Germany
and Brazil for the development of nuclear energy appear to indicate an adjustment toward equality in the character of relations.

Without prejudice toward the preceding, Brazil should now
try to create a special relationship with Japan in the economic
realm.[11] Brazil's traditional ties with the United States and
recently with Western Europe and Japan give plausibility to
the hypothesis that Brazil would constitute a kind of subim-
perialistic platform for the action of the capitalist powers.
Venezuela should be forming a special relationship with the
United States, owing to the strategic nature of the importation
of Venezuelan oil. This relationship should be reinforced by
the fact that the Venezuelan political regime corresponds to the
desirable North American political model for Latin America.
Mexico has had a special relationship with the United States,
since the installation several decades ago of its present political
model. The political stability of this model has succeeded in
permitting a permanent flow of North American investment
into the country. In addition, Mexico's abundant oil reserves

tend to reinforce the special relationship because of the nation's conversion into a potential exporter of gas and petroleum to the United States.

As a source of influence on the rest of Latin America, the United States' special relationship with Brazil, Venezuela, and Mexico has an ambivalent character. In effect, the Latin American country that has a special relationship with the United States also places itself in a special position vis-à-vis the rest of the Latin American countries. This can serve to increase the favored nation's influence over the others, help it to deal bilaterally with the Colossus of the North and, indeed, diminish prevailing anti–North American sentiments in the region that have made the relationship politically suspicious. In this last case, the special relationship will have a negative character unless the favored nation simultaneously assumes regional leadership (such as analyzed in propositions five and six) and arrests the demonstrated negative effect, thus reinforcing its regional influence.

Fifth, Argentine and Brazilian doctrines of national security have influenced the present regimes of Chile and Uruguay ideologically. Sporadically, Bolivia, Ecuador, and Peru have also been inspired in certain ways by these doctrines. Sixth, Venezuela, with an individual viability relatively inferior to that of Brazil, is creating a sphere of influence in Central America by means of oil credits and other actions and is also economically penetrating the New Caribbean.[12] However, by means of international actions of leadership and by its important role as a member country of the Organization of Petroleum Exporting Countries (OPEC), Venezuela is undertaking a significant role in the Third World bloc with global consequences in the North-South dialogue. In addition, it has exercised a degree of regional leadership by means of international actions such as its initiative with Mexico for the creation of the Latin American Economic System (SELA). Seventh, Mexico is creating its zone of influence in Central America by means of credits, investments, and technical advice, perhaps on a scale less than that of Venezuela, but through a sustained effort that dates back many years. It has also exercised regional influence and leadership with its initiative for the creation of SELA and the project of the Charter

of Economic Rights and Duties of States that was proposed in
UNCTAD III. Given its petroleum reserves, Mexico should also
increase its world power and influence.

Eighth, no country that lacks relative individual viability
presently has regional power and influence in any ambit, not
even through actions of international leadership. In this sense
Chile, which in the past exercised power and influence through
the international prestige derived from its democratic system,
from the excellence of its higher education, and from its international initiatives in various fields, has ceased to play a strong
role, producing a leadership vacuum that Venezuela and Mexico
are tending to fill. Nevertheless, Chile and other Latin American
countries could in the future exercise international leadership
despite their minor economic importance deriving from their
lack of relative individual viability. Ninth, Cuba, whose national
viability has been made possible through its membership in the
Council for Mutual Economic Assistance (COMECON) and
through the economic assistance of the Soviet Union, exercises
regional influence of an ideological type, has extended its power
to Africa, influences the unaligned nations within the Third
World and, at the world level, other revolutionary movements
and governments. Tenth, the countries of the New Caribbean
should acquire a certain level of influence in Latin America
through their voting power in the Organization of American
States, through their democratic regimes, and through their ties
with other regions of the Third World by means of the Africa-
Caribbean-Pacific (ACP) group and with the European Economic
Community through participation in the Lomé Convention.[13]

Latin America and the New World Order

In this section a third area of research is proposed, one centered on the study of Latin America with respect to the New
World Order.[14] Proposing an area of research in this field is
particularly difficult since the universe of study is as broad
as the future of human society. This necessarily obliges one to
be selective, to restrict the area to those matters of the greatest
significance. For this reason, propositions in this section should
be considered exploratory attempts to define a field truly relevant to our purpose.

When in 1975 the General Assembly of the United Nations adopted instruments 3201 (S-6) and 3203 (S-6), which approved the Resolution and the Program of Action to establish a New International Economic Order (NIEO), the futurological movement found itself fully flourishing, and it continues to do so today. The futurological movement originally sprung forth from a perception of illegitimacy, as did the NIEO later. But whereas the illegitimacy upon which the NIEO focused was the postwar economic system, its evident crises, and the necessity of creating a new, more egalitarian system for the economic development of the nation-states, the futurological movement—at least in some of its versions—had already diagnosed a more extensive and profound illegitimacy, that of the existing order in its broadest sense. It thereby proposed a New World Order (NWO) of an egalitarian nature that would make possible the integral development of each inhabitant of the planet.

The NIEO thus has had and has today a much more concrete character (although in itself it is also necessarily vague). However, its fundamental conception is based on the mechanisms and motivations of the existing order, which in turn are based on the proposition that the economic systems of the Third World can reach an egalitarian order in a new international economic system "that will continue extracting its dynamism from production for exportation and from the international currents of investment and of technological innovation."[15] NIEO development means for the Third World what it has meant for the countries that are today prosperous and industrialized—that is, the production and massive consumption that mutually stimulate one another. But the cyclical crises, the struggle for markets, the exploitation of the weak by the strong, the degradation of the human environment, and other disadvantages of this type of development would be attenuated by a mixture of planning, negotiation, and goodwill.[16] Although rhetorically the leaders of the Third World criticize the model of consumer societies, the premises on which the NIEO rests seem to be those we have indicated. In any event, the basic units of a NIEO-directed world would continue to be nation-states.

On the other hand, the NWO questions the very foundation of conventional development, postulates an "integral development" of human beings in all their potentialities, and proposes a development centered on the full expression of humanity rather than on the nation-state, although it does not deny the necessity of the latter as an instrument to achieve an end. NWO is based upon a cultural, social, economic, and political transformation, a true cultural revolution that would radically transform the motiviations of the existing order not only economically but also in terms of ideas, beliefs, symbols, and human values. NWO would produce change on a world level, mobilizing all social forces and altering human priorities.

A comparison of futurological models and their antecedents yields certain clear conclusions: (1) the NWO model constitutes a more or less grandiose utopia that necessarily includes a new international economic order, one that would be radically different from the official NIEO; (2) the NIEO model appears by its modest dimensions as a much more concrete utopia and therefore seems more realizable; (3) the NIEO is based on the conception of the crisis of the economic system; (4) the NWO model is based upon the presumption of the generalized crisis of human society; and (5) although recent declarations adopted at various international meetings suggest that both currents are complementary, the way in which they are juxtaposed in their declarations suggests a series of transactions between very different visions of human society and its development. There is an obvious need for efforts to define these concepts, with educators of differing positions working to find a common ground in the face of the present multifaceted international crisis. One cannot trace a dividing line between the partisans of one or the other current that separates the developed countries and the Third World; those who are part of one or the other are found on both sides of this line.[17]

Notwithstanding adjustments between the representatives of both currents, these compromises cannot hide the evident contradictions that exist between the two foci. For example, in agreement with the NIEO the developed countries should continue increasing their purchases of primary materials from the developing countries at stable and high prices, and they should

open their markets to the importation of Third World manu-
factured goods. On the other hand, the NWO would demand
that the developed countries utilize primary materials with
greater economy and that they leave a much greater portion of
them to satisfy the necessities of the developing countries. The
developing countries should also expand their manufactures,
especially for meeting the basic needs of their own inhabitants.
The NIEO implies that both groups should become increasingly
interdependent; the NWO suggests that they should become
more self-sufficient and considers the consequent restriction of
certain lines of growth not as a disaster but as a step forward.[18]

The preceding analysis confirms our earlier assertion that
enormous difficulties face the creation of a research agenda in
the area of futurological studies. Nevertheless, we will suggest a
proposed research area by selecting fields of study that appear
relevant to us. The criteria used for selection share the following
general propositions.

1. Whatever the current to which one adheres (NIEO or
NWO), it is unquestionable that the realization of either set of
objectives implies a transformation of the existing distribution
of world power—radical in the case of NWO, much more modest
and reformist in that of the NIEO—because the present international economic system is already believed to be in the process
of disintegration, as is the planetary system. Both rest on world
structures of power and neither structure is modified by the
generosity of its beneficiaries (groups and social classes of nations), but rather by a new correlation of historical forces that
tip the balance in favor of change. We therefore propose to
focus research on political aspects, on the structures of international power.

2. The vision of the NIEO that already draws support from
Third World governments can be enriched by the vision of the
NWO, thereby providing a basis for new proposals for international action that could be incorporated gradually into the
recovery of the Third World. This would require a vast inter-
disciplinary intellectual effort, one in which the academic
community and progressive social forces of the Third World
could play a significant role. This could be centered on selected
aspects: (a) an effort of a theoretical type destined to disen-

tangle the contradictions offered by both visions of the future;
(b) the identification of antagonistic and nonantagonistic contradictions between the two visions; (c) the enrichment of a
conception of the NIEO by the nonantagonistic aspects of the
NWO; (d) the conception and design of international strategies
of political and social mobilization in which the social forces
and progressive governments of the Third World could try to
raise the level of emerging consciousness of planetary problems.

3. For the investigation of political aspects of the NWO, we
suggest that the following topics be explored in order to identify
the alternatives that could be presented in the correlations of
international forces favorable or adverse to change in the distribution of world power: (a) the alternative scenarios of
détente in relation to the possibilities of international action of
the countries of Latin America and the Third World; (b) the
alternative scenarios of the transnational world in relation to
Latin America and the rest of the Third World; (c) identification of possible coalitions or alliances of international power
that Latin America could help to form or could participate in
regarding alternative scenarios of détente and of the transnational world. Let us examine each of these separately.

Alternative Scenarios of Détente. There has been little study
of the process of détente relative to Latin America and the rest
of the Third World, yet it is important to identify the scope of
this process and its future projections for the Third World.
The hearings on détente held in the U.S. Congress suggest that
a more-or-less nonpartisan consensus exists concerning this
issue. Conceived as a relaxation of tensions between the superpowers, détente is intended to avoid or to diminish substantially the danger of a nuclear war. Beyond this consensus, however, there are a variety of opinions regarding the degree of
détente advisable in economic, commercial, and scientific-
technological terms.[19]

Another issue in need of study is whether détente is a hegemonic instrument or a new kind of interaction between the
superpowers that generally favors the rest of the world. In
alleviating tensions, the understanding between superpowers
could free their hands with regard to weak countries or to lesser
intermediate powers. It could thus produce a new form of

dominion instead of being a new model for international cooperation that would facilitate a new distribution of world power and permit the restructuring of the international system. The second question refers to the possible existence of a preferential détente "in which one region would be pacified while in another an active conflict would be maintained."[20] This concept, under certain conditions, could be considered an expression of diversion of dominion.

Finally, a recent study suggests that in the future there could be three forms of détente: cooperative, competitive, or conflictual.[21] *Cooperative détente* would represent the scenario in which the process would reach its full maturity and consolidation, achieving a goal that would open the way to a new historic process, "progressing to a kind of entente, which in some ways would be reduced to the mutual advantage of the two superpowers, but which would affect at the same time in a positive form the majoritarian group of the remaining countries." This would produce certain effects from a global perspective favoring such processes as the "desatellization" of the dependent nations, the installation of functional authorities with world competence to face universal problems,[22] an economic ordering based on the predominance of multilateral over bilateral economic foci, the creation of a climate more propitious to democratic governments, and so on.

Competitive détente would represent the simple projection of present circumstances, characterized by an accentuated mobility and instability on the international scene, with fluctuations oscillating between tendencies of forward movement toward the form of cooperative détente sketched earlier and retrogressive tendencies toward the form of conflictual détente that will be analyzed below. The tensions of this type of détente would make the international system gravitate toward the status quo and would produce opposite effects of those shown in the scenario of cooperative détente.

Conflictual détente differs from competitive détente by the degree to which tensions would be expressed, carrying this form of détente toward a definitive crisis and opening the world to nuclear holocaust. The three categories of détente (cooperative, competitive, and conflictual) could be combined with other forms of this process—hegemonic détente and preferential détente—to form the basis for the design of international political strategies on the part of Latin America and the rest of the Third World. The purpose of these strategies would be to promote those forms of détente most favorable to the desatellization of these countries and the emergence of a climate favorable to the configuration of a new international order.

Alternative Scenarios of the Transnational World. The transnational world is composed of innumerable actors who operate on, above, and within nations. In a restricted sense, it includes only transnational corporations (TNCs), such as General Motors, IBM, Boeing, and Hitachi; in broader terms, it includes actors as diverse as universal religions and international labor organizations.

What is needed is a diagnosis of the actions of transnational actors with the object of determining: (1) the ambit and scope of their real power and influence in the economic, political, and cultural field; (2) the form in which each nation perceives the actor's actions in its territory; (3) the policies that each country follows to control these actions; and (4) the perceptions of transnational actors concerning initiatives tending toward the establishment of a new international order and the concrete actions based upon such perceptions. In this regard it can be shown that TNCs with bases in the United States have viewed the policy of détente as favorable to their interests in penetrating socialist economies. In following this policy they support forms of cooperative détente that encourage attitudes favorable to the new world order and promise greater freedom of action for the Latin American countries.

Nevertheless, it would seem that at the Latin American level the initiatives tending toward a new international order would prejudice the interests of the TNCs, since the new order presumably would contemplate multilateral control of their activities. Other transnational actors—or those affiliated with them—such as U.S. labor organizations (i.e., AFL-CIO), might, on the other hand, favor new forms of international ordering to reduce the export of jobs to Latin America and other regions of the Third World.

Identification of Potential Coalitions or Alliances. Changes in the existing distribution of world power will be made not by a gratuitous concession of present beneficiaries but by a new correlation of historical forces that will alter the present status quo in a manner favorable to the emergence of a new world ordering. Diagnoses of the present state of détente and of the transnational world, of its future scenarios in Latin America, and of the political strategies that Latin America generally could follow in the context of such scenarios need to be supplemented by a general model of analysis for the study of new international coalitions in which Latin America could participate.

The general working hypothesis is that the structures of world power are not monolithic. The flaws in the systems and subsystems of domination and dependency of which such structures are composed offer opportunities to the countries of Latin America to create new coalitions of international power that could, in turn, maximize the capacity of these countries for international negotiation. A typical example in this regard is the joint initiative of Venezuela and Saudi Arabia at the beginning of the 1960s, from which flowed the creation of OPEC (and of its subsystem, OAPEC). The agreement between OPEC and the Group of 77 made possible the constitution of the OPEC–non-oil-producing Third World alliance that obtained the United Nations resolution for the establishment of the NIEO and forced the industrialized capitalist world to enter into the North-South dialogue. It is possible that much room for innovation exists in the area of international coalitions. These possibilities need to be investigated systematically to identify potential new international "coalitions" of power from the Latin American point of view and from that of the rest of the Third World.

The report prepared for the Club of Rome under the direction of Nobel Laureate for Economics Jan Tinbergen—*RIO: Reshaping the International Order*—reaches the same conclusions concerning the necessity for new coalitions relative to the new order: "New structures of power can be constructed by means of the creation of new coalitions." These can be formed at a national and international level, with the objective of establishing new combinations of power and influence.[23] The single major formulation of the research agenda proposed in this chapter then gives plausibility to our thesis that the traditional analytic model for the inter-American system is obsolete and that the future of the system can be studied only within a global perspective, a perspective whose central lines of investigation we have sketched.

Notes

1. It can be argued that a subtle distinction exists between the terms "relations between the United States and Latin America" and "inter-American relations." The first term encompasses the totality of interactions that are produced between the two unities or regions, while the second refers to actions within the inter-American system—that is, the network of regional organizations, multilateral pacts, and collective norms by means of which relations between the United States and Latin America have been institutionalized. We use the terms interchangeably.

2. For a synthesis of relations between the United States and Latin America, see Federico G. Gil, *Latin American–United States Relations* (New York: Harcourt Brace Jovanovich, 1971). This work also has extremely useful bibliographic notes for the tracing of the evolution of inter-American studies.

3. Abraham F. Lowenthal, "The United States and Latin America; Ending the Hegemonic Presumption," *Foreign Affairs* 55 (October 1976): 199–213.

4. Here we are referring to the ideological basis of the hegemonic presumption, as expressed in Arthur P. Whitaker's classic *The Western Hemisphere Idea: Its Rise and Decline* (Ithaca: Cornell University Press, 1954).

5. On the reception given dependency theory in the United States, see Fernando Henrique Cardoso, "The Consumption of Dependency Theory in the United States," *Latin American Research Review* 12 (1977):117–124.

6. Jorge I. Domínguez, "Consensus and Divergence: The State of the Literature on Inter-American Relations in the 1970s," *Latin American Research Review* 13 (1978):115.

7. For example, see Julio Cotler and Richard Fagen (eds.), *Latin America and the United States: The Changing Political Realities* (Stanford: Stanford University Press, 1974). For an effort to apply a general theoretical model to the inter-American system, see L. Brock, *Entwicklung nationalismus und Kompradorenpolitik: Die Grundung der OAS und die Entwicklung der Abhangigkeit Lateinamerikas von den USA* (Main:

Maisenheim am Glan, 1975). Finally, for a global theoretical focus on international relations in Latin America, see G. Pope Atkins, *Latin America in the International Political System* (New York: Free Press, 1977).

8. Gustavo Lagos, *International Stratification and Underdeveloped Countries* (Chapel Hill: University of North Carolina Press, 1963).

9. The concept of national viability has been taken from the now-modified model proposed by Helio Jaguaribe, "El Brasil y America Latina," *Revista de Estudios Internacionales* 8 (enero-marzo 1975).

10. William Perry, *Contemporary Brazilian Foreign Policy: The International Strategy of an Emerging Power* (Beverly Hills: Sage Publications, 1976), p. 36.

11. Claudio Véliz, "Errores y omisiones: notas sobre la política exterior de los países de América Latina durante los últimos diez años," *Estudios Internacionales* 10 (octubre-diciembre 1977):9–10.

12. The New Caribbean designates a subregion of Latin America formed by English-speaking countries. It includes Belize in the west, Guyana in the southeast, and a chain of islands formed by the independent states of Trinidad and Tobago, Grenada, Barbados and Jamaica, and the semiautonomous associated states of the Lesser Antilles (Saint Vincent, Santa Lucia, Dominica, Antigua and San Cristobal, Nieves, Anguila, and the colony of Montserrat). All are formally or informally associated with the Caribbean Common Market (CARICOM).

13. The Lomé Convention is an economic cooperation agreement that links the countries of the so-called ACP group with the European Economic Community.

14. For the direction this research might take, see National Science Foundation, *The Study of the Future: An Agenda for Research* (Washington, D.C.: Government Printing Office, 1977), p. 3.

15. Marshall Wolfe, "Las utopias concretas y su confrontación con el mundo de hoy," CEPAL/DS/134, mimeographed (Marzo 1974).

16. Ibid.

17. Ibid.

18. Ibid.

19. Gustavo Lagos, *La détente y las crisis planetarias,* Serie de Publicaciones Especiales del Instituto de Estudios Internacionales no. 16 (Santiago, Chile, 1976), pp. 1–17.

20. "Kissinger's Point of View toward Détente and the Developing Nations," mimeographed (United States Information Service, May 14, 1974).

21. José Medina Echavarría, "América Latina en los escenarios posibles de la distensión," *Revista CEPAL,* Segundo Semestre 1976, pp. 9–87. Our analysis of these three types of détente is based on this text.

22. For a study of world agencies that might assume these responsibilities, see Gustavo Lagos and Horacio Godoy, *Revolution of Being: A Latin American View of the Future* (New York: Free Press, 1977), pp. 135–153.

23. Jan Tinbergen (ed.), *RIO: Reshaping the International Order: A Report to the Club of Rome* (New York: Dutton, 1976), pp. 105–107.

Part 2

United States–Latin American Relations: The Shape of Hegemony

4

The Political Mythology of the Monroe Doctrine: Reflections on the Social Psychology of Hegemony

Kenneth M. Coleman

This chapter analyzes the political mythology that has emerged among North Americans to justify the reality of U.S. hegemony in the Americas. This mythology appears to be in part a response to the curiously cyclical pattern of inter-American relations noted by Federico Gil.[1] A political mythology of U.S. national innocence is compatible with periods of disinterest in which Latin American behavior stays within acceptable limits; it is absolutely essential during periods when force must be employed to halt or deter behavior unacceptable to the United States.

History tells us that the persistent goals of U.S. foreign policy toward independent Latin America have included maximum U.S. geographic expansion and the establishment of political and economic hegemony. Hegemony—the establishment by a dominant power of limits for the behavior of other actors beyond which direct control by force will be invoked—implies an imposed homeostasis, i.e., so long as the behavior of the subordinate parties remains within prescribed limits, rule by force is not invoked. However, force is used when transgressions of the boundary between acceptable and unacceptable behavior occur; force is invoked in direct proportion to the perceived severity of the transgression.[2]

The assumption of the existence of a U.S. commitment to a hegemonic relationship might not go uncontested, although much recent scholarship seems to take this assumption for

granted.[3] The assumption would be attacked by those who
deny that the United States has sought to establish boundaries
for acceptable behavior. Events as distant as the reticence of the
United States to recognize an independent monarchical Mexico[4]
and as recent as the 1965 invasion of the Dominican Republic
belie this criticism. Other critics might contend that the relationship has been more imperial than hegemonic. It is true that
at various times the relationship between the United States and
Latin America might more properly have been characterized
as imperialistic than as hegemonic. The United States has engaged in direct rule by force on more than one occasion. However, these and other episodes of overt imperialism are indicative of the failure to achieve the goals of U.S. foreign policy—
to establish *indirect* U.S. control over the Americas. A constant
in the formulation of U.S. foreign policy toward Latin America
has been to develop and to maintain as much control as possible with the minimum employment of force.[5] When the
United States sends in its troops, erects an economic blockade,
or engages in covert intervention, its efforts to establish a workable hegemonic system have failed. The point is not to absolve
the United States of responsibility for imperialistic behavior,
but rather to distinguish between hegemony and imperialism.

Clarity about power relationships matters because the social
psychology of imperialism requires the projection of a different
type of political mythology than the social psychology of
hegemony. The predominance of hegemony as a goal of U.S.
policy has allowed the creation of a political mythology that
systematically denies the existence of U.S. self-interest as a
feature of inter-American relations. Were the creation of an empire an explicit goal of U.S. policy, the political mythology
would surely be different. The political mythology of a self-
consciously imperial power might deny self-interestedness, but
it cannot deny the facts of political and economic control.
Imperial control is too visible to be denied. The political mythology of hegemony is distinctive in that it denies the existence
of political and economic domination. It is similar to the mythology of imperialism in asserting that existing relationships are
just, appropriate, inevitable, or otherwise normatively defensible.
History provides the best approach to understanding the impor-

tance of this distinction, and it is to an analysis of the political mythology of the Monroe Doctrine that we now turn.

First, however, a definition is essential to our discussion. A political mythology (1) is an attempt to reconcile a contradiction between professed values and actual behavior, (2) is invoked more frequently in times of crisis, (3) can be invoked in normal times to reconcile the past with the present and the future, (4) is widely believed in response to social cues, and (5) acquires the character of a value-laden belief that (6) need be neither verifiable nor a valid reconstruction of the current world or of a world that once existed.[6]

The Monroe Doctrine: Misremembering the Past, Misconstruing the Present

Reconciling Contradictions

The Monroe Doctrine is an example of political myth creation that accompanied the establishment of North American hegemony over Latin America. Since its formulation in late 1823, the Monroe Doctrine has represented an attempt to reconcile the contradiction between the professed values of U.S. culture and the actual behavior of the U.S. government. Devised in response to a British proposal for joint action, the Monroe Doctrine was issued independently by the United States. The British proposal was for the United States and Britain jointly to warn the Holy Alliance to stay out of the Americas, at the same time committing both countries to cease territorial expansion in the New World. Although the independent statement by the United States left open the possibility of further territorial expansion,[7] rhetorical verbiage of disinterest and mutuality characterized James Monroe's response to the British proposal.

The text of the Monroe Doctrine, some three paragraphs in James Monroe's State of the Union Address in December 1823, was written under the predominant influence of John Quincy Adams, secretary of state and precandidate for the 1824 presidential nomination. It contained five key points:

1. It is in the national interest of the United States to advise European powers that the American continents should not

be considered open for future colonization by any European power.

2. The United States is interested in the affairs of Europe, but it does not intend to participate in wars among European powers nor in any other matter that exclusively concerns the European countries.

3. The systems of government of the Holy Alliance are fundamentally different from the republican forms found in the Americas and, for this reason, any attempt to extend European systems of government to the Americas will be considered a threat to the peace and security of the United States.

4. Any attempt to establish European control over the newly independent governments now recognized by the United States will be considered an unfriendly act by the United States.

5. It would be impossible to permit the extension of European political systems to any portion of the Americas without threatening the peace and happiness of the United States. It is obvious that Spain is never going to reestablish control over the ex-colonies. The United States would prefer to leave the resolution of disputes between Spain and the newly independent countries to the disputants; the United States would hope that other powers would behave similarly.

Upon reading the text of the Monroe statement, many reasonable people would have inferred that the United States was going to protect the new states of Latin America from foreign powers. Since Latin America was heavily populated with reasonable people, just such an interpretation was made by several Latin American governments. In the next three years, five explicit requests for U.S. guarantees of Latin American independence were directed to Washington. All were denied or evaded.[8] In addition, when France sent its navy to Haiti to extract indemnities in exchange for recognition of Haitian independence, Washington made no comment. The 1826 Congress of Panama envisioned a regional alliance against reconquest; but, because of congressional fears of entanglement the U.S. delegates arrived too late to participate. So Latin Americans soon discovered what had been made explicit in the private cabinet discussions preceding Monroe's 1823 speech: the United States would not take any actions that might lead to committing troops to the defense of Latin American independence.[10] The Monroe Doctrine was designed to give the appearance of extending a rather magnanimous offer of protection to Latin American countries. In fact it offered no protection.[11]

Similarly, a close reading of the historical record would justify suspicion of the professed self-abnegation of the United States in matters purely European. The principle of North American abstention from European affairs suggests a sense of mutuality and reciprocity: European restraint is demanded in exchange for promises of restraint from the United States. Yet we know from the records of cabinet debates that prominent North Americans—ex-President Thomas Jefferson, Secretary of War John Calhoun, and even James Monroe—were disposed to include recognition of Grecian independence from the Turks in the 1823 address. Only after strenuous efforts could John Quincy Adams convince the president to delete the passage from the later drafts of his message.[12] Adams prevailed in this portion of the message, but it would be difficult to suggest from the historical record the existence of a consensus among North American political leaders on the principle of nonintervention in European affairs. A number of U.S. officials were quite disposed to meddle in European politics.

Yet the situation was clear: the United States issued an independent statement because it wished to disguise its intentions to expand across the continent and perhaps into the Caribbean. In order to do so, it was advantageous to find a rhetorical vehicle through which to suggest not expansionist intent, but self-abnegation. But although a language of mutuality and reciprocity helped to obfuscate real intentions, the United States did not wish to forswear expansion into the vacuum created by the evaporation of the Spanish empire. The diplomatic dilemma confronting Monroe was that the United States was very much interested in the acquisition of former or current Spanish territory, Texas and Cuba, respectively. Hence it was better to proclaim disinterest in matters purely European than disinterest in European territory in the Americas. When confronted with alternative interpretations of what might be construed as reciprocity, U.S. officials knew to choose that variant which most favored their expansionist interests.

From its inception, then, the Monroe Doctrine has been a rhetorical vehicle designed to reconcile professed values of disinterest and self-abnegation with highly self-interested, expansionist intentions. The first defining characteristic of a political mythology is present.

Use in Time of Crisis

The most recent invocation of the Monroe Doctrine by the United States came in 1965, when President Lyndon B. Johnson sent troops into the Dominican Republic, ostensibly to protect U.S. lives. Subsequent analyses have demonstrated that the troops' principal purpose was to prevent a second social revolution in the Caribbean.[13] As José Moreno has observed,

> It is hard to ascertain what path the aborted revolution would have taken if American forces had not invaded. It was not a socialist revolution. It was, at best, a liberal-democratic revolution of the lower middle class whose advocacy of welfare reforms helped recruit the overwhelming support of the masses. One could not deny, however, the possibility that once under way, this petit-bourgeois revolution could have been steered into a more radical orientation. To foreclose that possibility, Washington ordered massive military intervention. The United States had learned its lesson in Cuba. Under no circumstances would another revolution, even a middle class revolution, be allowed.[14]

The State Department attempted to defend U.S. intervention by dusting off and modernizing the nineteenth-century proscription against introducing European forms of government in the New World. This time the alien form was Communism. It mattered little that the evidence of Communist participation in the uprising was negligible; the State Department fabricated a list of "known Communist" participants in the uprising with which it justified the intervention to the U.S. public.[15] Under the guise of collective security against an imaginary threat from forces external to the hemisphere, the United States then created an OAS peacekeeping force. The crisis was perceived as real by U.S. decision makers, and they rallied public support for intervention by invoking the Monroe Doctrine. Leaders and followers were willing partners.

Use in the Absence of Crisis

Myths help people to see the present as a continuation of a morally defensible past and as a step toward a justifiable future. This characteristic can be seen in the behavior of North Americans invoking the Monroe Doctrine in the absence of crisis. A dialogue between the U.S. ambassador to Mexico, Patrick J. Lucey, and a reporter for the Mexican newsmagazine *Proceso* illustrates the point. The interview occurred in October 1977, as Mexicans were debating whether to construct a gas pipeline to the U.S. border. The reporter asked Lucey: "What would the United States do in case of a security threat to protect the gas pipeline?"

> *Lucey*: People have put this question to me previously and I confess that I do not understand completely its significance. Why do you have to mention a war situation and connect it with the pipeline? Just thinking out loud, if there were a nuclear war between Russia and the United States, then naturally each one of these countries would try to intercept the supply of energy to the other, but I don't really understand why you ask the question. . . . Of course, in accord with the Monroe Doctrine, if Mexico were attacked, independently of whether it had the pipeline or not, Mexico could with confidence solicit the assistance of the United States for its own defense.
>
> *Proceso*: But we are not talking about a security threat to Mexico, rather a threat to the United States, what would the U.S. do in *this* case to protect the pipeline?
>
> *Lucey*: The United States would not do anything to protect the pipeline or any other natural resource which is found inside the sovereign territory of Mexico unless action were solicited by the government of Mexico.[16]

The ambassador's response was diplomatically correct, but at the same time it revealed little comprehension of Mexican history. That Mexicans might have some justification for fear of the United States, having lost over half of their national territory to it in a contrived war, seems to have been lost upon the ambassador.[17] Similarly, the fact that the United States had threatened to use troops to keep the supply of petroleum flowing during the Mexican Revolution seems to be *historia incognita* to the ambassador. As Glenn Price has observed, U.S. commentators have written about Mexico as if Mexican fears of the United States were not only unfounded but also indicative of the arrogance of an inferior who does not realize that tutelage by a superior is in his own best interest.[18] Hidden behind the ambassador's words is a refusal to admit that the United States aggressed against Mexico in the past. Implicit in his invocation of the Monroe Doctrine is a reconstruction of the past that suggests disinterested protection of Mexico by the United States. While the ambassador imagined future Soviet aggression, Mexican journalists were fearful of U.S. aggression in the form of protection. The ambassador had accepted the mythology.

Widely Diffused Belief; A Response to Social Cues

Salvador de Madariaga has captured both the socially cued nature of the Monroe Doctrine and the extent of its diffusion:

> I know only two things about the Monroe Doctrine: one is that no American I have met knows what it is; the other is that no American I have met will consent to its being tampered with. . . . I conclude that the Monroe Doctrine is not a doctrine but a dogma, . . . not one dogma, but two, to wit: the dogma of the infallibility of the American President and the dogma of the immaculate conception of American foreign policy.[19]

Evidence from surveys of public opinion suggests that U.S. citizens often exhibit deferential attitudes toward presidential initiatives in foreign policy.[20] Thus it is quite conceivable that presidential invocations of the Monroe Doctrine elicit a kind of conditioned response in which citizens demonstrate their allegiance to their nation. Obeisance to the Monroe Doctrine may well be a sort of minor national litmus test of citizenship in which one shows one's true colors. Since most citizens do not,

in fact, know what the doctrine says nor anything of the circumstances in which the doctrine was articulated, it is impossible for them to question the authority of presidential interpretation. Few citizens are capable of challenging presidential
invocation of the doctrine for the purpose of legitimating otherwise debatable policy choices.[21] In the long run, the U.S. public
will not accept an unwise policy merely by continued invocation
of the Monroe Doctrine, but invocation of the doctrine provides
North American statesmen with a tactical weapon to delay
criticism in the short run.

Value-Laden Belief

The Monroe Doctrine has survived because it carries a normative message—it tells U.S. citizens and officials that their current
causes are just, morally defensible, and in accord with the
highest principles of a political order superior to other political
orders. That the Monroe Doctrine was never intended as a guide
to behavior is revealed not only by the record of failure to in-
voke the doctrine on seemingly appropriate occasions but also
by the circumstances in which it has been invoked. The first
public reference to the doctrine by a U.S. president subsequent
to Monroe's address was in 1842, when James Tyler, in preparation for the annexation of Texas, recalled the Monrovian proscription against attempts to implant European forms of government in the Americas. He interpreted British and French preference for an independent Texas to be indicative of such an
attempt.[22] The object of Tyler's reference was twofold: first,
to warn Britain and France not to interfere in Texas and,
second, to convince U.S. citizens that the annexation of Texas
served a high moral purpose. Subsequent references to the
doctrine have served a similar function: to advise adversaries
of U.S. interests and at the same time to convince the domestic
political community that a defense of U.S. interests serves a
moral purpose beyond those interests. If a higher moral purpose
is served by the exercise of direct or indirect political control,
then to defend the interests of the United States is to defend
the interests of mankind. This is the most fundamental integrative myth of U.S. foreign policy, of which the Monroe
Doctrine is but one subsidiary manifestation. But both the

general case and the specific case reveal the value-laden nature of political mythology. The empirical world is interpreted in such a fashion as to produce a comfortingly positive normative assessment of one's actions.

Independence of Beliefs from Empirical or Historical Observation

A myth reconstructs the past and the current world not according to the demands of scientific observation, but in response to an underlying psychologic. The myth of the Monroe Doctrine lives not because it has protected Latin American states from alien forces, but because the United States has a need to believe that it has protected Latin America. The contradictions between professed values and actual behavior can be reconciled via mythology only when empirical observation is selective. Since psychological motivations exist to stimulate such selectivity, it is not difficult to achieve.

North Americans have an impressive capacity to read the historical record of the Monroe Doctrine selectively. In 1842, *El Venezolano,* a leading newspaper of Caracas, interpreted President Tyler's rediscovery of the Monroe Doctrine as a license for North American aggression against Mexico: "Words like these should open the eyes of all the hispanic republics. Do you want to be under the fatherly tutelage of Washington? Beware, brothers, the wolf approaches the lambs."[23] Yet, in an otherwise brilliant contribution to our understanding of the Monroe Doctrine, Ernest R. May has betrayed the blindness typical of North American citizens and officials:

> It is probably superfluous to say in conclusion that the decisions made were wise ones. During more than a century, Americans found the consequences of those decisions tolerable. Until the Doctrine was modified in the 1890s and later, the majority of nations of the world were not disposed to criticize the consequences either. Very few foreign policy decisions have survived such tests . . . It might be said that the Monroe Doctrine has represented the best of the foreign policy of Democracy.[24]

Even sophisticated scholars are capable of selectively reading the historical record to produce an assessment that reaffirms the presumption of a higher moral purpose as a guiding principle of the Monroe Doctrine.

Primary Myths of North American Foreign Policy

Melvin Gurtov has recently attempted to identify the underlying ideological tenets that contribute to "an American presumption that radical change in Third World politics is inherently inimical to U.S. 'interests' and must be prevented or resisted."[25] According to Gurtov, there are three interrelated axioms that constitute an interventionist "ideology of national interest": (1) the belief that "America's domestic tranquility depends on security and stability abroad," (2) the belief that "security and stability abroad for the forces of freedom depend on America's willingness to carry out the mission and responsibilities entrusted to it," and (3) the belief that the "fulfillment of the 'American Mission' depends on a willingness and ability to intervene in the domestic affairs of other peoples."[26]

The ideological perspective outlined by Gurtov has its roots in two political myths that are highly likely to be central elements in the belief systems of North American decision makers—two *primary myths* of U.S. foreign policymaking. These are (1) the United States has a special responsibility to lead the world in efforts at moral renewal, and (2) the interests of the United States are the interests of mankind.[27]

A Special Responsibility for Moral Renewal

In an earlier era, this myth might have been stated in a less secular form. José Fuentes Mares, Mexico's distinguished historian of U.S.-Mexican relations, has written insightfully of the importance the sense of being a people chosen by God had for continental expansion. The term that captured this sense of moral certainty in geographic expansion, Manifest Destiny, betrayed the comforting Calvinist certainty that God would reveal those who warranted His grace by making them prosperous.[28] Such a God would also reveal whom He wanted to occupy given parcels of land.

With time, however, the moral certainty of the United States found outlets other than those involved in geographic expansion, and they found expression in forms less overtly sacred. As Lance Bennett has suggested, "In the absence of dominant agencies of spiritual legitimation, spirituality attaches itself to temporal agencies, especially political institutions." Such a transformation marks the emergence of a civil religion. In discussing this transformation in North America, Bennett quotes Reinhold Neibuhr's suggestion that historically "the Puritans little by little changed their initial emphasis on the divine favor which the nation enjoyed to an emphasis on the virtues acquired by the nation as a result of divine favor." The distinction is subtle but important: the second version is more self-congratulatory than the first. After this historic change, continues Bennett, "a sense of mission and of grandiose purpose in [North] American politics contributed to moral embroilments beyond the national boundaries and produced recurrent millenial tendencies in domestic politics."[29]

Examples of the sense of moral mission are not difficult to find in the diplomatic history of the United States. Bennett encountered the phrase "moral renewal of mankind" in a speech before Congress by President Andrew Johnson in 1868. One might also cite the call of Woodrow Wilson to participate in the "war to end all wars," or the case of General Douglas MacArthur, who wished to "eliminate Communism in Asia" by extending the war in Korea to the Chinese mainland. John F. Kennedy's Alliance for Progress was conceived as the way "to transform Latin America pacifically so as better to avoid the evil of revolutions which produce socialist regimes." The conception and articulation of these grand designs were characteristically North American.

If these policies were all made under the influence of a political myth, in what sense were they attempts to resolve contradictions or to displace anxieties in the manner of a political myth? In the first case, Andrew Johnson made his speech less than three years after the termination of a destructive civil war and after the assassination of his predecessor. In such a context the utility of the search for an integrative moral mission ought to be clear. The function was to distract attention from the traumas the nation had recently experienced.

In the cases of President Wilson and General MacArthur, a

grandiose moral purpose justified the costs of war. President Wilson launched U.S. participation in the European war with a moralizing rhetoric about the need to restructure the world, which he later continued in his campaign for a League of Nations. MacArthur wanted to justify the cost of a limited war by pursuing a different moral crusade. For Kennedy the evil to be eliminated was identical, but the methods were more inclusive. When officials fear that desired goals cannot be achieved without extraordinary sacrifices from citizens, they are apt to justify their goals with calls to enlist in a moral crusade.[30] A moral crusade mobilizes political support. The public sense of moral certainty can then be invoked to relax normal ethical restrictions on behavior, restrictions that impede the accomplishment of the foreign policy goal. Kennedy clearly believed in the moral crusade of anti-Communism, just as much as did the citizens to whom he tried to sell his alliance. He believed so much in the morality of anti-Communism that he permitted an ill-considered invasion of Cuba by anti-Castro exiles and permitted various assassination attempts on the life of Castro himself.[31] The certainty of moral crusades often leads to lapses in good judgment.[32]

The United States is not the only country where political leaders have discovered the utility of moral crusades. But given the lingering sense that we are a chosen people, the sense of special responsibility remains strong. Gurtov summarizes the evidence of the persistence of this mythology:

> "History" would not "permit" Americans to live in isolation, John F. Kennedy said. "We are still the keystone in the arch of freedom, and I think we will continue to do, as we have done in the past, our duty. . . ." Lyndon Johnson . . . also relied on precedent and circumstances when he urged, "History and our own achievements have thrust upon us the principal responsibility for the protection of freedom on earth." One of his, and Kennedy's, chief advisers, Walt W. Rostow, agreed: "We cannot renounce our destiny. We are the trustees of the principles of national independence and human freedom all over the globe; and given our history, this is a proud and natural responsibility. . . ." In the Nixon Administration . . . the principle of America's destiny [was] upheld. Nixon told an interviewer in March, 1971 " . . . I want the American people . . . to do

what is needed to keep the peace in this world. We used to look to other nations to do this job once upon a time. But now only the United States plays a major role of this sort in the world."[33]

Although it might be assumed that missionary zeal would have abated in the post-Vietnam era, there is considerable evidence to suggest that the myth lies ready to reassert itself in times of crisis or threat to North American hegemony. Ole Holsti and James Rosenau have found little evidence of real attitude change in the lessons that North American opinion leaders drew from the Vietnam experience.[34] Many appear quite ready to reassert the propriety of a special responsibility of the U.S. public in a way that does not threaten either those who favored or those who opposed the war in Vietnam.[35] Perhaps most revealing of all was Senator George McGovern's suggestion in 1978 that the United States ought to seek UN intervention in Cambodia to prevent genocide. No stronger testimony to the staying power of political mythology could be given than its capacity to ensnare those who have themselves discredited the application of the myth in previous circumstances. Although action may or may not have been warranted by the United Nations, McGovern's call for action was clearly predicated on the assumption of the United States' special moral responsibility to initiate action, an assumption that McGovern had rejected in the case of U.S. participation in the Vietnamese civil war. McGovern's plea did not move the U.S. public, but such a plea would probably produce a sympathetic response were there a serious threat to U.S. hegemony. The myth may be in temporary abatement, but it has hardly disappeared.

The Interests of the United States Are the Interests of Mankind

The tendency to interpret almost any U.S. foreign policy action as an action that benefits all humanity was established in the colonial era. Yehoshua Arieli has argued that the North American colonists identified their new society as the New Jerusalem:

The religious vision of a morally renewed and purified society of the 17th and 18th centuries deepened the correlative belief that a new world was predestined for the happiness of a new man. The Puritans identified themselves with Israel: they thought of themselves as a Chosen People and of America as the Promised Land. Their messianic tendencies were given expression in a religious philosophy of history and progress. The future was the purpose of the movement of Mankind through history; and America was going to be the final stage in which people would be governed by "the Institutions, the Laws and Directives of the Word of God, not only in church governance but also in the administration and governance of all temporal matters of Mankind."[36]

If the United States represents the New Jerusalem, it is all but impossible to conceive of a situation in which the interests of mankind are not highly similar to those of the United States.

Given such a presumption, opposition to the Manifest Destiny of the New Jerusalem was no simple political opposition—it did not represent a mere difference of opinion. Rather it was a heresy against the people chosen by God Himself. The voices that protested the contrived war of expansion against Mexico—those of Representative Abraham Lincoln, Senator Thomas Corwin, Henry David Thoreau—were all easily ignored. President Polk and his supporters branded such protestors as traitors. If the authorities of the United States—the authorities chosen by the people favored by God Himself—were in favor of a given policy, then to criticize the justice or the morality of that policy was impossible.

In case after case in more recent times, the United States has behaved as if its interests could be assumed to coincide with those of mankind. Domestic critics who have opposed various expansionist or interventionist policies have repeatedly been labeled traitors ("dupes of Hanoi") or incompetents ("nervous Nellies"). Thus, even when the United States has not been involved in a moralistic foreign policy crusade, its foreign policy has often reflected the belief that other countries surely must be mistaken in opposing what the United States considers a just policy.[37]

Primary Myths, Secondary Myths, and
U.S. Hegemony in the Americas

Hegemony, just as much as empire, requires the creation of a legitimating mythology. The essential differences in such mythologies reflect the underlying power relationships. In imperial situations, the mythology must hold that "we rule you because it is your own best interest to be ruled by us." The variations on this theme can be many. In some cases it can be the white man's burden to civilize the heathen; in other cases foreign rule offers the opportunity "to become a Frenchman" (or a U.S. citizen, in the case of Puerto Rico). The underlying theme, however, is similar. In hegemonic situations, the mythology must generate the belief that existing relationships are mutually beneficial and that those who do not so perceive them are misguided or evil. Domination and control are denied; a community of interests is assumed.

For those who live in nations that dominate other nations indirectly via imposition of limits upon the behavior of the subordinate, the mythology is likely to take the form of a belief in national innocence. The two primary myths project such a belief. Both allow political leaders to mobilize public support for policies that would otherwise be questionable on such grounds as distributive justice (Who pays the cost of this intervention?), morality (Why should we intervene?), economic wastefulness (How much does this intervention cost and what other investments of these resources might we make?), or political wisdom (Is this the best way to achieve our ends?). Yet at the same time these myths serve to convince citizens and officials alike that each intervention is an exceptional case that the dominant power has a moral duty to resolve, rather than a part of a systematic pattern of control. Thus the CIA support for a Guatemalan counterrevolution in 1954, the Cuban invasion of 1961, the Dominican Republic invasion of 1965, and the credit blockade of Chile in the early 1970s are seen as separate instances, each warranted by exceptional threats. The U.S. response to each of these exceptional threats is explained by reference to the primary myths: the special responsibility of the United States, and the belief that the interests of mankind could not be favored by toleration of the presumed enemies of the United States. What is at stake, the primary myths suggest, is much more than the mere self-interest of the United States.

The Monroe Doctrine has survived in the political mythology of the United States because it applies the primary myths to the circumstances of U.S. hegemony in the Americas. If the Monroe Doctrine did not exist, a more compelling, contextually specific explanation for U.S. behavior would be required each time a Latin American government overstepped the bounds of acceptable behavior. In terms of social-psychological efficiency, the Monroe Doctrine is the secondary myth required by the fact of U.S. hegemony in this hemisphere. The idea of protecting the hemisphere from the alleged malevolence of extrahemispheric forces is central to the themes of the primary myths. Whether reference is made to the Monroe Doctrine or not, U.S. officials can be expected to continue to justify the maintenance of U.S. hegemony by reference to the inescapable burdens that power and moral authority thrust upon us. Should troops be employed in defense of U.S. hegemony once again, we should not expect that political leaders would take as sole recourse the secondary myth of the Monroe Doctrine. Statesmen never use the secondary myth without simultaneously invoking context-specific explanations for the commitments they have made on behalf of the nation. Nonetheless, political leaders will continue to find that the theme of protecting the hemisphere from external forces is capable of evoking deep support. The hegemonic presumption will not die easily.

Notes

1. Federico G. Gil, *Latin American–United States Relations* (New York: Harcourt Brace Jovanovich, 1971), pp. 284–85.

2. This distinction is similar to that proposed by Jorge Domínguez in "The U.S. Impact on Cuban Internal Politics and Economics, 1902–1958: From Imperialism to Hegemony" (Paper delivered at the 1976 Annual Meeting of the American Political Science Association, Chicago, Ill.).

3. Abraham Lowenthal, "The United States and Latin America: Ending the Hegemonic Presumption," *Foreign Affairs* 55 (October 1976): 199–213; Arthur P. Whitaker, "The American Idea and the Western

Hemisphere: Yesterday, Today and Tomorrow," *Orbis* 20 (Spring 1976): 163–64.

4. José Fuentes Mares, *Poinsett: historia de una gran intriga,* 4th ed. (Mexico: Editorial Jus, 1964).

5. For an analysis of the underlying ideological basis of the U.S. discomfort with the use of force, see Edward Weisband, "The Ideology of American Foreign Policy: A Paradigm of Lockean Liberalism," *Sage Professional Papers in International Studies,* no. 02-106 (Beverly Hills, Cal.: 1973).

6. This definition is discussed at length in Kenneth M. Coleman, "The Monroe Doctrine as Political Symbol," mimeographed (1977). Major sources used in creating the definition were Glenn W. Price, *The Origins of the War with Mexico: The Polk-Stockton Intrigue* (Austin: University of Texas Press, 1967), p. 9; Claude Lévi-Strauss, *Structural Anthropology* (New York: Doubleday-Anchor, 1963), p. 229; Ernst Cassirer, *The Myth of the State* (New Haven: Yale University Press, 1946), pp. 351–53; Murray Edelman, *Political Language: Words that Succeed and Policies that Fail* (New York: Academic Press, 1977), pp. 45–46; and idem, *Politics as Symbolic Action: Mass Arousal and Quiescence* (Chicago: Markham, 1971), pp. 14, 54.

7. Ernest R. May, *The Making of the Monroe Doctrine* (Cambridge: Harvard University Press, 1975), pp. 199, 202; Samuel Flagg Bemis, *The Latin American Policy of the United States: An Historical Interpretation* (New York: W. W. Norton, 1967), pp. 61–62.

8. Gil, *Latin American–United States Relations,* p. 62; Bemis, *Latin American Policy of the United States,* p. 68.

9. All of these events are discussed in greater detail in Coleman, "Monroe Doctrine." The published work that treats these events most wholly in accord with the spirit of this interpretation is Carlos Pereyra, *El mito de Monroe* (Buenos Aires: Jorge Alvarez, 1963).

10. May, *Making of the Monroe Doctrine,* pp. 221ff.

11. The oft-cited debate over whether the United States depended on the British navy for enforcement of the Monroe Doctrine misses the fundamental point about the doctrine. The United States had no intention of enforcing the doctrine on behalf of any interests other than those of the United States. If the British happened to behave in ways congruent with the doctrine, such behavior was neither motivated by a desire to enforce the Monroe Doctrine nor necessarily desired by the United States. And, of course, even Bemis has noted that the British themselves violated the manifest content of the Monroe Doctrine on a number of occasions.

12. Ernest May has noted that the presidential ambitions of Adams were best served by suppressing recognition of Grecian independence.

May, *Making of the Monroe Doctrine*, pp. 214–18, 228–40.

13. For evidence of the changing official interpretation of the need for U.S. intervention, see *Public Papers of the Presidents of the United States: Lyndon B. Johnson, 1965* (Washington, D.C.: Government Printing Office, 1966), 1:489ff, 461–62.

14. José A. Moreno, *The Dominican Revolution Revisited*, Latin American Monograph Series, no. 7 (Erie, Penn.: Northwestern Pennsylvania Institute for Latin American Studies, 1978), p. 32.

15. Theodore Draper, *The Dominican Report: A Case Study in American Policy* (New York: Commentary Report, 1968), pp. 80–96.

16. "Interview with Ambassador Lucey," *Proceso*, October 24, 1977.

17. On the contrived nature of the war, see Price, *Origins of the War*; Gastón García Cantú, *Las invasiones norteamericanas en México* (Mexico: Editorial ERA, 1970).

18. Price, *Origins of the War*, p. 197.

19. Salvador de Madariaga, *Latin America Between the Eagle and the Bear* (New York: Praeger, 1962), p. 74.

20. Morris Rosenberg, Sidney Verba, and Phillip Converse, *Vietnam and the Silent Majority: A Dove's Guide* (New York: Harper and Row, 1970), pp. 25–30. Compare Lee Sigelman, "Rallying to the President's Support: A Reappraisal of the Evidence," *Polity* 11 (Summer 1979): 542–61.

21. Note that Lyndon Johnson did not make explicit reference to the Monroe Doctrine in any of his three televised statements on the Dominican Republic invasion, but that State Department spokespersons did make reference to the doctrine.

22. Gil, *Latin American–United States Relations*, p. 65.

23. Benjamin Frankel, "Venezuela and the United States, 1810–1888" (Ph.D. diss., University of California, Berkeley, 1964), p. 387.

24. May, *Making of the Monroe Doctrine*, p. 260.

25. Melvin Gurtov, *The United States Against the Third World* (New York: Praeger, 1974), p. 2.

26. Ibid., pp. 4–8.

27. For a discussion of a third popular myth—that U.S. society offers equality of opportunity—see Kenneth M. Coleman, "Una reseña general de la mitología de la política exterior de los Estados Unidos" (Unpublished lecture delivered at El Colegio de Mexico, March 6, 1978), pp. 9–18.

28. The work of Fuentes Mares can be sampled in *La génesis del expansionismo norteamericano* (Mexico: El Colegio de Mexico, 1979). See also Darryl Baskin, *American Pluralist Democracy: A Critique* (New York: Van Nostrand, Reinhold, 1971), p. 112; Max Weber, *The Protestant Ethic and the Spirit of Capitalism*, trans. by Talcott Parsons (New York:

Charles Scribner's Sons, 1930), pp. 166, 170–72.

29. W. Lance Bennett, "Political Sanctification: The Civil Religion and American Politics," *Social Science Information* 14 (1975):83–85; Reinhold Neibuhr, *The Irony of American History* (New York: Charles Scribner's Sons, 1952), p. 70.

30. Or, as in the case of MacArthur, when generals feel that goals cannot be achieved by the observation of then-reigning moral standards of warfare, they are apt to intensify their attempts to depict current conflicts as moral crusades.

31. On the assassination attempts see Daniel Schorr, "Assassination: The CIA, Castro, and Kennedy," *New York Review of Books,* October 13, 1977, pp. 14–22.

32. Irving Janis discusses the deleterious consequences of excessive commitment to group harmony, a condition likely to be present in all moral crusades, in his provocative *Victims of Groupthink* (Boston: Houghton Mifflin, 1972).

33. Gurtov, *United States Against the Third World,* pp. 5–6.

34. Ole R. Holsti and James Rosenau, "The Lessons of Vietnam: Belief Systems of American Decision-Makers," *The International Journal* (Canada) 32 (Summer 1977):452–74.

35. Carter's appeal to return to a "foreign policy as good and as just as are the American people" is analyzed in Coleman, "The Monroe Doctrine as Political Symbol."

36. Cited in Bennett, "Political Sanctification," p. 84.

37. In the best of cases, U.S. foreign-policy makers seek to avoid conflict by educating the North American public as to the legitimate interests of other countries and how those interests have influenced bargaining between representatives of the United States and those other countries. A good example of such an attempt is Sol Linowitz, "The Panama Canal Treaties Are in the National Interest" (Speech delivered to the Chicago Council on Foreign Relations, October 18, 1977).

5

The Madness of the Method: The United States and Cuba in the Seventies

Enrique A. Baloyra

The Facts

During the past decade the United States and Cuba formalized their bilateral relations to a considerable degree. To be sure, this formalization fell substantially short of full-fledged diplomatic "normalization," but it provided a framework to end the state of informal belligerence that characterized the relations between the two countries in the sixties. Some of the issues resolved were really "threshold issues"[1] involving incidents and situations that had contributed to increased tensions in the past and could, in all likelihood, serve the same purpose in the future. The antihijacking agreement signed on February 15, 1973, two fishing agreements signed on April 27, 1977, and a treaty delineating the maritime boundaries between the two nations signed in December 1977 provided some ground rules in areas where considerable friction existed before.[2]

However, there were other developments that nibbled at the sorest spots in the relationship. On August 21, 1975, the United States relaxed some of the provisions of its economic embargo against Cuba.[3] "Interests sections" were simultaneously opened on September 1, 1977, in the Swiss embassy in Havana and in the embassy of Czechoslovakia in Washington, D.C., to represent the governments of the United States and Cuba respectively.[4] In 1978, unprecedented contacts took place in Havana between Cuban exiles and the Cuban government, culminating in the gradual release of Cuban political prisoners by the latter and in some 30,000 Cuban-Americans visiting their relatives on the island during the first months of 1979. This was hardly "business as usual."

Although serious obstacles remained, both sides showed a willingness to yield and to listen to each other. Despite denials of basic changes in policy, continued criticism of each other's failure to "show good faith" by refusing to accommodate the next set of demands, and protestations to the effect that no further moves would be possible unless such demands were met, both countries were closer in 1979 than at any point since they started drifting apart in late 1959.

It has been said, with good reason, that the basic objectives of the United States and Cuba were met with success during the sixties. The former prevented Cuba from creating many Vietnams in Latin America while the latter thwarted U.S. efforts to end the revolution.[5] If such was the case, how would one characterize a process of formalization that took place without the United States ending its economic embargo against Cuba and without Cuba getting out of the business of exporting revolution? Two explanations come to mind immediately. First, the embargo is not what it used to be, and Cuba has moved its act to a different continent. Second, the policies are not related in a causal sense, although they continue to be linked in the ongoing negotiations.

Leaving such concerns aside for the moment, a brief recapitulation of this process of formalization should provide some clues about what actually took place and should suggest possible developments in the future. This was, after all, a process that started during the Nixon administration, gained some impetus during the Ford administration, and came very close to normalization during the first year of the Carter administration. How did all this happen? Who set the process in motion?

The explanatory agenda is complex. At issue here is not just the question of whether U.S. policy toward Cuba follows a "rational" or a "bureaucratic-politics" model.[6] There are elements of both, but this would be a rather narrow focus given the multitude of interests and actors intervening in the process.

A number of third-party initiatives enhanced the framework of opportunities for negotiations that were then conducted by the protagonists. For example, Costa Rica, Colombia, Peru, Venezuela, and a number of Caribbean governments led a sustained effort to remove the sanctions enacted by the OAS against Cuba in 1964. The Nixon administration managed to neutralize the initiative on repeated occasions.[7] Finally, on July 29, 1975, the Ford administration joined fifteen other members of the OAS in voting to end diplomatic and commercial sanctions against Cuba. The lifting of the sanctions, plus the fact that countries like Venezuela—a target of Cuban subversion during the sixties—led the effort to rescind them, allowed the Ford administration to join in the initiative, neutralizing conservative criticism and saving face when, in August 1975, it relaxed some of the provisions of the U.S. embargo against Cuba.

The move was a victory for Cuba, which had long trumpeted that it would never return to the OAS, an organization that Cuban officials never ceased to condemn;[8] and it took advantage of the opportunity to heap praise on the governments voting against the sanctions and reestablishing diplomatic relations. In addition, Cuba took advantage of the new climate of opinion in Latin America to rejoin the Latin American caucus in international organizations and to participate in multilateral Latin American initiatives.[9] This all happened without Cuba rejoining the OAS.

Pressures from subsidiaries of U.S. firms and from their host governments also played a part. Perhaps the most published instance involved a deal between Argentine subsidiaries of GM, Ford, and Chrysler and the Cuban government for 44,000 vehicles worth between U.S. $130 and $150 million. The question had been "under study" for some time until the removal of the embargo allowed the Ford administration to grant the export licenses without creating too much trouble for itself. Licensing had also been a sore point in U.S.-Canadian relations. A Canadian subsidiary of Litton Industries, which had been denied previously the license to export office equipment to Cuba, was also granted one such license by the Ford administration.

With some of the more serious and respectable adversaries of the Cuban regime taking the initiative in these and other issues involving relations with Cuba, U.S. administrations could claim that they were responding to and not leading such efforts. In the case of OAS sanctions, it was the more democratic governments of the region, which had once joined in President Kennedy's call to "build a wall of dedicated men around Cuba," that led the drive to end such sanctions. On the other hand, in the case of the automotive transaction between Argentina and Cuba, it was not a maverick like Cyrus Eaton who was prodding the administration to change commercial policy toward Cuba, but rather some of the very pillars of U.S. capitalism. It was a question of redressing a situation in which U.S. businessmen were at a disadvantage in gaining access to a market that appeared very lucrative.[10]

Members of Congress, and especially the Senate, offered much advice but found little to consent to. Liberal criticism of the Cuban policy focused on the embargo. Senators Kennedy, Fulbright, Sparkman, and Church were most prominent in issuing periodic proposals for a reexamination of the objectives of the Cuba policy. Senator Buckley called for a national debate before "plunging into" relations with Cuba. Members of the House stole the thunder from Senate liberals on numerous occasions by issuing their own policy proposals. In January of 1973, twelve members of the House of Representatives issued the statement "A Détente with Cuba" urging the Nixon administration to normalize relations with Cuba. They saw the need and desirability for normalization (1) as a natural extension of the policy of détente practiced toward China and the Soviet Union, (2) as a recognition of the growing trend among Latin American nations to normalize their relations with Cuba, and (3) as reciprocity to Cuba's apparent softening of its intransigent foreign policy.[11] Faithful keepers of the "Cuba watch" could have told them that Cuba is not China[12] and that it would take more than principle and realism to make the administration change a policy perceived as relatively costless at that time.[13] Ironically, the embargo was having an impact on Cuba.

Congressional committees provided an arena for discussion and formulation of new strategies. On April 23, 1974, the Senate Foreign Relations Committee unanimously approved a resolution calling for an end to the embargo and a renewal of relations. Proposed initially by Senator Jacob Javits and adopted as a rider to a State Department appropriations bill, it was not binding on the administration. Pat Holt, a senior staff member of the committee, visited Cuba in the summer of 1974 and upon his return wrote a report that was published widely.[14] In May of 1976 the House Committee on International Relations produced its own report written by Barry Sklar, a senior researcher for the Library of Congress who had visited Cuba in the fall of 1975.[15] Sklar's report was aimed to serve "the continuing interest in Congress in Cuba policy."[16] On May 10, 1977, the Senate Foreign Relations Committee voted 10 to 6 to ease the trade embargo and enable Cuba to buy medicines, food, and agricultural products in the United States. This was a watered-down version of Senator McGovern's original proposal to end the embargo. The House responded 252 to 158, reaffirming its opposition to trade with Cuba while approving a foreign-aid bill that eliminated "outmoded restrictions" to aid foreign countries that trade with Cuba.

Visits to Cuba by congressional delegations or individual members of Congress produced similar statements and counter-proposals, while providing a useful avenue for a direct exchange of views with high-ranking officials, including Fidel Castro. In late September of 1974 Senators Jacob Javits and Claiborne Pell visited Cuba, engaging in a "very frank" discussion with Fidel Castro. Javits reported that he outlined U.S. objections to Cuban policies including the military connection with the Soviet Union, the human rights question, and the matter of compensation. Castro replied with an inventory of his objections to U.S. policies toward Cuba. Senator George McGovern visited the island in May of 1975, spent considerable time with Castro, and took up with him the matter of political prisoners. Upon his return, McGovern called for a suspension of the embargo and normalization of relations. Representative Jonathan Bingham went to Cuba in February of 1977, discussing these two concerns in meetings with Cuban Vice-president Carlos Rafael Rodríguez and President Castro.

In April of 1977, Senator McGovern returned to Cuba, accompanied by Senator James Abourezk, Representative Les Aspin, and a basketball team from the University of South Dakota. The Americans took advantage of the opportunity to raise the issue of Cuban troops in Africa, while General Raúl Castro, who praised the visit as "an important step toward the normalization of relations between the two countries," complained about reconnaissance flights over Cuba. President Castro, who had just returned from a visit to the Soviet Union, met with McGovern and added the issue of the Guantánamo base to his preconditions for normalization. In August of 1977, in what was described by the Carter administration as a visit of enormous importance, Senator Frank Church traveled to Cuba in an Air Force plane and spent three days on the island. The Cuban government reciprocated, allowing eighty-four U.S. citizens and their families to leave Cuba. Church and Castro spent considerable time together, and Church reported that the latter did not request any specific concessions from the United States. Church reportedly took advantage of the opportunity to criticize the Cuban presence in Africa.

In spite of editorializing to the effect that these visits were counterproductive and tended to confuse the objectives of U.S. policy toward Cuba, it is hard to conceive that these congressmen did not convey a sense of that policy to the Cubans. At least in the case of the Church visit, which took place shortly before the opening of the interest sections, the administration presumably took advantage of the opportunity to convey messages to the Cuban government.[17] To be sure, grandstanding and posturing occurred, but the visits fell short of having the impact of "shuttle diplomacy." If anything, they added to what seems to have been a very arduous and difficult process of negotiations that took place through different channels and levels. In addition, these contacts enabled the Cuban government to explain or at least justify their policies and gave the visitors an opportunity to gauge Cuban strategy for the process of formalization.

Congress was also an arena for criticism of U.S. and Cuban policies. Liberals were the most outspoken during the Nixon and Ford administrations, while moderates and conservatives were most vocal during Carter's. Although the cleavage produced by the issue of "relations with Cuba" had a marked ideological nature that tended to blur party lines, partisanship remained a relevant distinction.

Liberal proposals to end the embargo have been noted, as well as the 1977 House vote against any such initiative. The question of Africa was raised by forty senators who wrote a letter to Castro in December of 1977. On December 24, Castro rejected the letter and charged "the Carter administration" of blackmailing Cuba. The Republican minority, on the other hand, took exception to the opening of the interest sections. On June 3, 1977, Senator Robert Dole announced that he would introduce legislation restricting any further steps toward normalization, while Senator Howard Baker said that the move had been inopportune.

Congressional liberals also had the opportunity to criticize the Cuban regime on the issue of human rights. On August 28, 1976, Senator Edward Kennedy, for one, chided the Cubans for not allowing international organizations to observe the condition of Cuban political prisoners. Senator McGovern had criticized Castro in person during his 1975 visit for Cuba's failure to release the prisoners.

Congress was therefore much more than an interested and passive observer in the process of formalization. Even though the different administrations tried to retain their monopoly of Cuban policymaking, Congress forced its way in on a number of occasions.

Contacts between members of the Cuban community in the United States and the Cuban premier himself provided an unexpected arena for the discussion of issues of capital importance to the former. The unprecedented nature of these contacts could hardly be overemphasized. To be sure, the community remained very divided on the question of Cuban relations, but the fact that some prominent members of that community incurred the wrath of their neighbors attests to the high efficacy they attached to the contacts. Leftist members of the community had been visiting the island since the early seventies. Their presence had been more visible since February of 1978 when a contingent of students and young professionals created the Antonio Maceo Brigade and visited the island. However, the new contacts involved some segments of the mainstream of the community, including businessmen and clergy.

On September 11, 1978, President Castro met with eleven

Cuban-American reporters, most of them based in Miami, and expressed a willingness to release the political prisoners and widen the exchanges to include "representative elements" of the community. On October 24, 1978, the Cuban president received a delegation of exiles and accepted a "preagenda" document presented to him by the exiles. He agreed to (1) schedule a gradual release of the prisoners, (2) facilitate access to Cuba for Cubans living abroad, and (3) facilitate the reunification of Cuban families. Considering that Article 32 of the Cuban constitution approved on February 24, 1976, excluded many of the members of the exile delegation from the definition of "Cuban,"[18] Castro's willingness to meet with them and consent to their demands signified an unmistakable desire on the part of the Cuban government to get closer to the community.

On November 5, 1978, counselor Ramón Sánchez Parodi declared in Washington that most political prisoners would be eligible for amnesty and that Cuba hoped to hold discussions with exile representatives on family reunification and travel. In early December a delegation of 75 Cuban-Americans traveled to Havana and met with Castro and other Cuban officials, agreeing on the text of a joint declaration stressing the aforementioned objectives. The first group of 70 liberated prisoners arrived in Miami shortly thereafter. An additional group of some 400 prisoners was to leave on January 1, 1979; others would follow as soon as the Justice Department processed them and granted them permits to enter the United States. Some members of the delegation, as well as the Cuban government, criticized the slowness with which Attorney General Griffin Bell was proceeding to grant admittance to the United States to those released from jail.

Even though these exchanges had an unofficial nature, at least from the standpoint of the U.S. government, the Carter administration derived some benefits from an initiative adopted by more recalcitrant adversaries of the Cuban regime. It was very difficult to criticize the administration's decision to admit the prisoners, although some did not think Bell was proceeding "with all deliberate speed." Conservative criticism was absent in this regard, but members of the community charged, with good reason, that the price of the "tours" the exiles were purchasing to visit their families on the island was leonine. In addition many were routed through Jamaica, thereby wasting two of the seven days of the tour. Yet for the Carter administration, the informality of the arrangement provided some grounds to avoid criticism, since these efforts were concerted among the Cubans themselves and clearly coincided with the emphasis on human rights articulated by the president in his first years in office.

The momentum of the new initiative lost some steam when, in late April 1979, the Cuban government imposed restrictions on the amount of goods that exiles traveling to Cuba could bring. A deposit was required to guarantee that, upon their exit, they would take everything back. This irritated many who had made the down payments for their trips solely for the purpose of bringing their relatives certain items that could not be readily purchased in Cuba. Apparently the Cuban government was reacting to internal pressures on this issue. It became evident that there was domestic discontent with a policy that allowed the less-enthusiastic supporters of the regime, or those who still opposed it, to gain access to some consumer goods ordinary Cubans had not seen in some time.

If most of the initiatives leading to these steps toward formalization came from outsiders, what were the roles of the U.S. and Cuban governments in this process? Were they simply passive actors who waited for others to test and try out new strategies or did they have a hand in all this? Or was this perhaps a measure of the success with which the Cuban government had induced third parties to pressure the U.S. government into some concessions? Were the Cubans so crafty and astute that they were winning by turning the tables on the United States, leaving the Americans "behind" and isolating them from the more progressive elements within the OAS and other regional organizations? Was the U.S. government simply reacting to "constituency demands" for a new relationship with Cuba? Did the Ford and Carter administrations lose control of their Cuba policies?

The Madness

The governments of the United States and Cuba became very much involved in the maneuvering that led to a partial formalization of relations in the late seventies. Cuba, with more to win, adopted a more activist role, while the United States, which found it difficult to give up a relatively costless policy, was somewhat less active. In addition, it is inaccurate to say that both governments did not relate to each other. To be sure, their mutual exchanges were not always conciliatory or civil, but they made efforts to influence each other as well as the march of events. Despite the intermittent nature of the process, the heavy rhetoric utilized in the public channel of interaction, and the denials that anything substantive was taking place, the method produced results. There was no major "failure" of U.S. policy toward Cuba, nor was Cuba completely frustrated in its dealings with successive administrations. There was, after all, a method to the apparent madness.

The element of continuity in U.S. policy toward Cuba was provided by a strategy of "restrained hostility,"[19] of "economic denial"[20] implemented through the embargo. The complementary objective of isolating Cuba in order to prevent the spread of revolution into Latin America was as much a strategy of the United States as of those countries who voted to impose sanctions against Cuba in 1964. Changes in Cuban foreign policy toward Latin America provided the evidence and inducement necessary to convince those countries that the sanctions were no longer justified. As we have seen, the United States did not lead in this effort but joined in the vote to remove the sanctions and derived some benefits from it. However, so far as we know, Cuba never tried to export revolution to the United States and there was little need to move much further on this score, although the provisions of the embargo were relaxed somewhat.

The process of formalization could not really proceed beyond the initial stages of bargaining. U.S. policy continued to rely on the embargo as the only leverage with which it could extract some concessions from Cuba. The Cubans perceived the embargo as an act of hostility and made the removal of the embargo a precondition for normalization. The United States perceived Cuba's Africa policy as a new installment in the saga of exporting the revolution. "Linkage" between the two issues was the wrong formula to move the negotiations to the trade-off stage since neither side could yield.

Fidel Castro has repeatedly defined the embargo as a knife at the throat of the Cuban people. The embargo, the Cubans readily admit, has contributed to the disarticulation of the Cuban economy.[21] Every American official who has visited Cuba recently has left with the clear impression that *el bloqueo* ("the blockade"), as the Cubans call it, "has been elevated to a dominant place superseding and affecting conversations on all other issues."[22] There is no question, therefore, that this policy has been effective. It has been at least sufficient to arouse intense reactions among Cubans. However, since no U.S. administration seemed to have made a thorough review of the purposes of and the justification for the embargo—a strategy put in practice during the most belligerent stage in U.S.-Cuban relations—the Cubans assumed that the United States remained basically hostile to the Cuban revolution. Thus the element of continuity in U.S. policy toward Cuba was perceived by the latter as an act of hostility.

Conversely, one element of continuity in Cuban policy, assistance to allies involved in struggles of national liberation in the Third World, presented U.S. officials with a dilemma concerning the interpretation of Havana's true intentions. Cuba's export of the revolution to Latin America was clearly a policy of confrontation with the United States during the sixties. The fact that Cuba was promoting revolution in Africa during the seventies was proof of continued Cuban hostility toward the United States. The element of "personal pique"[23] was once again at work in U.S.-Cuban relations. The old image of "the inborn, inbred, ineradicable anti-Yankeeism of Fidel Castro"[24] once again dominated U.S. perceptions of Cuba.[25]

Profound psychological reasons prevented U.S. officials from granting any rationality to the Cuban presence in Africa or any credibility to the *direct* explanations offered by Cuban officials. Even though Secretary of State Henry Kissinger believed that Cuba had committed itself willingly to the Africa policy and had not been "forced" into it by the Soviet Union, he viewed the whole matter as irresponsible: "Who has ever heard of Cubans in Africa?" On June 5, 1977, with Carter already in office, Senate minority leader Howard Baker tried to dampen further moves toward reconciliation with Cuba, arguing that he could not believe for one minute that the Cuban presence in Africa represented an extension of Cuban foreign policy. A small nation was not supposed to do those things. The fact that the Soviet Union was also helping in the effort was conclusive proof that the Cubans were acting as surrogates for the former.

Attempts to link these two elements of continuity in the policies of both countries produced another stalemate in the process of formalization, but did not result in its ultimate demise. The fact that, during the seventies, the issues of the embargo and of Africa could not be linked to one another is no indication that normalization was impossible or that they cannot be linked to other concerns during the eighties. To be sure, Cuba will not accept this linkage, at least in the *form* that has been presented, for reasons that go at least as far back as the Platt Amendment.[26] It is difficult for the Cuban government to really justify the loss of young Cuban lives in Africa, and it may become even more so if Cuban troops stay there a long time. But the hagiography of 100 years of Cuban struggle for self-determination offers ample justification for adopting an apparently recalcitrant stance on the question of foreign interference with Cuban policies.[27] If Cole Blasier was correct in saying that the elimination of U.S. influence was one of the major achievements of the Cuban revolution,[28] it is very unlikely that the Cuban government will yield to open, defiant demands made by a U.S. administration. This type of pressure or, better, this style of applying pressure is irreconcilable to the Cuban conception of normalization.

Additional elements of unreality seemed to have influenced the demeanor of the protagonists and explain in part the tentativeness of some of their moves. The U.S. administrations acted as if it would be better "to let a sleeping dog lie." Anticipated negative reactions from domestic critics, the Latin American republics, and the Cuban community in the United States made the administration in power very cautious in its approach to Cuba. Yet we have seen that much of this failed to materialize and that, on the contrary, elements within the ranks of these traditional adversaries of Fidel Castro provided much of the impetus for formalization.

One of the dormant fleas on the dog may have been U.S. public opinion. However, the evidence suggests that during the seventies the matter of Cuban relations appeared to have taken on the character of a "valence" or consensus issue among the U.S. public. If anything, the mood of the U.S. public was for normalization of relations with Cuba. To be sure, Americans were not impressed with the Cuban experiment. In 1968 only 6 percent of Americans polled gave Cuba a positive rating,[29] while in 1976 the percentage of registered voters predisposed favorably toward Cuba did not exceed 15 percent.[30] In 1978, a Gallup study commissioned by the Chicago Council on Foreign Relations showed that the attitude of the U.S. public toward Cuba remained relatively cold.[31]

But this antipathy has not been translated into a jingoistic desire to "get Cuba,"[32] nor has it represented an obstacle to normalization. In early 1973, 71 percent of a national sample were in favor of sending Secretary of State Henry Kissinger to Havana to open a round of shuttle diplomacy.[33] Obviously, Richard Nixon was not predisposed to take this initiative— and probably Castro would not have been able to accept it— but the Ford and Carter administrations would have had little selling to do on the question of relations with Cuba. In late 1974, 63 percent of registered American voters would have been in favor of such an initiative even in the middle of an election campaign,[34] while 50 percent of the entire electorate would have supported such a move.[35] In 1977, in spite of the well-publicized Cuban involvement in Africa, 53 percent would have supported normalization.[36]

This evidence questions the conventional wisdom concerning the ease with which one could lose an election in the United States by favoring relations with Cuba. It may still be true in congressional or even senatorial races, but it is highly debatable in the case of a presidential race. The fact that Nixon would not entertain such a move, that Ford was never elected on his own, and that Carter's attempts came very early in his presidency may help explain the caution, but only in part. A phobia against provoking the electorate into a violent reaction seems to have been a major concern that has given a cyclical nature to the process of formalization, at least during the Ford and

Carter terms. Notice that most of the measures resulting from the process have come in odd years: the antihijacking agreement (1973), the relaxation of the embargo (1975), the agreement on fisheries (1977), the opening of interest sections (1977), the end of blacklisting against third parties (1977), and the agreement of maritime boundaries (1977).

This is not to say that there have been no other factors contributing to the cyclical aspect of the process or at least lending it an intermittent character. A safe candidate is the export price of Cuban sugar, which added its own measure of madness to the process. In 1974–1975, the bonanza in international sugar prices made Cuba a very attractive market, as witnessed by the U.S. $1.2 billion in credit Argentina granted to Cuba. This was followed by the brouhaha of the export licenses and the deal between the subsidiaries of U.S. automakers and the Cubans. The prospects for trade became so attractive that those who hurried into the action spent very little time pondering any linkage regarding compensation, where the Cuban government had shown flexibility before,[37] or any other issue.

Somewhat (but not entirely) surprising was the ease with which several different delegations from U.S. businesses went to Cuba, met with top Cuban officials, and were wined and dined. If the latter were trying to use these as conduits for stepping up the process of formalization they certainly fell short. The moment the Castro regime did not appear to have the disposable income that had been anticipated, these new-found friends dropped out of sight. The dash to Havana by U.S. businesses was ironic, for, twenty years before, they had responded to the Cuban revolution in a visceral fashion, demanding from the Eisenhower administration the destruction of the Cuban regime. They could have made amends for past mistakes, including their refusal to accept guarantees of payments for confiscated properties. At that time they believed they would not have to deal with Castro for long. In the late seventies they believed that they could make money in Cuba. They were wrong on both counts.

A "new" relationship with Cuba could not be justified on the grounds of great economic benefits for the United States. Although individual companies could derive substantial benefits from commerce with Cuba, the benefits to the U.S. economy would be more modest. Carmelo Mesa-Lago has shown that while such mutual benefits would not be spectacular, Cuba would probably benefit through reducing freight costs, eliminating triangular trade, exporting sugar and nickel to the United States, and increasing revenues from tourism.[38] Given Cuba's continued emphasis on capital expenditures plus the structure of the Cuban import trade, U.S. export potential to Cuba would stay at a modest U.S. $600 to $750 million annually.[39]

In short, the economic justification was not sufficient, and the haste and improvisation with which the argument was made could not have carried the day. It was foolhardy to try to justify formalization on the basis of priority for economic considerations. In addition, the economic incentive alone, powerful as it undoubtedly was and is, could not woo Cuba back. The Cubans knew perfectly well that their greatest advantage with COMECON was the ability to shield themselves from the cyclical fluctuations of their export prices. They could harbor little hope that capitalist countries could or would match the terms of their financial and commercial covenants with the socialist camp. The Cubans admitted their economic difficulties to all kinds of visitors, but they could scarcely be eager to fall under the tutelage of IMF and the World Bank.

If these attempts proved unreal, what are we to say of efforts to manipulate presidential election campaigns in this country in order to maintain the status quo in U.S.-Cuban relations? I of course refer to the Watergate affair and, indirectly, to the prolonged "secret war" of the CIA against Fidel Castro,[40] as well as to the response of some former participants in such activities to the process of formalization. Little can be added here to the now-voluminous literature on Watergate. As for the CIA, it is doubtful that the agency will be able to extricate itself from the legal restraints imposed upon it before relations with Cuba are restored in full. However, some of its former operatives have shown a willingness to continue on a war footing against Castro.[41]

Those involved in acts of hostility may find a justification for their intransigence in the ideals and actions of Cuban revolutionary leaders of the past 100 years. To them any attempt at dialogue or bargaining with the Cuban government would by definition be a sellout. Crooked politicians deal with each other through compromise, true revolutionaries remain loyal to their principles regardless of the odds.

Some of the initiatives adopted by members of the Cuban community in the United States have resulted in the gradual liberation of Cuban political prisoners and have made it less difficult to travel to Cuba. Even if these initiatives have tended to polarize opinion in the community, even if they have been abused and not given the credit they deserve, they have made it more difficult for the terrorists to justify their activities. Unfortunately, more lives will probably be wasted before they desist from their actions or are brought to justice.[42] The more successful the results of contacts between members of the community and the Cuban government, the more likely it is that the community will take a more active part in putting an end to terrorism. This will have to include resolute action against those who use their "patriotic" activities against Castro as a cover for drug trafficking and other illegal activities.

The process of formalization helped to debunk one additional misconception concerning the form and substance of reconciliation with Cuba. This involved the question of whether a republican or democratic administration is more likely to bring about normalization with Cuba. First of all, Gerald Ford and Jimmy Carter made use of "the method" of dealing with Cuba in fairly similar ways. They were subject to similar pressures, tried to handle them in similar ways, made similar mistakes, and produced some concrete results before reaching a new impasse in the negotiations. Undoubtedly Carter achieved more, but he had the benefit of a wider set of direct and indirect contacts with Cuba and was perceived more favorably by the Cubans, at least at the start of his presidency.

Second, a comparison of the rebuttals and denials uttered by the Ford and Carter administrations shows a marked identity in the obstacles that they claimed were preventing full-fledged normalization. On March 1, 1975, Secretary Kissinger remarked at a civic club gathering in Houston that there was "no virtue in perpetual antagonism between the United States and Cuba." According to Kissinger this could be ended if Cuba demonstrated a readiness to assume a mutuality of obligation and regard. The question of military ties with countries outside the hemisphere was also mentioned. In August, following the relaxation of some of the provisions of the embargo, the State Department identified some of the divisive issues that had to be solved. Among these were family visits in both directions, the release of U.S. political prisoners held in Cuba, and Cuba's failure to adhere to strict principles of nonintervention, as witnessed by Cuban activism on the question of Puerto Rico. President Ford expressed concern about Cuban involvement in Angola in December of 1975. Secretary Kissinger returned to the theme the following February. On February 28, 1976, Ford's characterization of Castro as an "international outlaw" was accompanied by an insistence on Cuban withdrawal from Africa, restraint on the Puerto Rico question, and nonintervention in Latin America's internal problems as preconditions for further talks. Kissinger's stern if vacuous warning of March 22 to the effect that the United States would not tolerate Cuban interventionism abroad appeared to have marked another impasse in the process of formalization.

It is important to stress that Castro tried to rebuild his links to the Ford administration following this vituperative exchange that marked the first half of 1976. Castro wrote a letter to Swedish Premier Olof Palme "in response to criticism of Cuba in the Swedish press," stating that Cuba would begin to withdraw its troops from Angola at the rate of 200 per week. Castro authorized Palme, who received the letter on May 21, to share its contents with Kissinger, who visited Sweden at that time. On May 25, the latter declared in Luxembourg that this was a positive development although the rate of withdrawal should be stepped up. The regime of Agostinho Neto turned out to be weaker than anticipated and the Cuban withdrawal had to be slowed. Nevertheless, this helped to ease tensions somewhat.

In addition, according to the testimony of former Assistant Secretary of State for Inter-American Affairs William D. Rogers, direct contacts between the Ford administration and the Cuban government began in November of 1974. Lawrence Eagleburger, executive assistant to Secretary Kissinger, telephoned the Cuban mission to the United Nations and explained the desire of the Ford administration to hold private talks. Following a series of meetings at which the initial negotiating positions of both countries were disclosed, a series of steps were taken by both governments to indicate their seriousness and goodwill. The last meeting took place in late November of 1975 between Rogers and a Cuban envoy from Havana. Therefore, Carter inherited from Ford a much better situation on relations with Cuba than had Ford from Richard Nixon.

Carter on his part renewed the informal contacts, this time between Terence Todman, Rogers' successor, and Pelegrín Torras, the Cuban deputy minister for foreign affairs. Carter's complaints about Cuba were made public on February 16, 1977. He linked improved relations with the island to human rights, family visits, the release of political prisoners, and the question of Cuban interference in Angola. On March 5, he repeated these concerns during a call-in radio broadcast. On June 2, White House press secretary Jody Powell qualified the announcement concerning the opening of interest sections by saying that this was simply a "procedural step" and that substantial differences still existed. He added the issue of compensation for confiscated properties to Carter's previous list. On June 9, Castro dismissed as insufficient the measure adopted by the Senate Foreign Relations Committee that would ease embargo restrictions a bit further, while saying that although Carter's intentions were good, full diplomatic ties could not be restored soon. On September 28, Castro reiterated that the removal of the embargo remained a precondition for normalization, and he asked for the devolution of the Guantánamo base as an additional precondition.

During 1978, an election year, the Carter administration was under considerable pressure to undo much of what had been accomplished by the process of formalization. On March 23, National Republican Chairman Bill Brock asked for the expulsion of the Cuban diplomats from Washington and for the recall of counselor Lyle Lane and his entourage from Havana. Senate majority leader Robert Byrd echoed the proposal, perhaps anticipating a nonbinding interpretation of the Senate resolution (53 to 29) calling for the suspension of all relations with Cuba. To his credit Carter resisted the onslaught, although he found means and opportunity to make criticisms of his own. On May 14 he mentioned his concern over Soviet domination of Cuba and the lack of human rights. This was not as harsh as Ford's "outlaw" statement, but it marked the low point in the cycle.

In November, after the elections, the administration saw an improvement of relations over the following winter. This may have come by way of closer contacts between the Cuban community and the Cuban government. It was Castro's turn to bid. On May 18, 1979, during a visit to Mexico he complained that relations were as abysmal as ever, that the United States continued with its miserable boycott, and that Carter could not criticize Cuba on the question of human rights. Perhaps he was venting his frustration, anticipating that nothing of substance could occur until the presidential campaign of 1980 would clarify who was to occupy the White House.

The Method

This account of the process of formalization between Cuba and the United States may sound all too cynical. It is not. If anything, I have tried to show that there was a method to the madness of U.S.-Cuban relations in the seventies. There were mistakes and miscalculations; both sides continued to misinterpret one another; some opportunities were lost. At the end of the decade Fidel Castro did not really understand the United States any better than his U.S. visitors understood him and his revolution. Critics continued to refer to the embargo as ineffective, outmoded, anomalous. Cuba's export of the revolution was still attacked on grounds of irresponsibility, irrationality, and warmongering. However, what made this decade different was that *substantial progress was made* and most of the gains were retained.

What are the lessons that can be drawn from this process, and what kinds of improvements might be suggested for the future? The most important lesson is that a series of contradictions remain and they will be very difficult to resolve. The basic problem will be adjusting to the creative tensions of these contradictions and not confusing the problems they create with the basic antagonism between Cuba and the United States. In addition, both sides, or at least the United States, will have to clarify what is being pursued. The anomaly of nonrelations can no longer be argued, for *there are relations.*

> CONTRADICTION 1: If the essence of the Cuban revolution is the permanent defiance of the imperialist government of the United States,[43] then the regime of Fidel Castro cannot afford normalization with the United States.

As far as political systems go, Cuba and the United States follow models that are mutually exclusive. That is obviously not the main problem, however, since the United States has relations with Communist countries, including small ones, and Cuba has relations with capitalist countries, including large ones. The real issue is whether the Cuban regime, as presently constituted, can survive the contaminating effect of relations with the United States. In spite of the process of institution building that occurred in Cuba during the seventies, the Cuban regime still retained its *fidelista* ("Castroite") essence by the end of the decade. Notwithstanding the emphasis on economic development that the regime began publicizing in the seventies, the Cuban regime derives its legitimacy from political criteria. Among these, the heroic-leadership style of Fidel Castro and the political accomplishments of the revolution are paramount. The struggle against the United States provides incentive to both.

> CONTRADICTION 2: The essence of the policy of embargo does not respond to a consideration of economic denial alone. The embargo illustrates a fundamental ambivalence with respect to Cuba on the part of the United States. Maintenance of the embargo responds to a series of concerns (including economic ones), but even more importantly, to a desire to elicit a respectful attitude from Cuba toward the United States.

The reasons why Cuba perceives the embargo as hostile have been noted as well as the ineffective attempts to link the embargo to changes in policy from Cuba, which have occurred of Cuba's own accord. However, since there is little question that the embargo will not destroy the Cuban revolution, what is really being served by its continuation? At bottom, I believe that the best explanation was provided some time ago by a U.S. president and repreated almost verbatim by his secretary of state on several occasions: "As long as Castro is adopting an antagonistic, anti-American line, we are certainly not going to normalize our relations with Castro."

The problem is that the president who made this statement was never known for his evenhandedness with Cuba. Given his basic hostility toward Cuba, Richard Nixon did not have to justify his continuation of the embargo—a cornerstone of normalization—with much diplomatic cosmetology. This, I believe, remains a very central concern of the basic presidential attitude toward Cuba. The indicators of Cuban hostility toward the United States may change, but U.S. presidents will need many public gestures of Cuban respect for the United States before normalization can take place. In addition, normalization is deeply intertwined with classic concerns about who wins and who loses in a negotiation between adversaries. A U.S. president could probably live with a Cuban regime claiming the abolition of the embargo and the return of Guantánamo base as major victories for Cuba. However, it would be very difficult for a U.S. president to yield on these issues before a relatively prolonged interval of amicable relations between both countries. This leads to a third contradiction that is by now very familiar.

CONTRADICTION 3. Since Cuba demands the total abolition of the embargo as a precondition for normalization, and since the United States links normalization to a change in Cuba's basic attitude toward the United States, the embargo is likely to remain linked to normalization for the foreseeable future.

I have no doubt that normalization cannot be produced without the United States returning Guantánamo. By normalization I mean cordial, warm relations existing between both countries. However, we have just seen that the reasons for the continuation of the embargo, although not the justification for it, may be more profound and lasting than the Cuban presence in Africa. I must stress that I have focused on the embargo here because it has been the most stable Cuban precondition for normalization and has been the one objective repeated with the greatest vehemence by Cuban officials. The Guantánamo issue could come next in line and the argument would still hold. Only the issue would be different; the concerns would remain on both sides.

CONTRADICTION 4: Since the embargo or *bloqueo* has been utilized by the Cuban regime as a justification and rallying point to mobilize the Cuban people for the task of socialist construction, the Cuban regime could not justify in the immediate future a noticeable change in its attitude toward the United States unless the embargo were abolished.

This is the point on which Cuba could insist that the United States yield, so that the regime could have more success in selling normalization to its supporters at home. The abolition of the *bloqueo* would give the Cubans a moral victory, and they have shown that they can get much mileage out of a victory like this. More importantly it would show the Cuban people that the United States no longer wants to destroy the revolution, although it may remain unsympathetic to revolutionary methods. However, the Cuban regime has done little to prepare Cubans for this kind of an attitude, partly because it has not had much reason to do so, and partly because it will prove very difficult. In addition, in view of Contradiction 2, the Cubans could very well afford to tone down their rhetoric as a gesture of goodwill, even if they continue to appear as radical in the United States. There is little to gain from continued vituperation.

Most successful political experiments are based on contradictions. That is why I see no major reason for gloom or despair concerning the future of U.S.-Cuban relations. Fidel Castro has shown a remarkable ability to deal with contradictions, and he will eventually meet his match when a U.S. administration musters the resolve to take advantage of a conjunctural moment. But let us not forget that there *are* relations. They were restored during the seventies as a result of the practice of traditional diplomacy between the two countries, conducted through secret or private channels utilized by middle-level officials. Enough instruments are in place to allow for continuing negotiations on issues of bilateral interest, including further relaxation of the *bloqueo,* without the need for immediate normalization.

But what is really meant by normalization? Do people refer to the status quo ante between Cuba and the United States and if so, what historical period do they have in mind? It seems absurd to talk about normalization except in terms other than "cordial relations." That seems to be the only logical and reasonable standard applicable. But, like the phoenix, cordial relations must rise from the ashes. Can this normalization be achieved in the short run? Can we do away with the four contradictions by fiat? Can the removal of the embargo, either in part or in full, and the deescalation of Cuban intervention in Africa produce normalization?

Normalization must be preceded by more negotiations, or "conversations" as the Cubans call them, within a framework of formalization. The process has worked, and not many things between the United States and Cuba have in the last two decades. Formalization has produced results. They may not look like much, but when contrasted to the situation that existed in the sixties, they are impressive. Formalization provides some deniability with which to allay criticism of the hard-liners on both sides. More time is needed for formalization to produce further results along the lines of the agenda suggested by William Watts and Jorge Domínguez,[44] for example, so that the legitimacy of the process is accepted by broader sectors. After all, this does not seem to be far from Castro's game plan during the seventies. He tried to get the most while yielding the least. He engaged in negotiations but admitted only that they were conversations. He exchanged ambassadors but insisted on calling them "counselors." He protested that he would not negotiate unless his preconditions were met, but he negotiated. Can he, or we, afford to call the new formalized relations "normalization" when they are yet far from cordial?

One actor likely to increase in relevance in the future is the Cuban community in the United States. The release of the political prisoners removed the *most* difficult obstacle to rapprochement between the community and the Cuban government. South Florida and Metropolitan Dade County, in particular, should receive additional congressional seats from the reapportionment that follows the 1980 census. Cuban Americans could well win at least one of these seats. Electing one of their own to the U.S. Congress should increase their political leverage both in Washington and in Havana and provide them with their own representative to defend their interests in the ongoing process.

One supreme irritant has been removed—the community now has its own direct links with the Cuban government and does not need to rely on the opinion of any Yankee "expert," whether a revolutionary tourist or an "informed" conservative, to get the facts on Cuba. The community needs no intermediaries other than its own members who want to participate in a dialogue with Cuba. But the community cannot label what has occurred as normalization, for it still falls short of the mark. More time is needed to produce further results, involve more people, gain more concessions from Cuba, and make relations more cordial.

One remaining question concerns the Cuban connection with the Soviet Union, which gives rise to a major contradiction for which I do not have even a difficult cure. It has frequently been said that one of the goals of U.S. policy toward Cuba is the elimination of that connection.[45] I do not foresee that Castro will disengage from the Soviets' military and economic ties completely, nor that U.S. policy initiatives will create enough incentives for him to do so. On the other hand, I do not think the Soviets forced him after the 1974 Brezhnev visit to mend fences with the United States, although they certainly suggested to him that it would be in Cuba's interest to do so. In other words, I believe that the Soviet connection is as permanent as Cuba's commitment to socialism.

I have long subscribed to the *lo de comunistas fue sólo un truquito*[46] theory of the Cuban revolution. Thus, I reject any notion of stages or of an irreversible configuration in the structure of the Cuban regime until we have seen the end of the beginning—that is, some kind of reconciliation between Cuba and the rest of those hemispheric regimes that first opposed the Cuban revolution. To be sure, a "return to the fold" or a full-fledged normalization between Cuba and her former adversaries has not been anticipated. We have yet to see the consequences and ultimate implications that formalization may produce in Cuba, but it may mark the end of the beginning, closing an initial cycle of twenty years in the Cuban revolution.

In looking at the present structural configuration of the Cuban regime in 1979, I conclude that Fidel Castro and his immediate collaborators seriously intend to build a socialist system in Cuba. This poses a great contradiction for the United States as well as for Cubans who live in this country. The question is how two antagonistic systems can relate to one another in terms other than an adversary relationship. How can they have cordial and intimate relations without undermining their foundations? Even more to the point, how can U.S. Cubans relate to a system with which they are in fundamental disagreement? More importantly, can the Cubans resolve a problem whose solution has so far eluded us in the twentieth century—namely, that of creating a society in which social equality and civil liberties are equally important? Can Cuba become a *truly open* socialist society? How can the members of the Cuban community in the United States collaborate in such an effort without doing violence to their principles?

If my theory is correct, this would be a good opportunity for Fidel Castro to show his true priorities. He insists that he is a Communist, that he is finally giving an important role to a Communist party organized along Soviet lines, and that he is deeply committed to the socialist camp. Obviously, if his main motive is to create a profound contrast between Cuba and the United States he certainly has succeeded. If socialism offers him a *comprehensive* solution to the problems facing Cuba, then why is he so insistent in his attempts to rebuild bridges? To be sure, his socialism has many unique features and obviously leaves ample room for improvement. U.S. Cubans have had the experience of trying to preserve their identity while living in the Colossus of the North; perhaps they have something unique to say about what it means to be Cuban.

There is no need to stress the fact that this contradiction cannot be reconciled; one can only observe that political life is full of contradictions. The method of formalization shows, however, that we can live with them. Knowing who we are is the first indispensable step. Knowing why we should try to approach one another may tell us how.

Notes

1. This is the description of former Assistant Secretary of State for Inter-American Relations William D. Rogers, who participated in direct negotiations with Cuban officials between late 1974 and late 1975. I presume he was referring to procedural matters and to some substantive matters as well, although of secondary importance.

2. The first contacts between the two governments on the matter of hijackings occurred in March of 1970. Cuba returned one hijacker in September of that year as a gesture of "good faith." Shortly thereafter Cuban Foreign Minister Raúl Roa and Cuban Ambassador to the United Nations Ricardo Alarcón declared that Cuba was ready to negotiate the issue on a bilateral basis. Formal talks did not take place until November of 1972. The agreement was signed on February 15, 1973, in Havana and Washington, D.C., simultaneously. On April 27, 1977, the then Assistant Secretary of State for Inter-American Affairs, Terence A. Todman, signed the fishing agreements in Havana, becoming the first high-ranking U.S. diplomat to visit Cuba since 1961.

3. The relaxation included four different aspects: (1) licenses would be granted to allow commerce between U.S. subsidiaries and Cuba for trade in foreign-made goods; (2) nations whose ships and aircraft carried cargo to Cuba would no longer be penalized by withholding U.S. assistance to them; (3) such ships and aircraft would be allowed to refuel in the United States; and (4) legislation would be introduced to repeal Public Law 480 that prohibited food assistance to any country trading with Cuba.

4. Each interest section would be headed by a "counselor," an official with a rank below ambassador or minister. The sections would perform all the work of an embassy except for protocol functions. Each section was expected to engage in discussions of bilateral issues with its respective host.

5. Jorge Domínguez, "Taming the Cuban Shrew," *Foreign Policy* 10 (1972):94–98; John Plank, "We Should Start Talking with Castro," in Richard B. Gray, ed., *Latin America and the United States in the 1970s* (Itasca, Ill.: F. E. Peacock, 1971), pp. 241, 245.

6. See John Spanier and Eric M. Uslaner, *How American Foreign Policy is Made*, 2nd ed. (New York: Holt, Rinehart and Winston/Praeger, 1978), p. 103, for a clarification of terms.

7. Discussions about Cuba took place at the following meetings of the OAS: June 25–July 8, 1970 (Washington, D.C.); April 12–21, 1972 (Washington, D.C.); April 4–5, 1973 (Washington, D.C.); February 21–23, 1974 (Mexico City, Mexico); April 19–May 1, 1974 (Atlanta, Georgia); November 8–12 (Quito, Ecuador); and at the San José, Costa Rica, meeting

of July 17–29, 1975, where the sanctions were lifted. The United States was under very intense pressure from proponents and opponents of the motion to end the sanctions. The former were very bitter and critical of U.S. "neutrality" at the Quito meeting, which, they said, was really a position of antagonism.

8. These vituperations were accompanied by praise for those governments supporting the end of the sanctions and by offers to those governments to renew diplomatic relations with them. This two-fisted approach that characterized Castro's overall attitude during the process of formalization was obviously not new in international relations. However, Cuban statements expressing very extreme and opposite points of view succeeded each other with such speed that they did more than convey messages to friends and foes; the messages, in effect, added to the natural ambiguity and confusion of a process of reconciliation between former adversaries.

9. On January 29, 1975, Cuban Ambassador Alarcón joined the formal caucus of Latin American envoys to the United Nations, ending a thirteen-year absence. Cuba was also active in the creation of SELA, the Latin American Economic System, which was supported by twenty-five Latin American and Caribbean nations. SELA was created on October 17, 1975, at Panama City, Panama.

10. A delegation of 200 Argentine businessmen had visited Cuba, concluding a series of commercial agreements and obtaining U.S. $1.2 billion in credits from their government to finance the transaction. U.S. businessmen felt handcuffed at the time.

11. Lester A. Sobel, ed., *Castro's Cuba in the 1970s* (New York: Facts on File, 1978), p. 48.

12. Edward González, "The United States and Castro: Breaking the Deadlock," *Foreign Affairs* 50, no. 4 (July 1972):722–37.

13. Domínguez, "Taming the Cuban Shrew," p. 111.

14. U.S., Congress, Senate, Committee on Foreign Relations, *Cuba, A Staff Report,* 93rd Cong., 2d sess. (Washington, D.C.: U.S. Government Printing Office, 1974). The value of the Holt report is primarily symbolic since it contains a number of factual inaccuracies that diminish its value.

15. U.S., Congress, House, Committee on International Relations, *United States–Cuban Perspectives—1975: Conversations on Major Issues with Cuban Officials* (Washington, D.C.: U.S. Government Printing Office, 1976).

16. Ibid, p. v.

17. In early December of 1977 two congressmen, Frederick Richmond and Richard Nolan, gave Castro a message from Jimmy Carter urging Cuba to withdraw from Angola. On December 5, Castro said that Cuba's presence in Africa was not negotiable and could not be linked to normalization.

Even though the outcome was unsuccessful, Richmond and Nolan's "mission" illustrates my point, namely, that members of Congress provided the administration with useful conduits of information to Cuba.

18. Sections (a) through (e) in the article defined the conditions leading to the loss of Cuban citizenship. All the members of the delegation were included under section (a), which deprives "those who become citizens of another country" of Cuban citizenship. Some of the delegates probably fell under four of the five sections.

19. Abraham F. Lowenthal, "Cuba: Time for a Change?" *Foreign Policy* 20 (Fall, 1975):68.

20. Roger W. Fontaine, *On Negotiating with Cuba* (Washington, D.C.: American Enterprise Institute for Public Policy Research, 1975), pp. 48–50.

21. Domínguez, "Taming the Cuban Shrew," p. 111.

22. Committee on International Relations, *United States–Cuban Perspectives,* p. 6.

23. Lowenthal, "Cuba: Time for a Change?" p. 68.

24. Herbert Lionel Matthews, *Revolution in Cuba* (New York: Scribner's, 1975), p. 431.

25. Castro visited Africa on two occasions, in March of 1976 and in March of 1977. A picture of Castro atop a Land Rover surveying the landscape of a wildlife preserve in Tanzania was perhaps too much to bear. He had now appropriated the role of "great white hunter." This was the ultimate transgression!

26. Introduced as a rider to a 1901 army appropriations bill, the amendment was offered by Senator Orville Platt. The amendment, an act of a foreign legislature, had to be accepted by Cubans so that U.S. occupation of Cuba would terminate and a Cuban "republic" be inaugurated. The amendment had a number of deleterious consequences for Cuban domestic politics and sovereignty. It created the impossible contradiction that any act of a Cuban government compromising the sovereignty of Cuba would be considered illegal by the United States. The amendment itself represented such an act. It was finally repealed in 1935.

27. More specifically, any act of the U.S. Congress that may be billed as an attempt to restrain Cuba will not be acceptable to the Cubans. If I have argued that Congress had a positive role to play, it could nonetheless erect an insurmountable obstacle to normalization by insisting on some unilateral measure such as a "De Concini" or "Platt" type of amendment. Fidel Castro's personal authority would evaporate if he accepted anything of this sort.

28. Cole Blasier, "The Elimination of United States Influence," in Carmelo Mesa-Lago, ed., *Revolutionary Change in Cuba* (Pittsburgh: University of Pittsburgh Press, 1971), p. 43.

29. Gallup Special Study (February 7, 1968).

30. Gallup Study 959K (September 24–27, 1976).

31. John E. Rielly, *American Public Opinion and U.S. Foreign Policy* (Chicago: Chicago Council on Foreign Relations, 1979), pp. 16–17. It should be noted that the Gallup studies utilized the ten-point Stapel scalometer to measure positive or negative feelings toward Cuba, while that commissioned by the Chicago Council on Foreign Relations used the "thermometer" technique, which measures the warmth of feeling respondents indicate toward a particular person or object.

32. For the record, it should be stressed that ever since Fidel Castro came to power in 1959, U.S. public opinion has followed the directives of presidential initiatives toward Cuba and has been both supportive and restrained in this sense. For example, in early 1962, while 63 percent of the public was against trading with Cuba as long as Castro remained in power and 44 percent were in favor of helping anti-Castro forces with economic and military resources, only 24 percent were in favor of a direct military intervention by the United States in Cuba (Gallup Study 643A [April 28–May 3, 1962]). Later that year, on the eve of the missile crisis, only 31 percent were in favor of armed U.S. military intervention in Cuba (Gallup Study 663K [September 20–25, 1962]).

33. Gallup Study 864K (February 16–19, 1973).

34. Gallup Study 917K (October 18–21, 1974).

35. Gallup Special Study (December 16, 1974).

36. Gallup Study 971K (March 21–28, 1977).

37. Cuba had settled the issue of compensation with French and Swiss nationals. Although these claims were modest as compared to those of U.S. nationals, the precedent had been made and there was no reason to believe that Cuba would stonewall in coming to terms with U.S. claims. However, it would certainly drive a hard bargain.

38. Carmelo Mesa-Lago, "The Economics of U.S.-Cuban Rapprochement," in Cole Blasier and Carmelo Mesa-Lago, eds., *Cuba in the World* (Pittsburgh: University of Pittsburgh Press, 1979), pp. 203–07.

39. Ibid., pp. 212, 214.

40. See Taylor Branch and George Crile, III, "The Kennedy Vendetta, How the CIA Waged a Silent War Against Castro," *Harper's*, August 1975, pp. 49–63, for a very adequate journalistic discussion of the topic.

41. One such instance was the bombing of a Cubana airliner over Barbados that, on October 6, 1976, took the lives of all seventy-three passengers and crew. The incident led the Cuban government to announce that it would not honor the agreement on hijackings past April 15, 1977. Castro added that he would be willing to discuss the renewal of the agreement with a new administration provided all acts of hostility against Cuba ceased.

42. On April 28, 1979, Carlos Muñiz, a member of the Antonio Maceo Brigade, was shot in San Juan, Puerto Rico. Muñiz died of his wounds shortly thereafter. A group identifying itself as Comando Cero claimed responsibility for the shooting. Muñiz had been active in organizing trips to Cuba, first as a member of the brigade and later as coowner of Viajes Varadero, a travel agency that had been involved in promoting tours among the Cuban community of Puerto Rico.

43. González, "The United States and Castro," p. 732.

44. William Watts and Jorge I. Domínguez, "The United States and Cuba: Old Issues and New Direction," *Policy Perspectives from Potomac Associates* (Washington, D.C.: School of Advanced International Studies, 1977), pp. 47, 53.

45. Fontaine, *On Negotiating with Cuba,* p. 85; Domínguez, "Taming the Cuban Shrew," pp. 104–05; Lowenthal, "Cuba: Time for a Change?" pp. 68–70, 79; Andrés Suárez, "¿Cuál es la política norteamericana hacia Cuba?" *Nueva Generación* 22 (Marzo):11; Matthews, *Revolution in Cuba,* pp. 409–10.

46. Roughly, the turn to Communism was more in response to short-term political tactics than to a grand ideological strategy.

6

Democracy and the
Imposition of Values:
Definitions and Diplomacy

John D. Martz

"Democracy," according to our dictionaries, signifies a form of government in which all classes, including the lowest, have a voice either directly or through their freely chosen representatives. *Demokratia,* its Greek derivation, is termed popular government. Further elucidation is drawn from *demos* and *kratien.* The former is described as the people of a country, with particular reference to the common people or the lower classes. An additional meaning of *demos* speaks of the lower classes in the sense of an irresponsible, uncontrollable rabble. The suffix *kratien* denotes a form of rule or government. Given the sense of elitist snobbery such semantic roots project, it may be argued that they tell us more about the ancient Greek polity than about contemporary concepts of democracy. Certainly the connotations placed upon the word are susceptible to varying and even conflicting ideas. Without undertaking an extended excursion along the paths and byways of democratic theory, there are broad general notions that are necessary in guiding our thinking. At least two overarching traditions run through the literature.

In purer and more idealistic tradition, democracy extends beyond the realm of the political. It must assure the realization of such social values as freedom, equality, and justice. Among its products is the emergence of the rational citizen. A less sweeping view holds that democracy is fundamentally a political means of regulating conflict and power. Alexander Wilde uses the following language:

> "Democracy" can be defined in more restricted, procedural terms as
> those rules that allow (though they do not necessarily bring about)
> genuine competition for authoritative political roles. No effective
> political office should be excluded from such competition, nor
> should opposition be suppressed by force. More specifically, such
> rules would include freedom of speech, press, and assembly, and the
> provision of regular institutional mechanisms for obtaining consent
> and permitting change of political personnel (normally, elections.)[1]

It is the latter, more constrained interpretation that has most
often inspired the United States to call upon Latin America to
cleanse itself of nondemocratic practices and to institutionalize
electoral constitutionality.

It is perhaps unsurprising that periodic bursts of U.S. missionary zeal in the Americas are themselves characterized by
contradictions and inconsistencies. In its formulations and
implementations of policies designed to export democracy to
the republics of Latin America, the United States has experienced widely divergent approaches. Fredrick Pike puts it in
tellingly cogent terms. "Periodically, the United States passes
through alternating cycles of trying to make the world safe for
its type of democracy and of endeavoring to make its type of
democracy safe from the world. It alternates, that is, between
periods of defending its liberal institutions and political culture
by trying to propagate them in foreign lands and of rejecting
crusades for liberalism in order to remain liberal at home."[2]
Illustrations are manifest, ranging from the moralistic righteous-
ness of Woodrow Wilson to the born-again innocence of Jimmy
Carter's preinaugural self-assurance and interspersed with the
harshly Calvinistic anti-Communist zeal of John Foster Dulles
and the stylistically elegant pragmatism of John F. Kennedy,
himself a product of the Cold War era.

As Kenneth M. Coleman writes in Chapter 4, broadly fluctuating expressions of North American policy in the hemisphere
are unfailingly justified on the grounds of "primary myths."
The special responsibility of the United States toward universal
moral renewal is writ large, as is the insistence that its interests
are identical to those of Humankind. A fundamental component
of this foreign policy litany is an unalloyed faith in democracy.

However the concept is defined, it is invoked as a panacea through which Latin America may progress and, moreover, may be expected to serve the national interest of the United States. From this perspective diplomacy represents an effort to impose values upon other societies, ones whose cultural outlooks and historical roots are often decidedly different. Democracy, in short, can be and is subjected to varying understandings. But as a rhetorical cornerstone of U.S. interests in the Americas, it has provided a solid foundation for a wide array of policies.

The fundamental problem may be summarized thusly: (1) U.S. diplomacy attempts seriously to encourage democracy only when geopolitical security interests are not presumably imperiled by so doing; (2) its constricted definition of democracy ignores, indeed insults the more basic components of the concept; (3) ethnocentric assumptions about Latin American society and politics produce paternalistically distorted expectations; and (4) Latin American perspectives on democracy are themselves injuriously twisted as a result of historical experience. In considering the practical and definitional implication of U.S. policy, then, our attention must first be directed to selected snapshots from the past. This in turn will lead to a consideration of both the intellectual and political inconsistencies that result. The burden of the argument is not to denigrate the concept of democracy or its meaning for Latin America, but rather to suggest the hypocrisy and dysfunctionality that has accompanied U.S. diplomacy. If, as might be wished, the United States has dedicated itself to the proposition of helping men and women become free, neither its vision nor its understanding has been adequate to the challenge.

Democracy in the Practice of U.S. Diplomacy

The cyclical nature of inter-American relations has already been identified as a prominent feature in its history. Federico Gil has observed that "periods of rising interest in and concern with Latin America on the part of the United States have invariably been followed by periods of declining interest, increasing conflict, and almost total disregard for the fate of these nations."[3] Among the consequences is the Latin American

contention that U.S. interest in the quest for hemispheric solidarity emerges only when specific geopolitical security questions
are raised. Two administrations powerfully committed in their
rhetoric to democracy and individual freedoms and separated
by nearly a half-century from one another were those of Woodrow Wilson and John F. Kennedy. A brief recollection of their
hemispheric policies can enrich an understanding of our subject.[4]

Upon entering office in 1913, Woodrow Wilson undertook a
paternalistic effort to promote democracy and constitutionalism. Intertwining the principles of liberalism with the practice
of military intervention, he assumed that external pressure from
a mature United States might discourage that endemic instability
displayed by presumably immature Latin American states. It
was within this context that Wilson advanced his views on the
nonrecognition of revolutionary governments. The intention
was translated into a withholding of diplomatic relations from
regimes lacking constitutional bases. Washington, of course, was
to be the judge. In juridical terms, Wilson's thinking was remi-
niscent of Ecuadorian diplomat Carlos R. Tobar, who in 1907
proposed that constitutional regimes refuse to recognize de
facto governments that obtain power by toppling constitutional
regimes through violent measures. The major expression of the
so-called Tobar Doctrine came at the Central American Peace
Conference held that very year in Washington, where the sig-
natories pledged not to recognize "revolutionary" governments
until free elections had led to a constitutional reorganization
of the country.[5]

The Wilsonian record in pursuit of his ideals is all too familiar.
Open and direct intervention in Mexico was an important element during its revolutionary era. U.S. warships at one point
bombarded Veracruz, while the expeditionary force under
General John J. Pershing was dispatched across the border onto
Mexican soil for punitive purposes. Marines were sent to Haiti,
the Dominican Republic, and Nicaragua. Throughout his
administration, Wilson pursued his self-conceived civilizing and
democratizing mission with an ardor that guaranteed hostility
and criticism throughout the Americas. Unpopular governments were driven to seek sustenance from external sources
as the effects of what some called negative intervention effec-

tively added the tool of diplomatic nonrecognition to the North American arsenal of financial and military involvement.

More than four decades later, a more pragmatic "developmentalist" orientation toward the imposition of democratic values emerged in the government of John F. Kennedy. Coming to office as a sharp critic of his predecessor's sympathetic policies toward Latin American dictatorships and anti-Communist military authoritarianism, yet susceptible to prevailing anti-Communist sentiment and anxious to respond to the Cuban challenge, Kennedy soon announced the Alliance for Progress. The Preamble to the Charter of Punta del Este, signed on August 17, 1961, called for "accelerated economic progress and broader social justice within the framework of personal dignity and political liberty." Furthermore, the itemization of the alliance's twelve basic objectives was preceded by the requirement of a cooperative effort by all the nations of the hemisphere in order to achieve "maximum levels of well-being, with equal opportunities for all, *in democratic societies adapted to their own needs and desires*" (emphasis added).[6] The intention was clearly to place the quest for economic development and social reform within a North American framework of democratic regulations and procedures. In his statement of personal commitment, moreover, Kennedy envisaged the stimulation of democratic reforms as serving the national interest in providing a counterweight to the radical solutions being advanced by Cuba.

The U.S. policy of strengthening democratic governments and condemning threats to their existence was tested by a series of military *golpes de estado* ("coups") in seven nations from 1961 through 1963. Washington's responses were revealing; in the interests of brevity, consider only Peru, Ecuador, and the Dominican Republic. The Peruvian coup of 1962 took the form of military intervention in the wake of electoral irregularities and controversies. The United States reacted by recalling its ambassador, suspending military assistance, and cutting off economic aid. Other nations failed to join the boycott, however, and the provisional regime in Lima capitalized domestically upon what was depicted as unwarranted Yankee intervention in Peruvian affairs. A new ambassador was eventually posted and both economic and military assistance were restored, conditioned on a pledge that elections would be held. They were indeed conducted in June of 1963 but, notwithstanding U.S. claims for the efficacy of its actions, it is questionable whether U.S. tactics were more than marginally instrumental in the convening of the elections.

The 1963 *golpe* in Ecuador was also a somewhat ambiguous case.[7] The civilian chief of state—who had been elected vice-president in 1960 only to overthrow his senior running mate eighteen months later—was forced into exile after several episodes of public drunkenness, during the last of which his insults had singled out the North American ambassador and the president of Grace Lines. The Central Intelligence Agency had been concurrently active behind the scenes, motivated by its suspicion of leftist infiltration of the government.[8] The subsequent military junta that ruled Ecuador from 1963 to 1966 received diplomatic recognition promptly. The same practice, in fact, had also followed swiftly on the heels of the military ouster of elected authorities in Guatemala the same year.

If the Kennedy administration found itself increasingly harried by the difficulty in consistent application of policies without disregarding its perception of security interests, this did not prevent efforts on behalf of a democratic regime in the Dominican Republic. In the wake of the May 1961 assassination of Generalissimo Rafael Leonidas Trujillo, Washington consciously sought to nurture a fledgling democratic system based on constitutional rule and national elections. One widely publicized measure was a naval show of force in the waters off Santo Domingo on November 15, 1961, which helped discourage a projected *golpe de estado* by two brothers and a son of the slain dictator. By 1962 large sums of aid were arriving under the Alliance for Progress, and the December election of Juan Bosch brought to office a man seen in Washington as politically akin to such acceptably sanitized democratic reformers as Rómulo Betancourt of Venezuela and Costa Rica's José Figueres. Bosch's tenure proved ill-fated and brief. His temperamental rejection of political dialogue, his willingness to permit the return of Dominican Communists, and his inability to co-opt military leaders to his cause combined to produce his ouster on September 25, 1963 after only eight months in office. This occurred despite explicit North American efforts at dissuasion. In the days preceding the widely rumored coup, embassy officials had pleaded with Bosch and other civilian leaders for greater flexibility and accommodation, while military representatives threatened their Dominican counterparts with diplomatic and economic sanctions.

Such pressures were unavailing, and the United States carried through with its threats by severing diplomatic relations, suspending Alliance for Progress programs, and withdrawing its military and economic aid officials. Secretary of State Dean Rusk enunciated the Kennedy principles, declaring that the establishment and maintenance of a representative and constitutional government remained an "essential element" in the Alliance. Preconditions for renewed ties included a demand for observance of civil liberties and—predictably—a pledge to hold popular elections and restore constitutional rule. As the result of White House deliberations shortly before Kennedy's murder, relations were reestablished effective December 14, 1963, based on a promise of elections within the next twenty-four months. Early in 1964 assistance funds were made available to the military-backed provisional government, and the flow was still continuing when the April 1965 fighting led to civil turmoil and the ultimate landing of 21,500 North American troops on Dominican soil on the directive of Lyndon Johnson.

The efforts of the Kennedy administration, then, neither prevented the toppling of Bosch nor led to the prompt convening of national elections. The earlier show of naval power, to be sure, had annulled any possible resurrection of *trujillismo* at that juncture. However, both the Kennedy and Johnson actions failed to introduce American-style democratic values into the Dominican Republic. The best that could be said was that the official perception of a Marxist threat had led to measures that avoided "a second Cuba" in the Caribbean. Considered in conjunction with the preceding examples, the Kennedy approach could be said to have manifested an early zeal and energetic proselytizing in seeking to strengthen civilian-elected governments in Latin America. Tools designed to realize this commitment ran the gamut from private persuasion, cajolery, and threats of economic deprivation to the breaking of official relations to ultimate displays of military force and old-fashioned gunboat diplomacy. Yet the cycle of military ousters of elected regimes continued throughout the period and afterwards.

As a practical matter, North American policymakers eventually accepted the ineffectiveness of many such efforts, bending their announced scruples in the interests of geopolitical considerations. Differing understandings and interpretations of democracy permit sporadic shifts in the priority it was originally assigned by Washington. As a collaborator of Kennedy later recalled, the president concluded that

> The military often represented more competence in administration and more sympathy with the U.S. than any other group in the country. To halt work on the Alliance in every nation not ruled by a genuine democracy would have paralyzed the whole program. Some military usurpers in Latin America, moreover, . . . were neither unpopular nor reactionary; and those able and willing to guide their countries to progress he wanted to encourage. Unfortunately, he had learned, many of the more progressive civilian governments in Latin America (as elsewhere) were less willing or less able to impose the necessary curbs on extravagant projects, runaway inflation and political disorder. They were more likely to frighten away local and foreign investments and to ignore the less vote-worthy rural populations.[9]

Ultimately, attempts by Kennedy to impose conditions such as elections and constitutional procedures were erratic and inconsistent. "Both economic aid and diplomatic relations were cut off, restored, or not cut off without any discernible pattern in a situation which itself had little discernible pattern."[10]

Although similar illustrations of North American ethnocentrism in policy formulations and ineffectiveness in practical implementation might be extended ad infinitum, the lessons seem clear. The imposition of democratic values is subject to differing conceptual understandings and diverse forms of policymaking, yielding when necessary to purportedly pragmatic considerations of the national interest in the Américas. On a more profound plane, moreover, efforts to stimulate and promote democratic values have been curtailed by the more restricted and regulatory view of political democracy as translated into elections and constitutional rule. From the Latin American perspective, North American definitions and applications fueled the negativism with which the term "democracy" was endowed. The implications of this assertion lead us to an examination of Latin American intellectual and political views.

Intellectual Perspectives on the Dissonance of Democracy

Having considered examples of U.S. diplomacy embodying diverse applications of democratic ideals, we now turn to the views of Latin American intellectuals and political leaders. Here too there is a plurality of interpretations. The extent to which Latin Americans perceive the concept of democracy from their own particularistic historical experience further underlines the arbitrary quality of the external imposition of values derived from U.S. history. As is so often the case, there is enlightenment to be acquired from the writings of the Liberator.

In analyzing the failure of the first Venezuelan republic in 1812, Simón Bolívar criticized what he regarded as an impractically visionary attempt to construct a federal system of government. "Popular elections . . . set another obstacle in the way of the smooth functioning of the federation . . . for the peasants are so ignorant that they vote without knowing what they are about, and city dwellers are so ambitious that everything they attempt leads to factions."[11] Six years later he further cautioned against efforts to emulate and copy North American political forms.

> I must say that it has never for a moment entered my mind to compare the position and character of two states as dissimilar as the English-American and the Spanish-American. . . . Does not *L'Esprit des lois* state that laws should be suited to the people for whom they are made; that it would be a major coincidence if those of one nation could be adapted to another; that laws must take into account the physical conditions of the country, climate, character of the land, location, size, and mode of living of the people; that they should be in keeping with the degree of liberty that the Constitution can sanction respecting the religion of the inhabitants, their inclinations, resources, number, commerce, habits, and customs? This is the code we must consult, not the code of Washington.[12]

Over a half-century later another famed revolutionary hero was to issue a similar complaint. Thus, in the words of José Martí,

> Spanish America owes its inability to govern itself entirely to those of its leaders who sought to rule nations that have conquered their identity through violence with laws based on four centuries of free-dom in the United States and nineteen centuries of monarch in France. . . . Government must grow upward from the land itself. The spirit of a government must be based on the true nature of the country.[13]

Following upon this traditional strain of reasoning, the writings of many other Latin Americans have continued to consider and sometimes to question the applicability of democracy within the cultural milieu and ambience of Hispanic traditions and values. The debate has been a lively one, and from the revolutionary era to the present, it has resisted intellectual resolution.

This tendency to view democracy in the context of cultural, geographic, and historical forces has long endured in Latin American political thought. It is cogently posed by the remarks of Mexico's Porfirio Díaz to a North American interviewer on the eve of the great revolutionary upheaval in that country.

> I believe democracy to be the one true, just principle of government, although in practice it is possible only to highly developed peoples. . . . Here in Mexico we have had different conditions. I received this Government from the hands of a victorious army at a time when the people were divided and unprepared for the exercise of the extreme principles of democratic government. To have thrown upon the masses the whole responsibility of government at once would have produced conditions that might have discredited the cause of free government.[14]

Other Latin American political thinkers and activists have reflected upon these attitudes, sometimes arguing that the dominion of such classic caudillos as Díaz is explainable by socioeconomic conditions and political reality. A prominent Venezuelan writer has voiced its contemporary expression thusly:

> They [the historic strongmen] were the products of the land, of tradition, and of historic necessity. . . . The historic *caudillo* was the native reply to the power vacuum. Latin America saw the emergence of a form of social organization that was contrary to the republican ideas that had been fashioned in Europe, but that perfectly suited the American economic and social structure. . . . Men like Don Porfirio or Rosas emerged because they reflected the thoughts, the inclination, the deep feelings of the majority of their people; in the fullest sense of the term, they were their spokesmen, their representatives, the symbol of the dominant collective feeling of their time.[15]

In recent times there has been a growing sense of Latin American disillusionment over the concept of democracy. Owing in part to U.S.-imposed versions in recent years, democracy has come to bear a negative connotation, as Silvert has explained.

> ["Democracy"] has come to symbolize hypocrisy. Democracy is only for those who can afford it; it is a luxury that comes at the end of a long process of economic development. The world's democratic countries may be partially democratic for themselves—"bourgeois" democracies—but for the poorer parts of the world, they are only the extractors of surplus value, the imposers of colonialism, the buyers of local elites, the prompters of worldwide dislocation, as they move about in the ceaseless search for economic advantage and military security.[16]

Consequently, as is true of "liberalism," "democracy" carries overtones of external control and economic exploitation. Thus the attitude Silvert notes may constitute less a rejection of the concept than of the international practice of democracy. Its impact, however, is no less profound. It also bespeaks the influence exerted by the forms of democracy seemingly espoused by the United States and pressed upon Latin America.

This externally induced negativism toward democracy in both conceptual and practical terms is well documented in the work of contemporary Latin American social scientists. The rise in recent years of dependency theory is accompanied by a striking silence on the issues of freedom and liberty. Democracy in its ethical sense has been largely excluded from the agenda of

social scientists. Patterns of dominance are diagnosed, with prescriptive formulas rich in socioeconomic interpretations and
class analyses but impoverished on questions of human rights
and civil liberties. It is illuminating to note, for example, that
an influential and widely quoted multiauthored study on U.S.–
Latin American relationships devotes almost no direct attention
to the topic. The phrases and catchwords that inform and orient
its selections are "imperialism," "ideological monolithism,"
"foreign capital and technology," "forms of control," "semi-
colonial accumulation," and the like.[17]

The emergence of both the bureaucratic-authoritarian and
the corporativist schools of thought further testify to the intellectual disuse and disregard into which the concept of democracy
has fallen. The former, whose most creative and penetrating
spokesman has been Guillermo O'Donnell, swiftly shredded the
arguments of those North Americans who attempted to equate
socioeconomic development with political democracy. Wielding
his scalpel with surgical precision, O'Donnell moved toward
different theoretical and conceptual dimensions of analysis.
Responding at least in part to his particular concern with
authoritarianism in the Southern Cone, he then developed new
paradigms and frameworks within which individual freedoms
and rights are given no more than minimal treatment.[18] Corporativist interpretations, predominately the work of North
American scholars, similarly proceed along analytic paths that
largely eschew considerations of democracy.[19]

For a host of reasons, then, the consideration of democracy
stands low on the agenda of many intellectuals. The political
events of the era have borne some of the responsibility, with
scholars seeing a lack of convergence between democracy and
development. To cite but one instance, Candido Mendes draws
upon the post-1964 military technocracy in Brazil to suggest
that confrontation is endemic to the relationship. He questions
the degree to which the mechanisms of democracy, "designed
to recognize special interests and to conciliate divergent social
aspirations," have truly been tested. In the course of dissecting
what he terms the old populist model, Mendes replies in the
negative. "Insofar as Latin America is concerned, the attempt to
direct the body politic toward national consensus within the

classic formulas of political alignment was unsuccessful."[20] This attitude has become generalized among Latin American scholars and students.

The weight of the preceding, in short, confirms the contention that contemporary intellectual perspectives on democracy are shaded by skepticism and disbelief. Reasons of history, perceptions of North American policy interests, and the manifest failures of democracy as experienced in Latin America have all contributed to this outlook. In addition, the values and norms presumably expressed by the United States add credence to the impression that it is the mechanistic definition that prevails. Its restricted emphasis upon procedural and regulatory patterns constitutes the image that has been transmitted to Latin America. This is what was described earlier as a minimal definition presenting as its criteria the freedoms of association and speech; nonviolent competition among leaders; provisions for participation—largely electoral—of all members of the political community; and the right to articulate and promote political alternatives. Emphases are thus eminently political, with less concern for social relationships, economic justice, and equality of occupational and educational opportunities. Crucial nonpolitical values are ignored or underemphasized, with the human democratization of society all too often relegated to the dustbin of forgotten or unrealized ideas, dreams, and aspirations.

Fantasies and Realities of Electoral Democracy

Despite frequent rhetorical obeisance paid to the ideals of democracy as a fundamental diplomatic objective, U.S. policymakers have customarily given highest priority to elements other than the implantation of democratic values. They have exaggerated or misunderstood the differences between meaningful participatory democracy and controlled or nonrepresentative elections, especially when this is convenient to the exigencies of geopolitical and security demands. Gil has put it clearly: "The policy of the United States has had two unchanging objectives: to prevent the influence of extracontinental powers in the Western Hemisphere and to make Latin America a special sphere of influence of the United States, the latter to be accomplished by a variety of means, among which have been trade and investment, diplomacy, and military objectives."[21] Even with such administrations as Wilson's and Kennedy's, the concern with democracy and constitutionality has been bent or distorted when necessary for the support of the nation's perceived geopolitical and security interests. Franklin D. Roosevelt, the great good neighbor, encountered little difficulty in praising Nicaragua's strongman Anastasio Somoza as "an SOB, but *our* SOB." His administration also had few qualms in pressuring Ecuador to accept the loss of territory taken by force of Peruvian arms, in order that hemispheric solidarity not be disrupted on the eve of World War II. In the past, such practical rationalizations by the United States have rarely been foreign to the minds of policymakers, nor are they absent today.

This is not to deny that the history of U.S. policy and attitudes toward the Americas has often reflected a subtle blend of childlike naiveté with expressions of pragmatic self-interest. The inordinately misleading democracy-versus-dictatorship syndrome has long endured. To be sure, it has been recognized that elections, while presumably desirable and necessary, are less than sufficient in and of themselves to assure meaningful democracy and the honoring of constitutional freedoms and human rights. Nonetheless, this recognition has been accompanied by a surrealistic idea that the seemingly cyclical nature of regime changes across the hemisphere can be explained by unrefined and ill-considered generalizations. For instance, with the fall of a host of authoritarian regimes toward the close of the 1950s—including Pérez Jiménez, Batista, Odría, and Rojas Pinilla—it was felt that this "twilight of the tyrants" constituted a watershed beyond which lay a new and permanent democratic order.[22] Washington also developed a mentality that projected vastly overgeneralized perspectives toward the domestic political trends of the Americas. A succession of panaceas was cited as evidence of a magical transformation from authoritarianism to representative democracy.

For some years it was an act of faith in the United States that the decisive and determining model was that of democratic reformism—the so-called Democratic Left, constituted by such figures as Rómulo Betancourt, José Figueres, Luis Muñoz Marín, and their political parties. When it later appeared that such social democratic movements had outlived their stay and were on the wane, renewed enthusiasm was elicited by the rise of Christian Democracy. The 1964 victory in Chile of Eduardo Frei—whose movement, we now know, was sufficiently favored by the United States to receive funds from the Central Intelligence Agency for a decade—was taken as heralding a new wave of democracy in Latin America. Further impetus was provided in 1968 with the triumph of Rafael Caldera in Venezuela. By the early 1970s however, the Christian Democratic "solution" to democracy and social justice had also fallen in esteem. As with the Democratic Left, Washington found Christian Democracy to be an insubstantial chimera.

Well before the advent of Richard M. Nixon in the White House, U.S. policymakers showed themselves willing to overlook or to forget democracy when their other interests were threatened. The Johnson administration in 1964 demonstrated as much in Brazil, for example. Suddenly the United States seemingly discovered the presumably positive attributes of military authoritarianism. The same attitude servived the transition from Johnson to Nixon, with the latter publicly praising Brazilian military rule as constituting a model to be emulated elsewhere. The icy wrath of such democratic governments as Venezuela, Costa Rica, and Colombia were little noted. Only later, with the subsequent demise of the widely publicized "new dialogue" and the departure of Henry Kissinger from office, did the wheel spin back toward official encouragement of constitutionality and democracy. The inauguration of the Carter administration in January of 1977 reincorporated into U.S. policy with a vengeance the rhetoric of democracy and human rights.

Official spokesmen argued for a recrudescence of democracy, elections, and individual liberties in the Americas—few with greater conviction than the president himself. The particular emphasis on human rights, described at length in other chapters, produced a record that has become and will remain a subject of controversy and dispute for many years. At the same time, the new administration expressed the wish that democracy and constitutionality might also be enhanced. The most obvious manifestation in its eyes was that of national elections. However, a characteristically oversimplistic understanding of practical political realities and of constricted definitions of democracy was to plague the Carter policy, as it had those of so many of his predecessors. Democracy was again defined in basically procedural terms while the administration overpublicized its commitment as indicative of its missionary responsibility for its neighbors. A brief if selective review of the record since 1977 is useful.

Let us consider four disparate cases: Venezuela, Brazil, Ecuador, and Bolivia. In the first two, elections have been conducted regularly for fifteen to twenty years, although the quality of democracy is fundamentally dissimilar. With the latter Andean states, the armed forces after an extended period of power committed themselves publicly to a restoration and reestablishment of civilian, constitutional, elected government. Both Ecuador and Bolivia were strongly encouraged by Washington, and even officially singled out as marking a renaissance of democracy in Latin America, to the credit of the United States. The fantasies of policymakers and the dynamic political realities of these cases provide further evidence of the flawed perceptions of democracy and their meaning as regards forms of exportation to Latin America from the United States. We turn first to the only one of the four cases in which the principles of democracy were fairly and meaningfully served.

The December 1978 Venezuelan elections marked the fifth consecutive national exercise in suffrage since the 1958 establishment of the present pluralistic democratic system. A shade under 90 percent of eligible voters cast their ballots, resulting in the victory of Luis Herrera Campins for the social christian party, the Comité de Organización Política Electoral Independiente (COPEI). In defeating his closest rival by a margin of some 46 to 43 percent, Herrera became the third successive opposition candidate to wrest the presidency from the incumbent party. Moreover, a once fragmented multiparty system dominated by Acción Democrática (AD) had evolved into a two-party arrangement in which COPEI and the AD dominated the competition. In 1973 their two presidential nominees had received 85 percent of the vote, and this total reached 90 in

1978. The continuation and extension of the Venezuelan democratic experience were marked by a public vigor and political vibrancy unparalleled in Latin America. Certainly by the close of the 1970s the country stood among the most representative and participatory of systems in the hemisphere.[23]

The Venezuelan pattern had emerged following the 1958 ouster of General Marcos Pérez Jiménez, whose ruthless dictatorship had been cordially embraced by the United States. Such acts as the awarding of the highest U.S. decoration to Pérez Jiménez by Dwight D. Eisenhower had contributed to the widespread resentment that in 1958 sparked the near-fatal Caracas demonstrations against then Vice-President Richard Nixon. Although the Kennedy administration subsequently established warm and supportive ties with the democratic administration of Rómulo Betancourt, it could scarcely be said that Washington was responsible for the evolution that had culminated in 1978 elections. Although Carter termed outgoing president Carlos Andrés Pérez his closest adviser on Latin American policy, it was also true that Venezuelan democracy, with all its successes and failures, stands as a monument to its own political leadership. It owes little to the United States.

In Brazil the situation has been much different.[24] There the armed forces toppled civilian constitutional rule in 1964. Prominent political figures and existing parties were proscribed at the outset, while authority was exercised through a series of so-called Institutional Acts. New constitutional procedures, a legislative body, and a pair of hybrid parties failed to mask the authoritarianism of military rule. Four consecutive general-presidents served as chiefs of state prior to 1978, when the incumbent Ernesto Geisel reiterated his earlier preoccupation with "democratization" and "institutionalization." He opted for reforms that purportedly broadened the system but that, for all practical purposes, curbed the rise of opposition sentiment. The identity of the new president was known well in advance of elections, as Geisel and his close associates selected General João Baptista Figueiredo, formerly the head of the Servico Nacional de Informações (SNI). His choice was confirmed by the electoral college in October 1978. Although the opposition Movimento Democrático Brasileiro (MDB) subsequently defeated progovernment forces in the November 15 congressional elections, its impact was merely to narrow somewhat the regime's comfortable majority in the Senate and Chamber of Deputies.

Even should the military extend its cautious flirtation with less-authoritarian structures and processes, this would in no sense reflect a response to U.S. policy preferences. Public and private pressures from Washington following the inauguration of President Carter were met with anger and resentment from the Brazilian government. Following the period in which Brazil had been viewed by the Nixon-Ford-Kissinger policy as Washington's most congenial and sympathetic hemispheric ally, underlined by the executive agreement signed by the secretary of state in February 1976 at Brasilia, the Carter policy came as a startling and unwelcome change. Washington's efforts to dissuade West Germany from pursuing its nuclear power agreements with Brazil, followed by the Brazilian cancellation of the joint Brazilian-U.S. military commission and the rejection of U.S. military assistance credits, signaled a marked deterioration in bilateral relations. Separate visits by both Mrs. Carter and her husband were marked by frostily distant Brazilian attitudes. By the close of 1977 U.S. human rights adviser Patricia Derian complained publicly about a lack of responsiveness from the Brazilians. Itamaraty's international posture became more avowedly independent than in the past, with Washington's influence on domestic affairs approaching a nadir. Whatever the precise form of democracy presumably being advocated by the United States, its promotion and advocacy enhanced neither North American policy interests nor the substance of freedom and liberty in Brazil.

With the instances of Ecuador and Bolivia, the announced intention by both military regimes to restore elected civilian rule was welcomed by the Carter government as the harbinger of a new day for democracy in Latin America. Its preference for civilian over military and elected over nonelected governments underlined the narrow and formalistic concept of democracy; there were precious few indications of any awareness that such regime changes were unlikely to alter the lives of the vast majority of Ecuadorians and Bolivians. In the former case, the January 1976 ouster of General Guillermo Rodríguez Lara by a junta of military colleagues was accompanied by a pledge to restore elected government within twenty-four months. Yet by the spring of 1979 this had not yet taken place, and the ultimate completion of a tortuously long and complex process remained uncertain. Two full years had passed before Ecuadorians voted to choose between two constitutional drafts on January 15, 1978. This in turn led to July 16 presidential elections in which an antisystem opponent of the government, Jaime Roldós Aguilera of the populistic Concentración de Fuerzas Populares (CFP), won a six-man race with 31 percent of the vote.

Four months passed while the electoral tribunal, encouraged by the military to press for annullment of the vote, delayed in announcing official returns. When the results were eventually proclaimed, there remained a runoff between Roldós and his closest competitor to produce a president-elect. The addition of congressional races allowed the armed forces to delay the new election until late April, with inauguration of a civilian government scheduled for August 1979. Such footdragging on the part of the military, actively promoted by significant elements of the commercial and exporting sectors of the country, stood in tacit defiance of public and private pressures from Washington. The inclusion of Ecuador on Rosalynn Carter's 1977 itinerary was explicitly based upon the desire to encourage the withdrawal of the military. Two successive North American ambassadors in Quito further urged fulfillment of the January 1976 pledge, as did U.S. military representatives during periodic visits to the country. Even the completion of the heralded "juridical restoration of the state," as the military termed the process, was at best a flawed reflection of procedural democracy, however. Despite the provisions of the new constitution, illiterates remained disenfranchised; several legitimate parties were banned from official participation; and would-be candidates from diverse political sectors were barred from participation, including the man universally regarded as a certain winner, Asaad Bucaram.[25]

This preponderance of form over substance was even more evident in Bolivia, where the completion of a military return to the barracks is, even as these words are written, also uncertain and where, again, the significance for the citizens of the country is minimal. General Hugo Banzer called elections for July 9, 1978, in preparation for his own withdrawal after some seven years in power—an exceptionally long period of rule by Bolivian standards. Following massive electoral fraud on behalf of his chosen successor, General Juan Pereda Asbun, the latter seized power by force and promised a new round of elections for July 1980. This decision provoked widespread opposition from the military as well as from aspiring civilian politicians, producing in turn another *golpe de estado* in late November. General David Padilla Arancibia promised new elections for July 1, 1979, after which the military was to withdraw from the presidential palace. As with Brazil and Ecuador, two circumstances were undeniably manifest: the influence of Washington had not been decisive, and democracy was not on the ascendency, except perhaps in the very narrowest meaning of the term.

Washington had actively encouraged and pressed General Banzer to carry out his promise of free and honest elections. In the confusion following the vote, policymakers were divided and indecisive. After initial threats to suspend all U.S. assistance programs, Washington opted for more private suasion on behalf of the prompt rescheduling of elections. In the meantime, economic and military aid continued at a more modest level. Whatever the eventual outcome of the process, there was little basis to argue that Washington's preferences were paramount for the Bolivians. The unfolding of events was primarily responsive to shifting military attitudes, the incessant reformulation of civilian alliances, and related pressures eminently domestic in character. Few Bolivians saw any reason to anticipate significant change in basic political realities, let alone overriding social and economic policy needs. Even the procedural manifestations of democracy in Bolivia were weak and in no sense could be ascribed to the articulation and implementation of policy from Washington.

Conclusions: Diplomacy and the Democratic Ideal

The preceding argument might be interpreted as a call for the United States to abandon its concern with democracy in the

Americas. We have examined the constricted definition of democracy and the inclination of U.S. diplomacy to encourage democracy only when geopolitical security interests are not thereby imperiled. Furthermore, it is evident that Latin American views of democracy are themselves diverse and are further distorted by the periodic hypocrisy of U.S. policy. As a consequence, an extension of the argument might contend that the very concept of democracy is alien to the Latin American heritage and psyche. This, however, is not the basic thrust of my remarks, for they are intended rather as an indictment of provincial ethnocentrism and hypocritical paternalism on the part of North American authorities. Rather than denigrating democratic values and individual freedoms for Latin America, I insist that the historical record amply demonstrates that authoritarian governments, whatever the alleged commitment to progress, to improvement, to a betterment of life for their citizens, have rarely maintained themselves for more than a few years. Remarks about the limits of procedural democratic concepts as mirrored by electoral exercises in contemporary Latin America are not designed to portray such undertakings as a sham, but rather as linked to mechanisms inadequate in and of themselves to liberate the individual from systemic (as opposed to merely political) oppression.

Similarly, criticism of North American diplomacy does not constitute a dismissal of defensible political norms and values. National traditions should not be disregarded, nor can they be discarded, because of unsatisfactory incorporation into the operation and application of foreign policy. Like it or not, North Americans are deeply imbued with the conviction that their country has a higher mission than the sheer pursuit of its national interest. As Stanley Hoffmann recently observed, "American idealism will not go away."[26] Neither may it be forgotten that, from a more pragmatic vantage point, the injustice and repression found in authoritarian systems are guarantors of the instability and revolutionary turmoil running contrary to orthodox U.S. preferences for stability and predictability. Critics and advocates alike must concede the deeply rooted commitment in the United States to democratic ideals, however distorted or imcomplete their practical realization. Consider the following:

It is not true men are born free and everywhere they are in chains.
Men are born infants, dependent and therefore unfree. . . . Only as
they become thinking animals can they become responsible for their
actions, and thus able to free themselves from the accidents which
have planted them in the hands of their parents, their lands, and
their material conditions. The United States has dedicated itself to
the proposition of helping men to become free as they attain competence. This vision, always difficult to define let alone realize, has
ever been under attack. Never made real for everyone, it has still
always been partially true for some. The rich successes of [North]
America have now brought this country to the point at which democratic freedoms can be extended to all members of the society; the
ethic of the American Revolution is ours to complete.[27]

The author of these words further contends that the United
States and Latin America share a common problem in confronting the necessity of developing and channeling the use of reason through accountable institutions. The structured institutionalization of reason requires a higher level of comprehension
and dedication from citizens of all polities. Given the inevitable
and seemingly indestructible character of hemispheric interrelationships, North American diplomacy will continue to seek
a favorable reception in Latin America. It will also incorporate
a component of normative appeals directed at the enshrinement
of democratic values, however narrowly or inadequately defined.
If the vision is circumscribed by the blinders of selfishly conceived national interests, the task then becomes that of extending horizons and broadening policy perspectives. The ultimate
objective, notwithstanding the utopianism of such idealized
goals, has been described by a pair of Latin American social
scientists as constituting a humanist society "in constant process of construction, through the conscious free will of its
members, . . . to face the social order in which they find themselves as beings capable of controlling and modifying it so as to
make it more human every day."[28]

In our argument we have stressed the disinclination of U.S.
diplomacy to prize democratic values above security interests;
the inadequacy of limited conceptual definitions; the ethnocentrism of assumptions about Latin American society and politics; a formalistic perception of electoral politics; and the conse-

quent devaluation of democracy in the eyes of many Latin Americans. Nonetheless, North and Latin Americans alike might well heed the words of Kalman Silvert, a critic of unrealized or faulty understandings of democracy throughout the Americas but, more importantly, an eloquent and impassioned advocate of classical democratic values.

> It is theoretically possible for profound and positive social change to come about in the absence of violence and blind coercion. It is practically possible in the near future in probably only a very few countries—those with a high degree of national cohesion, many socially sensitized citizens, and a stock of ideological commitments accepting human freedom as the virtue from which flows the essential means for a self-fulfilling social order. Even there, however, there must be a broad recognition that the practice of freedom is the purpose of freedom, as the end of humanness is reached by being human.[29]

If this perfect dream of the democratic ideal can never fully be realized, it nevertheless stands as a shimmering inspiration for all those of the Americas who would be free.

Notes

1. Alexander W. Wilde, "Conversations among Gentlemen: Oligarchical Democracy in Colombia," in Juan J. Linz and Alfred Stepan (eds.), *The Breakdown of Democratic Regimes: Latin America* (Baltimore: Johns Hopkins University Press, 1978), p. 29.

2. Fredrick B. Pike, *The United States and the Andean Republics: Peru, Bolivia, and Ecuador* (Cambridge: Harvard University Press, 1977), p. 303.

3. Federico G. Gil, *Latin American-United States Relations* (New York: Harcourt Brace Jovanovich, 1971), p. 284.

4. Portions of these illustrative passages were included in my paper "Democracy and Human Rights in Latin America: The Limits of U.S. Influence" (delivered at the April 1978 International Conference of the Center for International Studies at North Carolina Central University).

5. Gil, *Latin American-United States Relations*, p. 76, presents a succinct summary.

6. Characteristic views of the alliance at its inception are set forth by

one of its architects in Lincoln Gordon, *A New Deal for Latin America: The Alliance for Progress* (Cambridge: Harvard University Press, 1963). The work also includes the texts of documents approved at Punta del Este. The phrases quoted above are found on pp. 118 and 119.

7. One of the relatively few case studies of an individual coup is Martin C. Needler, *Anatomy of a Coup d'Etat: Ecuador 1963* (Washington: Institute for the Comparative Study of Political Systems, 1964). A more detailed treatment, placed within a broader theoretical and chronological framework, is John Samuel Fitch's splendid *The Military Coup d'Etat as a Political Process: Ecuador, 1948-1966* (Baltimore: Johns Hopkins University Press, 1977).

8. Philip Agee, *Inside the Company: CIA Diary* (New York: Stonehill Publishing, 1975), pp. 99–317.

9. Theodore C. Sorensen, *Kennedy* (New York: Harper and Row, 1965), pp. 535–36.

10. Ibid, p. 536.

11. "Memoria dirigida a los ciudadanos de la Nueva Granada por un caraqueño" (December 15, 1812), in Vicente Lecuna (ed.) *Proclama y discursos del Libertador* (Caracas: Litografía y Tipografía del Comercio, 1939), 1:22.

12. This, the so-called Angostura Discourse, was delivered to the Venezuelan congress on February 15, 1819, in the city today known as Ciudad Bolívar. For the text, see Harold A. Bierck, Jr., and Vicente Lecuna (eds. and comps.), *Selected Writings of Bolívar* (New York: Colonial Press for the Banco de Venezuela, 1951), 1:179–80.

13. José Martí, *Nuestra América* (1891), as cited in Carlos Rangel, *Del buen salvaje al buen revolucionario* (Caracas: Monte Avila Editores, 1976), p. 180.

14. Díaz's interview with James Creelman, published in the March 1908 issue of *Pearson's Magazine,* is excerpted in Lewis Hanke (ed.), *History of Latin American Civilization: Sources and Interpretations,* vol. 2, *The Modern Age* (Boston: Little, Brown, 1967), pp. 258–59.

15. Arturo Uslar Pietri, "El caudillo ante el movelista," *El Nacional* (Caracas), May 11, 1975, p. D-1.

16. Kalman H. Silvert, *Essays in Understanding Latin America* (Philadelphia: Institute for the Study of Human Issues, 1977), p. 58.

17. Julio Cotler and Richard R. Fagen (eds.), *Latin America and the United States: The Changing Political Realities* (Stanford: Stanford University Press, 1974).

18. For his first major statement, see Guillermo A. O'Donnell, *Modernization and Bureaucratic-Authoritarianism: Studies in South American Poli-*

tics (Berkeley: Institute of International Studies, 1973), especially pp. 1–53 and 166–201. For a later refinement of O'Donnell's views, see his "Reflections on the Patterns of Change in the Bureaucratic-Authoritarian State," *Latin American Research Review* 13, no. 1 (1978):3–39.

19. It is notable that a major compendium of such studies has no entries whatever under "democracy" in its seven-page index. Compare James M. Malloy (ed.), *Authoritarianism and Corporatism in Latin America* (Pittsburgh: University of Pittsburgh Press, 1977). For an incisive review of the work that also delineates the several streams of corporativist thought, see Charles W. Anderson in the *American Political Science Review* 72, no. 4 (December 1978):1478–79. An important case study superbly built upon corporativist theoretical bases is Alfred Stepan, *The State and Society: Peru in Comparative Perspective* (Princeton: Princeton University Press, 1978).

20. Candido Mendes, *Beyond Populism*, trans. L. Gray Cowan (Albany: State University of New York at Albany, Graduate School of Public Affairs, 1977), p. 40.

21. Gil, *Latin American–United States Relations*, p. 283.

22. For a knowledgeable journalistic account that nonetheless shared this optimism, see Tad Szulc, *Twilight of the Tyrants* (New York: Praeger, 1959).

23. For detailed discussion and analysis, see Howard R. Penniman (ed.), *Venezuela at the Polls* (Washington: American Enterprise Institute, 1979), especially the introduction and conclusions by John D. Martz and David J. Myers respectively. Also see Martz and Myers's *Venezuela: The Democratic Experience* (New York: Praeger, 1977).

24. For a thoughtful and perceptive treatment of systemic factors and their interactions both before and after the events of 1964, see Alfred Stepan, "Political Leadership and Regime Breakdown: Brazil," in Juan J. Linz and Alfred Stepan (eds.), *The Breakdown of Democratic Regimes: Latin America* (Baltimore: Johns Hopkins University Press, 1978), pp. 110–38. Among other treatments considering the nature of the contemporary regime, see Alfred Stepan (ed.), *Authoritarian Brazil: Origins, Policies and the Future* (New Haven: Yale University Press, 1973).

25. A detailed analysis of the process is John D. Martz, "The Chimera and Facade of Ecuadorian Democracy: The 'Juridical Restoration of the State,' " forthcoming. A related study is idem, "Marxism in Ecuador," *Inter-American Economic Affairs* 33 (Summer 1979):3–29.

26. Stanley Hoffman, "Rights and Diplomacy," *The New York Times*, December 31, 1978, p. E-17.

27. Kalman H. Silvert, *The Reason for Democracy* (New York: Viking Press, 1977), p. 1.

28. Gustavo Lagos and Horacio H. Godoy, *Revolution of Being: A Latin American View of the Future* (New York: Free Press, 1977), p. 92.

29. Kalman H. Silvert, *Man's Power: A Biased Guide to Political Thought and Action* (New York: Viking Press, 1970), pp. 162–63.

Part 3

Human Rights and U.S. Policy
Toward Latin America

7

U.S. Diplomacy and Human Rights in Latin America

Lars Schoultz

During the course of the 1970s, a remarkable transformation occurred in the content of U.S. diplomacy on the issue of human rights violations in Latin America. Prior to 1977, U.S. diplomatic activity sought to legitimize the hemisphere's most repressive regimes, to protect them from assault by other forces, particularly the United Nations and the U.S. Congress, and on occasion to prod them quietly to moderate the intensity of their human rights violations. Within a few months of the inauguration of President Carter, however, diplomacy became a major foreign policy tool to attack Latin American regimes characterized by high levels of repression. The purpose of this chapter is to analyze the differing policies of the Nixon-Ford and the Carter administrations and then to describe how these policies were implemented by U.S. diplomats.

U.S. Policy Toward Human Rights in Latin America

Although some administrations clearly place greater emphasis than others on the promotion of human rights, in no case has a commitment to improve the impact of human rights considerations in U.S. foreign policy been to deny the legitimacy of other competing values. In every administration the importance of human rights is a function of their influence upon policymakers relative to all the other potential interests and values that impinge upon any given policy decision.[1] Thus the question U.S.

policymakers address is not whether to incorporate human rights into the decision-making process but rather *how much* influence human rights should have in relation to a host of other potentially conflicting variables. The question is not human rights versus no human rights; instead it is human rights versus national security versus friendly relations with existing regimes versus economic benefits to the U.S. economy and U.S. investors versus humanitarian aid to impoverished people. At the perceived extreme—the mass extermination of Caucasians, perhaps—there would probably be a near-perfect consensus in any administration that U.S. policy ought to emphasize human rights values above all others. In most cases, however, differing circumstances and disparate assessments of the importance of human rights in U.S. foreign policy encourage differing human rights policies.

Most of the witnesses who appeared at the initial human rights hearings by the Fraser subcommittee in 1973 noted that the Nixon policy was to denigrate humanitarian values in foreign policy making. Fresh from a tour as the U.S. representative to the UN Commission on Human Rights, Rita Hauser told of how "we speak out against violations of countries we are not particularly close to . . . and we are largely silent . . . when human rights violations occur on the part of our allies." Richard Falk lamented that human rights maintained such a low priority that they were all but excluded from foreign policy decision making. This evaluation was echoed by a second specialist in international law, Tom Farer, who characterized human rights as "the stepchildren of United States foreign policy." "The best guarantor of an aborted career in the defense and foreign policy establishments," he observed, "is a marked concern for the humanitarian consequences of national behavior."[2]

The issue of U.S. policy toward human rights violations in Latin America was never directly confronted in public by President Nixon. This in itself is significant, for a presidential address serves as one of the principal mechanisms by which a president informs the executive branch of the concerns he wishes to emphasize. The importance an administration wishes to attach to nearly any issue can be gauged at least in part by the public attention it receives from the president. When President Nixon did approach the subject of human rights indirectly, he emphasized his greater interest in other potentially competing values, particularly the stability of existing relationships: "The United States has a strong interest in maintaining cooperation with our neighbors regardless of their domestic viewpoint. . . . We hope that governments will evolve toward constitutional procedures but it is not our mission to try to provide, except by example, the answers to such questions to other sovereign nations. We deal with governments as they are."[3] Except for this comment and a similar one near the end of his presidency, Mr. Nixon was silent on the issue of human rights in Latin America.[4]

The primary Nixon administration spokesperson on the human rights component of U.S. foreign policy was Secretary of State Henry Kissinger. Until 1975 he commented upon the issue only in response to direct questioning. At his 1973 confirmation hearing, Mr. Kissinger was asked about the administration's intentions in light of the increasing level of repression among U.S. allies. Mr. Kissinger responded: "In our bilateral dealings we will follow a pragmatic policy of degree. If the infringement on human rights is not so offensive that we cannot live with it, we will seek to work out what we can with the country involved in order to increase our influence. If the infringement is so offensive that we cannot live with it, we will avoid dealing with the offending country."[5] At the same time Mr. Kissinger was making this argument, the level of human rights violations in many countries with which the United States was allied (Chile, Indonesia, Iran, the Philippines, South Korea, Uruguay) was reaching new levels of barbarity. When he and the president failed to make an issue of these violations, the foreign policy bureaucracy concluded correctly that the administration wished to emphasize values other than human rights in its relations with repressive governments. In July 1974, the particular issue of diplomatic intervention on behalf of human rights appeared to be settled for the duration of the Nixon-Ford administration. In that month the U.S. ambassador to Chile, David Popper, broached the subject of torture and other abuses during the course of a meeting with the Chilean minister of defense. In the margin of the cable describing the discussion, Secretary Kissinger scrawled an instruction to his aide: "Tell Popper to cut out the political science lectures."[6]

But then, in mid-1975, the Ford administration began to propose a change in the importance of human rights in U.S. foreign policy. Once again, Secretary of State Kissinger was the principal administration spokesperson. During his final year and a half in office, he asserted repeatedly that there were limits to the extent to which governments engaged in the systematic repression of their citizens' human rights could be "congenial partners" with the United States.[7] The impetus for this changed rhetoric is uncertain, although many factors probably contributed; certainly congressional pressure would have been among the most prominent of these. And many observers would agree with David Weissbrodt, the legal scholar who has chronicled the Kissinger human rights policy most carefully, that the secretary's "rhetoric may not have been translated into his policies."[8] Yet the fact is that the human rights policy enunciated by the "late" Kissinger differed substantially from that of the "early" Kissinger.

The most vivid example of this difference came at his June 1976 speech on "Human Rights and the Western Hemisphere" presented at the Sixth General Assembly of the Organization of American States (OAS) in Santiago, Chile. He began: "One of the most compelling issues of our time, and one which calls for the concerted action of all responsible peoples and nations, is the necessity to protect and extend the fundamental rights of humanity."[9] The secretary's speech touched upon no other subject than human rights. There exists no parallel to this address in the first seven years of the Nixon-Ford administration. The message to U.S. diplomats was that the value of human rights in U.S. policy toward Latin America had increased considerably.

It is of absolutely crucial importance to note, however, that throughout the 1969–1977 period Secretary Kissinger consistently enunciated the belief that human rights concerns must remain secondary to the maintenance of peace and world order. The best example of his understanding of this subordinate relationship appeared in a 1976 speech in which he acknowledged that

It is our obligation as the world's leading democracy to dedicate ourselves to assuring freedom for the human spirit. But responsibility compels also a recognition of our limits. Our alliances . . . serve the cause of peace by strengthening regional and world security. If well conceived, they are not favors to others but a recognition of common interests. They should be withdrawn when those interests change; they should not, as a general rule, be used as levers to extort a standard of conduct or to punish acts with which we do not agree.[10]

Overall, then, the message from the secretary of state to his diplomats was that human rights, although deserving of greater attention, should not distract the U.S. government from the pursuit of its more traditional national security interests.

Once out of office, Mr. Kissinger placed this position in sharper focus in commenting upon the obvious difference between his human rights policy and that of the Carter administration. Speaking as a private citizen in 1977, he warned the Carter policymakers to "maintain the moral distinction between aggressive totalitarianism and other governments which, with all their imperfections, are trying to resist foreign pressures or subversion and which thereby help preserve the balance of power in behalf of all free peoples."[11] This statement appears to confirm Rita Hauser's evaluation that under the Nixon administration the United States had friends—"free peoples" in Mr. Kissinger's lexicon—whose human rights practices were irrelevant to U.S. policy because these allies were engaged in a struggle to maintain a higher value, the balance of power. The human rights behavior of "aggressive totalitarianisms," conversely, was morally distinct: their abuses could not be counterbalanced by the value of maintaining freedom. It is upon this logic that U.S. policy toward the international protection of human rights was based during the Nixon and Ford administrations.

If one were to search for the single most prominent difference between the foreign policy of the Carter administration and that of its immediate predecessors, surely the distinction would be the policy on human rights protection. Candidate Carter's first major speech emphasizing human rights and foreign

policy came during his September 8, 1976, appearance before
the national convention of B'nai B'rith: "We cannot look away
when a government tortures people, or jails them for their
beliefs or denies minorities fair treatment or the right to emi-
grate. . . . We should begin by having it understood that if any
nation . . . deprives its own people of basic human rights, that
fact will help shape our own people's attitude towards that
nation's government."[12] During the second preelection debate
in October 1976, Mr. Carter accused the Ford administration
of ignoring "in our foreign policy the character of the American
people" and of acting "contrary to our longstanding beliefs
and principles." Responding to President Ford's statement that
the United States "does not condone . . . repressive measures"
in South Korea, Mr. Carter noted "that Mr. Ford didn't comment on the prisons in Chile," where "his administration overthrew an elected government and helped to establish a military
dictatorship."

Thereafter, statements about human rights became a prominent feature of the Carter campaign. By the time of his inauguration, no one was startled to hear him assert that "our commitment to human rights must be absolute." Perhaps the most-
quoted passage from his initial presidential address concerned
human rights: "Because we are free, we can never be indifferent
to the fate of freedom elsewhere. Our moral sense dictates a
clearcut preference for those societies which share with us an
abiding respect for individual human rights."[13] Even if President Carter had done nothing else on the issue, he would have
been noted, as Deputy Secretary of State Warren Christopher
observed, for bringing human rights "to the center of diplomatic exchange."[14] After January 1977, U.S. diplomats knew
that the value of human rights as a component of U.S. foreign
policy had risen dramatically.

Once human rights had come out of the closet, the perennial
question arose over their relative value. One administration official observed that "those of us who had been outside came in
with lots of ideas about what was wrong and about what ought
to be, but not many ideas of how to go about it."[15] Gingerly,
they groped their way. At his February 8, 1977, news conference, the president noted that he was "reserving the right to

speak out forcefully whenever human rights are threatened," but then he finished this sentence by adding "not every instance, but when I think it's advisable." This, of course, suggested that his administration had a relative rather than an absolute commitment to increasing the value of human rights in U.S. foreign policy.

The question then became the same one that had faced all previous administrations: How much of a commitment? The first attempt at an answer was made by Secretary of State Cyrus Vance when he appeared before the Senate Appropriations Subcommittee on Foreign Operations on February 24, 1977. He announced that the Carter administration planned to reduce aid to Argentina, Ethiopia, and Uruguay because of their gross violations of human rights. Absent from the secretary's statement was any suggestion that human rights had the absolute value the president had mentioned in his inaugural address. Instead Mr. Vance noted that although human rights considerations would receive greater attention, as with previous administrations they would be incorporated in U.S. policy on a country-by-country basis: "In each case we must balance a political concern for human rights against economic or security goals."[16]

In March 1977, at his initial appearance before the UN General Assembly, President Carter made his first major speech on behalf of human rights. Here again, however, their relative value in U.S. foreign policy was emphasized by a carefully worded statement that human rights would not interfere with progress in certain other areas, especially arms control. The important point, though, is that the president actually addressed the issue of human rights and pledged the support of his administration for improved human rights practices. These presidential affirmations have continued over the course of the Carter administration. One of the strongest occurred in December 1978, when the president took advantage of the thirtieth anniversary of the Universal Declaration of Human Rights to emphasize his commitment:

> As long as I am President, the government of the United States will continue throughout the world to enhance human rights. . . . No force on earth can separate us from that commitment. . . . Our

human rights policy is not a decoration. It is not something we have adopted to polish up our image abroad, or to put a fresh coat of moral paint on the discredited policies of the past. . . . Human rights is the soul of our foreign policy.[17]

From the beginning, then, it was obvious that the president and his major advisers held a near-perfect consensus that human rights should be given a greater relative value than they were during the Nixon-Ford years. The answer to the question, "How much emphasis?" was "Quite a bit more."

Once this had been determined, a number of ancillary issues had to be clarified before U.S. diplomats could implement the administration's policy. One such issue—the selection of the type of human rights to be given major emphasis—was settled by Secretary of State Vance at his Law Day speech at the University of Georgia in April 1977. The Carter administration, he declared, would concentrate upon, first, the right to be free from governmental violation of the integrity of the person; second, the right to the fulfillment of basic human needs; and third, the right to enjoy civil and political liberties. Noting that problems might arise over which of these rights should be given the greatest importance in U.S. foreign policy, he indicated that the first set of rights was mentioned first because they were to be treated by U.S. diplomats first:

We may justifiably seek a rapid end to such gross violations as those cited in our law: "torture, or cruel inhuman or degrading treatment or punishment, or prolonged detention without charges. . . ." Just last week our ambassador to the United Nations, Andrew Young, suggested a series of new ways to confront the practice of torture around the world.

The promotion of other human rights is a broader challenge. The results may be slower in coming.[18]

After this address, there was little question as to where U.S. diplomats should concentrate their efforts on behalf of the international protection of human rights.

A second issue—the relationship between terrorism and governmental human rights violations—had particular significance for Latin America. It too was clarified by Secretary Vance, this time at the 7th General Assembly of the Organization of American States in June 1977. In that forum Mr. Vance presented a vigorous rebuttal to the contention that human rights abuses were an unfortunate but necessary concomitant of the war against terrorism. In direct contrast to the position of his predecessor, the secretary of state declared it "would be incorrect to take a position which would indicate that one combat terrorism with counterterrorism."[19] He continued:

> If terrorism and violence in the name of dissent cannot be condoned, neither can violence that is officially sanctioned. Such action perverts the legal system that, alone, assures the survival of our traditions. The surest way to defeat terrorism is to promote justice in our societies—legal, social and economic justice. Justice that is summary undermines the future it seeks to promote. It produces only more violence, more victims, and more terrorism.[20]

At the same meeting the United States cosponsored a resolution that reflected the Carter administration's refusal to recognize terrorism as an excuse for repression.

Finally, the manner in which the Carter administration handled four specific events in 1977 and early 1978 served to clarify for U.S. diplomats the limits of the new U.S. emphasis upon human rights in Latin America. First, any fears that the president would project a fundamentalist view of human rights protection were put to rest on March 9, 1977. A day earlier Brady Tyson, a Methodist minister, history professor, and aide-de-camp to UN Ambassador Andrew Young, appeared at a Geneva meeting of the UN Commission on Human Rights and expressed "our profoundest regrets" at the role of public and private U.S. groups in the overthrow of the Allende government in Chile. He further expressed sorrow that such regrets could not "contribute significantly to the reduction of suffering and terror that the people of Chile have experienced." Tyson was immediately called home for instruction in diplomatic procedures.[21]

At his news conference the following day, President Carter repudiated both Tyson and his own charge in October 1976 that the United States "overthrew an elected government and

helped to establish a military dictatorship" in Chile. Between
October and March he discovered the lack of "any evidence that
the U.S. was involved in the overthrow of the Allende government in Chile." He said little about the human rights violations
of the Pinochet government. To U.S. diplomats, the content
of this message was, in part, that the United States would not
attempt to atone—or even apologize—for human rights abuses
to which it may have contributed. To avoid such responsibility
it was permissible to ignore earlier statements.

The second event was the September 1977 ceremonial signing of the new Panama Canal treaties, attended by nearly all
of the hemisphere's chiefs of state. President Carter spoke individually with each of the leaders, including Chile's Pinochet
and Argentina's Videla, thereby signaling his belief that the
need for hemispheric solidarity on other important issues—
in this case, the canal treaties—was of sufficient importance to
override the damage done to human rights by such meetings.

The third event was a letter sent by President Carter to
Nicaraguan President Somoza in July 1978, praising his improvements in the area of human rights. The letter, drafted by a
National Security Council staff whose inexperience in Latin
American affairs was only exceeded by its self-confidence,
evoked strong opposition from the Department of State. But
the U.S. ambassador was ordered to deliver the letter, and every
United States diplomat learned it was the Carter policy to give
enthusiastic praise for minor reductions in human rights abuses.

The fourth and surely the most widely received human rights
message to the U.S. diplomatic corps came in the form of a
demonstration of what happens to half-hearted participants.
The individual in question was Assistant Secretary of State
for Inter-American Affairs Terence A. Todman, a career diplomat. Under his direction, the Bureau of Inter-American Affairs
(ARA) initially opposed the use of public diplomacy to pursue
aggressively the protection of human rights in Latin America.
In fact, Mr. Todman's public statements constituted something
of a reverse human rights policy. This was demonstrated clearly
on two major occasions. Upon completion of a trip to Chile in
October 1977, he remarked that the Department of State was
encouraged "by recent evidence that the trend away from

democracy may be ending," citing as an example of this trend the Chilean government's "public commitment to a timetable" for elections. No such timetable existed.

Within a week, the State Department took the unusual step of presenting a detailed rebuttal to Todman's statement. It noted that the assistant secretary "has tried to emphasize the readiness of our Government to recognize progress" and "to avoid the development of a sterile adversary relationship." However, the department argued that "at no time did he allege that the human rights situation in the Southern Cone countries was satisfactory," and even if he did give that impression, "the Department continues to be disappointed with the lack of political freedom in Chile."[22]

Todman's second major break with the Carter administration came in February 1978. During the course of a speech at the Center for Inter-American Relations in New York, he presented a list of ten "tactical mistakes" that the United States must avoid "if we are truly to help and not hinder the cause of promoting human rights and alleviating suffering." Among these were the practices of "condemning an entire government for every negative act by one of its officials" and of "holding entire countries up to public ridicule and embarrassment." Shortly thereafter, Mr. Todman was asked to leave his post and accept the ambassadorship to Spain.[23] His replacement, Viron "Pete" Vaky, ceased Todman's opposition to the use of public diplomacy as a foreign policy tool to protect human rights.

The general message that emerged from these events and actions was that human rights would have a significant place in nearly all decisions regarding U.S. foreign policy, but that the *amount* of significance would depend upon (1) the nature of other variables involved, (2) the type of human rights violations, and, therefore, (3) the countries involved. As it happened, many of the truly egregious human rights violators were outside the U.S. sphere of influence—the United States had no diplomatic relations with Cambodia or Uganda, for example. Other major violators were of such importance to U.S. strategic and economic interests that administration officials concluded that human rights values could not be pursued vigorously. In this category were the repressive governments of Indonesia, Iran, the Philippines, and South Korea.[24] This left the nations of Latin America—linked to the United States by two centuries of intimate intercourse and, with the possible exceptions of Brazil and Mexico, lacking any of the strategic significance that exempted other nations from U.S. diplomatic pressure on behalf of human rights.

Once the Carter administration recognized that a universal standard of human rights would conflict with other foreign policy values to an intolerable extent—once the administration adopted a case-by-case approach to human rights abuses—attention shifted to the nations of Latin America. By the end of 1977 it was clear to the U.S. diplomatic corps that U.S. efforts to protect human rights were to be concentrated upon Latin America's repressive governments. With the policy direction set, U.S. diplomats began to implement their superiors' directions.

Policy Implementation

Bilateral Diplomacy

Within the Department of State the two bureaus charged with using diplomacy to implement U.S. policy on human rights in Latin America are the Bureau of Inter-American Affairs (ARA) and the Bureau of Human Rights and Humanitarian Affairs (HA). The former bureau is responsible for the day-to-day diplomatic interaction, the staffing of embassies and consulates in Latin America, and the general observation of activities in the region that might affect U.S. interests. ARA's primary task is the maintenance of smooth relations with the various governments of Latin America.

Because of the nature of the bureau's duties, the officials of ARA have always been reluctant to raise publicly the issue of human rights abuses. Thus the following statement by the Nixon administration's assistant secretary of state for inter-American affairs, Jack Kubisch, verbalizes a widely held attitude: "It is one thing for our newspapers or for private citizens to make charges or make complaints or appeal to the Chileans. It is something else for U.S. Government officials or the Executive branch to lean hard publicly on a regime since to do so might make them feel that they are required to dig in their heels and resist us publicly, or not have anything to do with us, or discuss the matter with us."[25] It is doubtful that this attitude is simply a manifestation of an ideological affinity between ARA and the hemisphere's right-wing repressive regimes.[26] Although it could reflect a willingness to accept repression as an alternative to disorder and revolution, it is at least as plausible to suggest that the attitude stems from the simple perception that, as Kubisch stated, if the U.S. publicly presses a Latin American government too hard on a sensitive issue such as human rights, the government might indeed decide "not to have anything to do with us." Should that occur, ARA would have failed in its primary mission of maintaining smooth relations.

Because the officials of ARA have as their principal task the preservation of effective working relationships with all recognized Latin American governments, regardless of their level of repressiveness, the bureau has always preferred a special type of diplomatic interaction called quiet diplomacy. Quiet diplomacy is to ARA what foreign military sales credits are to the Defense Security Assistance Agency or what volunteer placement is to the Peace Corps—the standard means of conducting relations with Latin American governments. But there are various types of quiet diplomacy. During the Nixon-Ford years, diplomatic interaction over human rights issues was of a perfunctory nature. Secretary Kissinger's Assistant Secretary of State for Inter-American Affairs William D. Rogers liked to compare his marital experience and the Nixon-Ford administration's activities on behalf of human rights. He contended that he was much more willing to accept his wife's criticisms of his social misbehavior if she waited until they were alone in bed rather than chastising him publicly. Following this approach, Rogers argued, he could be more successful by tactfully suggesting rather than by openly demanding that a repressive regime relent.[27]

The validity of this analogy would be an interesting topic to pursue, but it is not the point to be made in this context. What needs to be emphasized here is that the quiet diplomacy ARA had in mind under the Nixon administration was not modeled after George and Martha's connubial interaction in *Who's Afraid of Virginia Woolf?* For example, when Senator Frank Church inquired whether ARA had expressed the concern of the U.S.

government over the evidence that the Brazilian dictatorship was systematically exterminating all dissent, William Roundtree, the U.S. ambassador to Brazil, halfheartedly responded: "To the Government, yes. I might say that the Department of State here in Washington has mentioned its concern to the representatives of Brazil, and the various members of the mission . . . have indicated concern regarding these stories."[28] To the Nixon-Ford administration, quiet diplomacy on behalf of human rights involved only the most circumspect protestations.

This style of quiet diplomacy contrasts vividly with that which has occurred under the Carter administration. For example, in 1978 Deputy Assistant Secretary of State for Inter-American Affairs Richard Arellano was asked the same question as Ambassador Roundtree regarding the repressive activities of El Salvador's White Warriors Union. He responded by describing a far more aggressive form of quiet diplomacy: "Repeatedly, upon instructions from Washington, the Embassy has made formal demarches, sent protest notes and otherwise actively sought to impress upon Salvadorean authorities and others the abiding concern of the American people and Government with the human rights ramifications of developments in El Salvador."[29] It is worth noting that few of the national security concerns that might have prompted a relatively mild approach to the Brazilian government's human rights violations apply to tiny El Salvador. But even in those instances where national security was a minor consideration—Uruguay, for example—the Nixon-Ford administration's form of quiet diplomacy was notably lacking in aggressiveness.

Despite these differences in tone and aggressiveness, it should be emphasized that under any administration ARA strives to conduct diplomatic relations in such a way that relations are not strained. Although under the Carter administration the bureau tended to accept occasionally the risk of straining relations, even then its opposition was apparent. In fact, by late 1977 the bureau had developed a reputation for renitence on the human rights issue. Much of this reputation was undeserved, for the bureau used its favorite foreign policy instrument, quiet diplomacy, over and over again in defense of human rights. But its quiet diplomacy often went unnoticed, and thus ARA's reputation came from its efforts to protect existing programs, especially economic and military assistance, for the sake of maintaining contact, access, and influence with repressive governments. Given its responsibilities, it is difficult to imagine how the bureau could have behaved otherwise. Its often-criticized "curator mentality"—the desire to protect existing relationships—will probably never disappear from ARA or, indeed, from any of the State Department's regional bureaus.[30]

The Bureau of Human Rights and Humanitarian Affairs, the second executive branch bureaucracy responsible for implementing U.S. policy toward human rights in Latin America, is a new organization whose present structure and functions date from the mid-1970s. The idea of creating a human rights bureau grew out of a 1968 recommendation by the Commission on the Observance of Human Rights Year that the president appoint an assistant for human rights. The following year Senator Edward Kennedy's Judiciary Subcommittee on Refugees advocated the creation of a bureau of humanitarian and social services. Soon thereafter, the President's Task Force on International Development urged the establishment of such a bureau, and in 1971 the Nixon administration included in its foreign assistance message a recommendation that Congress authorize its creation. The administration was not upset when Congress ignored the request.[31]

The subject next received attention in 1973, when Representative Donald Fraser introduced a resolution (H.R. 10455) to establish a bureau for humanitarian affairs in the Department of State. Although the House failed to give his proposal serious consideration, in the same year Senator Kennedy convinced the Senate to add to its version (S. 1443) of the Foreign Assistance Act of 1973 a statement urging the State Department to create a bureau of humanitarian and social services. The House bill contained no such provision, and the conference committee rejected Kennedy's initiative.[32] The Senate tried again in 1976, and this time the House accepted its suggestion. Thus the International Security Assistance and Arms Export Control Act (P.L. 94-329, Sec.301[b]) authorized the position of the coordinator for human rights and humanitarian affairs, providing it with responsibility for advising the secretary of state on

"matters pertaining to human rights and humanitarian affairs
. . . in the conduct of foreign policy." Congress indicated the
importance it wished to attach to this position by stipulating
that the coordinator was to be appointed by the president with
the advice and consent of the Senate.

Prior to the creation of the Office of the Coordinator, the
responsibility for the diplomatic aspect of human rights protection rested with the State Department's Bureau of International
Organization Affairs (IO) and, to a lesser extent, with the Office
of the Legal Advisor. This reflected the State Department's
conception of its human rights duties as primarily technical: the
preparation of instructions for U.S. representatives to international human rights commissions and the creation of U.S.
policy toward international human rights agreements. At the
time of the initial Fraser subcommittee hearings in 1973, IO
had assigned one foreign service officer to work full-time on
human rights, assisted part-time by a junior officer. In the
Office of the Legal Advisor, there was one assistant legal advisor
for human rights.[33]

Soon after the hearings were completed, a human rights officer was designated in every regional bureau. It is not known
whether the purpose of this move was to please congressional
critics or to promote a larger role for human rights in U.S.
foreign policy. But it is instructive to note that, initially, each
of these new human rights officers was expected to continue
with his or her previous tasks (most were labor specialists) and
to perform human rights functions as well.[34] In addition to the
creation of these regional human rights officers, IO's human
rights officer was upgraded to become deputy director of the
UN Political Affairs Office, and another officer was assigned to
work as his assistant. Finally, in April 1975, the State Department anticipated Congress' directive and appointed a coordinator for humanitarian affairs in the Office of the Deputy Secretary of State.[35] The 1976 congressional action mentioned above
changed the title of the coordinator, made the position subject
to Senate confirmation, and, most importantly, guaranteed the
position could not be abolished without congressional approval.

Despite these structural changes, the human rights officials
had little impact on policy determination during the Nixon-

Ford administration.[36] The coordinator for humanitarian affairs, James M. Wilson, Jr., was noted for his low visibility during his year-and-a-half tenure. Most of his first year in office was devoted to the problem of Vietnamese refugees; thereafter he spent much of his time attempting to convince Congress not to pass human rights legislation. In his only public statement on human rights and diplomacy, he offered an opinion of diplomatic interaction that differed not at all from that of his colleagues in ARA:

> In every instance . . . human rights problems are likely to be a unique result of a special set of circumstances. There will be few general prescriptions that will apply equally well to all countries. A case-by-case approach . . . is essential. . . . Bilateral diplomacy remains the basic weapon for promotion of human rights. . . . This requires deft diplomacy of the highest order. We have to retain contact and influence and yet try to persuade governments who feel fiercely beseiged [by terrorists].[37]

Responding to congressional demands for an activist human rights policy that would include the use of a variety of foreign policy tools, Wilson urged instead that the United States concentrate upon "quiet and friendly persuasion" to combat human rights abuses.[38]

At the initiative of the House of Representatives, in mid-1977 Congress included in its Foreign Relations Authorization Act (P.L. 95-105) an amendment upgrading the position of the coordinator to that of an assistant secretary of state, a move that was strongly endorsed by the Carter administration. The Bureau of Human Rights and Humanitarian Affairs (HA) quickly became the center of human rights activities in U.S. foreign policy and proved to be an unusually aggressive State Department bureaucracy. Most of HA's considerable bureaucratic strength stemmed, of course, from President Carter's emphasis that, as noted above, was most evident in U.S. policy toward Latin America. Because of this commitment, HA's staff grew by both quantitative and qualitative measures. The two-person staff under the Ford administration was almost immediately augmented by five new human rights officers, including a deputy assistant secretary of state for human rights, and further additions were made as needs became identified. By the end of 1978, HA had at least one expert covering each aspect of U.S. policy toward Latin America.

In qualitative terms, two individual appointments were particularly significant. As the first assistant secretary of state for human rights and humanitarian affairs, Patricia Derian set the tone of HA's activities. A civil rights activist, a founder of the Mississippi Civil Liberties Union, and an organizer of the biracial Loyalist Mississippi Democratic party that successfully challenged the all-white Mississippi delegation for seating at the 1968 Democratic party convention, Ms. Derian is a person of unusually strong will. If President Carter wanted an assistant secretary who could present forcefully the case for human rights and who was not intimidated by established bureaucratic procedures, there could have been few better choices than Derian.[39] Her principal associate was Mark Schneider, the deputy assistant secretary for human rights. Through Schneider, HA enjoyed extremely close relations with several members of Congress who had been working for years to enlarge the human rights component of U.S. foreign policy. A former Peace Corps volunteer with service in El Salvador, Schneider had worked as an aide to Senator Edward Kennedy, where he performed most of the staff work that resulted in a number of Senate-sponsored hearings, resolutions, and some legislation on repression in post-1973 Chile.

Under Derian, HA concentrated on building its staff and its expertise in specific policy areas, particularly foreign aid programs. But interspersed with these activities was an ongoing attempt at direct bilateral diplomacy on behalf of human rights, including a number of meetings with the leaders of Latin America's most repressive governments. Unlike officials at ARA, whose demarches and private conversations have expressed profound concern over human rights violations without going so far as to offend foreign leaders, HA was willing to push the issue beyond the bounds of normal diplomatic intercourse. Derian characterized her diplomatic conversations with leaders of repressive governments as "a very serious kind of thing. It's not just talk. It is always extremely tense."[40] She is one of the few U.S. diplomats to elaborate publicly upon her discussions:

What happens is that we begin a meeting, and this is at the official level, with long statements about the concern and affection and importance of human rights to the country involved. All countries say that they are great defenders of and believers in human rights. Then we have a kind of pause in the discussion and they explain whatever the crisis is in the country that causes them to violate human rights. No country really admits it is a human rights violator. All countries, or representatives of countries, profess to care as much as we do. They often hold up their own constitutions and pronounce them better than ours. Then they explain their crisis, which threatens their society, and next say that as soon as they get on the other side of this crisis they will begin to observe human rights again, but during this interval it is necessary for them to take extraordinary measures.

Then I talk respectfully about what they mean by extraordinary measures. There is ordinarily a great breakthrough because I use the word "torture" in places where this is applicable, and it is applicable in far too many places. I talk about the specific kinds that they do, the names of places where people are detained, the names of people who are missing, the names of people who are no longer in detention but are not [at liberty], who have suffered various kinds of abuses and mistreatment.

Then we come to a kind of reality facing. Mostly an explanation that they are not responsible, that we have to understand things are so terrible and intense in the place that people at a lower level are moved by their own overriding emotions to take these actions on their own. Then I talk about responsibility. If you hold high office you must take the full responsibility and the blame. Then we generally start all over again and go through the whole thing again. That is generally the end of the first encounter.[41]

To Latin American leaders accustomed to exchanges with U.S. diplomats that emphasize the maintenance of smooth relations, Derian's brand of quiet diplomacy must have come as a surprise.

Multilateral Diplomacy

In addition to their bilateral activities, U.S. diplomats work through the United Nations and the Organization of American States to implement U.S. policy toward human rights. For most of the Cold War period, however, multilateral diplomacy has not been a favored tool of U.S. policymakers. In 1974 Louis

Henkin lamented that "the United States has remained largely outside the international human rights program. It has been for this country a peripheral aspect of its United Nations activities, themselves increasingly peripheral, and conducted by officials peripheral to the seats of power and the major concerns of United States foreign policy."[42] This is not to suggest that the United States has always ignored the United Nations in address-ing its human rights concerns; indeed, the United States domi-nated the early human rights activities of the United Nations. Under the strong leadership of Eleanor Roosevelt, the first U.S. representative to the UN Commission on Human Rights, the United States provided the major impetus for the human rights provisions in the UN Charter and much of the initiative for the Universal Declaration of Human Rights and the Genocide Con-vention. In addition, the United States was instrumental in urg-ing the creation of the UN Commission on Human Rights, and it enjoys an excellent but largely unrecognized record of spon-soring improvements in the commission's procedures. But all of these activities occurred before the rise of Brickerism. Given the Cold War attitudes of U.S. policymakers and the decline of U.S. hegemony in the United Nations, it was probably inevitable that U.S. participation in UN human rights activities would peak early. Still, the decline in U.S. interest in multilateral diplomacy to protect human rights was impressive in its dimen-sions. Only in the late 1970s did the United States reverse some-what its two-decade record of obstructing the development of multilateral efforts to protect human rights.[43]

The general policy of the Nixon-Ford administration toward human rights issues in the United Nations was to protect U.S. allies from criticism.[44] Since the only major Latin American human rights issue to arise in the United Nations during the 1970s was that of Chile, it is upon the U.S. position on this single case that the entire record of the Nixon-Ford administra-tion stands. There is some question as to the content of that position. In his March 1976 testimony before Congress, Secre-tary of State Kissinger asserted that at his direction the U.S. representatives "voted in the United Nations with the majority on the issue of human rights in Chile."[45] However, contrary to the impression the secretary may have left with Congress, what he probably meant by this statement was not that the

United States consistently voted with the majority, or that it regularly voted with the majority, but that it *once* voted with the majority. The record is fairly unambiguous, and it indicates that the Nixon-Ford administration obstructed the efforts of the United Nations to assess the situation in Chile and to promote increased respect for human rights. This position appears congruent with what is already known about that administration's policy toward post-Allende Chile.

To begin, in early 1974 the Social Committee of the UN Economic and Social Council (ECOSOC) adopted its first resolution on Chile, a mild statement calling upon the government of Chile to "restore and safeguard basic human rights." The measure passed by a vote of forty-one to none, with two abstentions: Chile and the United States. The resolution was then passed to the parent ECOSOC, where it was adopted by consensus. According to one active observer, California Supreme Court Justice Frank Newman, in the ECOSOC deliberations the main contribution of the United States to the resolution "was to make it as weak as conceivable."[46]

In October 1974, the General Assembly's Social, Cultural and Humanitarian Committee voted eighty-three to nine to urge the Chilean government to restore human rights and to free political prisoners. The United States abstained.[47] The following month the General Assembly passed two resolutions on human rights in Chile. One called upon the government of Chile "to release all persons who have been detained without charge or imprisoned solely for political reasons." The resolution passed by a vote of ninety to eight. The United States abstained, calling the resolution "unbalanced." The second resolution requested freedom for Clodomiro Almeyda, Chile's foreign minister under Allende and the president of UNCTAD III. Again the United States abstained. Finally, on November 11, 1975, the United States voted with the majority on an issue of human rights in Chile, when the General Assembly's Social, Cultural and Humanitarian Committee recommended eighty-eight to eleven that the General Assembly express its "profound distress at the constant, flagrant violations of human rights, including the institutionalized practice of torture" in Chile.[48]

As part of the general increase in interest in human rights that was noted above, by late 1975 the Ford administration had begun to distance itself from the Pinochet government. The Chilean junta was a particularly vulnerable target for a variety of reasons: its unusual brutality, its 1975 decision to support (and later abstain on) the UN resolution equating Zionism with racism, its refusal to permit a UN human rights investigating team to enter Chile, and its decimation of domestic opposition (which consequently lowered the risk that the regime could be weakened by UN and OAS attacks). Of additional consequence were the negative connotations of an association with the Chilean junta during the upcoming presidential election year and, perhaps, a belief that the United States should speak out on the question of human rights abuses.

Thus in his June 8, 1976, speech to the foreign ministers of the OAS, Secretary of State Kissinger addressed with unusual frankness the subject of human rights in Chile. First he acknowledged that a report by the Inter-American Commission on Human Rights had noted that "the infringement of certain fundamental rights in Chile has undergone a quantitative reduction" and that "Chile has filed a comprehensive and responsive answer [to the commission's charges] that sets forth a number of hopeful prospects." But then Kissinger expressed the dismay of the U.S. government that violations continued to occur:

> In the United States, concern is widespread in the executive branch, in the press, and in the Congress, which has taken the extraordinary step of enacting specific statutory limits on United States military and economic aid to Chile. The condition of human rights . . . has impaired our relationship with Chile and will continue to do so. We wish this relationship to be close, and all friends of Chile hope that obstacles raised by conditions alleged in the report will soon be removed.[49]

Except for the periodic vilification of Cuba, this was, at the time, the strongest formal statement any OAS member had made against the internal human rights violations by another member of the OAS. Aside from this activity in support of human rights in Chile, however, the Nixon-Ford administration demonstrated little interest in using multilateral diplomacy to promote the observance of human rights in Latin America or elsewhere.

In their use of multilateral diplomacy as a foreign policy tool to promote human rights, there is little to differentiate the Nixon-Ford and the Carter administration. To date, the major difference in the United Nations has been the level of rhetoric. On March 17, 1977, President Carter chose the UN General Assembly as the site for his first major foreign policy speech as president. Although he spoke on several topics—the global economy, arms control, specific trouble spots—his remarks were noted for their emphasis on human rights:

> The search for peace and justice means also respect for human dignity. All the signatories of the UN Charter have pledged themselves to observe and to respect basic human rights. Thus, no member of the United Nations can claim that mistreatment of its citizens is solely its own business. Equally, no member can avoid its responsibilities to review and to speak when torture or unwarranted deprivation occurs in any part of the world.
>
> The basic thrust of human affairs points toward a more universal demand for fundamental human rights. The United States has a historical birthright to be associated with this process. We in the United States accept this responsibility in the fullest and the most constructive sense.[50]

To demonstrate this commitment, the president indicated that he would sign and seek Senate ratification of the two UN human rights covenants and that he would continue his predecessors' attempts to obtain ratification of both the Genocide Convention and the Treaty for the Elimination of All Forms of Racial Discrimination. In addition, he pledged to encourage the United Nations to give increased attention to human rights matters by improving its human rights machinery. Specifically, he proposed moving the UN Human Rights Division back to UN headquarters from Geneva, and he promised to support the efforts to establish the post of UN high commissioner for human rights.

Beyond this initial policy statement, the Carter administration has not emphasized the use of UN forums to promote respect for human rights in Latin America. This reflects in part the desire to address the issue of Latin American human rights violations in the OAS, where U.S. diplomatic power is far greater than in the United Nations. But even on non–Latin American human rights issues, the Carter administration appears to view the United Nations as a relatively unimportant arena. For example, the administration has continued to appoint part-time representatives to the UN Commission on Human Rights and, more often than not, these individuals are selected because they are underemployed party loyalists, particularly recently defeated members of Congress, rather than experts in the field of human rights or persons with a significant influence on U.S. foreign policy.[51] In the area of human rights and Latin America, the Carter administration has initiated little of significance in the United Nations.

Less than a month after his initial speech to the UN General Assembly, President Carter addressed for the first time the Permanent Council of the OAS. Unlike some of his predecessors who have taken advantage of their first appearance at the OAS to announce a new Latin American policy, President Carter's speech was basically a catalog of problems affecting inter-American relations, nearly all of which were economic in their nature. Special emphasis was placed upon human rights, however. He told the delegates that

> Our values and yours require us to combat abuses of individual free-
> dom, including those caused by political, social, and economic
> injustice. Our own concerns for these values will naturally influence
> our relations with the countries of this hemisphere and throughout
> the world. You will find this country eager to stand beside those
> nations which respect human rights and promote democratic values.[52]

In addition to this relatively mild statement, the president signed the Inter-American Human Rights Convention on June 1.

The Carter administration's use of the OAS as a tool of multilateral diplomacy to encourage respect for human rights can best be pictured not as a continuation but as an extension of the policy begun in 1976 by the Ford administration. The major effort to date occurred in mid-June 1977 at the organization's Seventh General Assembly on the Caribbean island of Grenada. The human rights issue totally dominated that meeting. As discussed above, Secretary of State Vance went far beyond the Kissinger statement at Santiago in 1976, presenting a strong rebuttal to the popular contention that human rights abuses were a necessary part of the war against terrorism. In addition, the United States cosponsored (and helped obtain the necessary votes for) a resolution that stated in part that "there are no circumstances which justify torture, summary executions or prolonged detention without trial contrary to law."[53] The secretary of state then proceeded to link the provision of U.S. aid to each recipient's level of respect for human rights, noting that U.S. aid would be useless in an environment of extreme repression. Finally, Mr. Vance met privately with the foreign ministers of nearly all OAS member states, urging the representatives of repressive regimes to take seriously his public comments. Each of these statements was a significant extension of the OAS human rights policy of the preceding administration.

But beyond this initial effort in 1977, multilateral diplomacy through the OAS has not been a prominent tool for implementing U.S. policy toward human rights. OAS members soon became aware that the Inter-American Commission on Human Rights was fully supported by the United States and that the reports of the commission could no longer be ignored as they had been for years. The necessary resolutions and declarations were made. Other than action against a specific nation for egregious violations, there was little more that the OAS could do to promote human rights. And there was never a question about the possibility of the OAS sanctioning an individual member. Most Latin American governments, repressive and nonrepressive alike, have always considered human rights questions as internal political matters. In addition, many nations were understandably suspicious of the role of the United States in the human rights effort. One need not know much about U.S.–Latin American relations to understand why Latin Americans might be wary of the motivations behind yet another U.S. crusade in Latin America. So although Latin America's repressive regimes could not prevent the United States and several hemispheric allies from making human rights the major issue in the OAS, they could make concrete action extremely difficult to accomplish. Recognizing this, the Carter administration decided to invest its scarce diplomatic resources in bilateral efforts to promote human rights in Latin America.

Conclusion

Two conclusions from this analysis of U.S. policy toward human rights violations in Latin America during the 1970s deserve further discussion. One is that U.S. policy—in both substance and implementation—appeared to change dramatically over the course of the decade. It is possible to contend, however, that the change was merely cosmetic, that words are cheap, and that the fundamental values orienting U.S. policy, particularly the maintenance of U.S. hegemony, remain unaffected. What changed during the 1970s, some critics might suggest, was the need for the United States to support repressive regimes in the major countries of Latin America. Were President Carter to perceive a threat such as that which Lyndon Johnson discerned in Brazil or Richard Nixon sensed in Chile, perhaps values other than human rights would characterize his administration's policy toward Latin America.

There is little in the discussion on the preceding pages to confirm or reject this hypothesis. By its nature, diplomacy is primarily a verbal interaction, mere words. The efficacy of the tool depends entirely upon the perceptions by repressive Latin American governments of the costs involved in ignoring the words. The words, then, have only a latent content: they communicate threats. They can be threats to reduce military or economic aid, to oppose loans in multilateral development banks, to interfere with private economic transactions, or to initiate covert actions. In this sense, diplomacy is the means whereby a threat is communicated; it is not the threat itself. Thus the test of whether any diplomatic initiative is genuine or cosmetic will be determined by measuring the extent to which these threats are carried out when diplomacy is ignored. That, unfortunately, is beyond the scope of this chapter. Yet until a systematic analysis of the linkage between words and deeds is completed, it is inappropriate, in my view, to denigrate as meaningless U.S. diplomacy on behalf of human rights. It simply is not known at present whether this diplomacy serves

only to distract attention from underlying structural relationships that continue unaffected, thereby supporting the repression diplomats are superficially attacking. Such may be the
conclusion of analysts blessed with an ideological insight that
permits them to interpret all aspects of U.S. policy toward
Latin America without having to examine the facts. For the rest
of us, however, judgment must await the collection and interpretation of the data. But clearly the history of inter-American
relations provides us with every reason to be suspicious of the
motivation behind U.S. human rights initiatives. The burden of
proof rests with the Carter administration.

The second conclusion from this discussion concerns the
alleged difficulty in converting policy statements into policy
action. A common feature of the literature on U.S. foreign policy
making is a description of our diplomats' tendency to avoid
doing as they are told. Instead of implementing the policies of
a given administration, diplomatic personnel are said to be
engaged in "cookie pushing" or in operating their "foreign
affairs fudge factory." Relating to the diplomatic corps is likened
to "pushing on a marshmallow" or "shaking a bowl of jelly."[54]

Understandably, most citizens are distressed to think that
U.S. diplomatic initiatives are being handled by people who are
most frequently likened to various kinds of junk food. Thus we
tend to sympathize with principal foreign policy officials like
Arthur Schlesinger, Jr., who lamented that he and his president
were kept from accomplishing their admirable goals in Latin
America because the State Department hired persons "for
whom the risks always outweighed the opportunities."[55] After
investment banker Earl E. T. Smith completed his on-the-job
training in diplomacy as President Eisenhower's ambassador to
Cuba, he wrote: "I have reached the conclusion that the structure of organization in the State Department is faulty by law.
No President, no Secretary of State, no matter how sincere and
purposeful, can protect the United States from the damage of
this day-to-day operation by the lower officials. These men . . .
protect each other as though they belonged to a fraternity."[56]

The material presented in this chapter indicates that such
pejorative characterizations of the foreign policy bureaucracy
are incorrect. They suggest that foreign policy failures result

from malfunctions in the system when, as we have seen in the case of human rights, the system is functioning quite well. U.S. diplomats ably implement whatever policy high-ranking officials decide to pursue. Their premier characteristic appears to be their responsiveness, their willingness to adapt to changing policy orientations. Viewed from this perspective, malfunctions in U.S. foreign policy probably result from incomplete or incompetent *direction* of the foreign policy bureaucracy. Thus it is wrong to assert that obstructionist diplomats are to blame for the Kennedy administration's failures in Latin America. That responsibility rests with Schlesinger and his fellow New Frontiersmen, the leaders who could never surrender to their admirable instincts. Of the Dominican crisis in 1961, the president told Schlesinger: "There are three possibilities in descending order of preference: a decent democratic regime, a continuation of the Trujillo regime or a Castro regime. We ought to aim at the first, but we really can't renounce the second until we are sure we can avoid the third."[57] Ambassador Smith's own record indicates that U.S. policy toward the rebellion against the Batista government was unusually ambiguous. Had their policies been less ambivalent, perhaps Schlesinger and Smith would have reached a different conclusion about the efficiency of the U.S. diplomatic corps. Under the very different but similarly purposeful direction of both the Nixon and Carter administrations, U.S. diplomats ably implemented their instructions in the area of human rights in Latin America.

Notes

1. Richard B. Bilder, "Human Rights and U.S. Foreign Policy: Short-Term Prospects," *Virginia Journal of International Law* 14 (Summer 1974):598.

2. U.S., Congress, House, Committee on Foreign Affairs, Subcommittee on International Organizations and Movements, *International Protection of Human Rights*, 93d Cong., 1st sess., 1973, pp. 233, 250, 113.

3. U.S., Congress, Senate, Committee on Foreign Relations, Subcommittee on Western Hemisphere Affairs, *United States Policies and Programs in Brazil*, 92d Cong., 1st sess., May 4, 5, and 11, 1971, p. 290.

4. U.S., President (Nixon), *U.S. Foreign Policy for the 1970's: Shaping a Durable Peace. A Report to the Congress*, May 3, 1973, p. 118.

5. *International Protection of Human Rights*, p. 507. This position is not significantly different from that advanced by the administration of Lyndon Johnson. James D. Cochrane, "U.S. Policy toward Recognition of Governments and Promotion of Democracy in Latin America since 1963," *Journal of Latin American Studies* 4 (November 1972):278.

6. *New York Times*, September 27, 1974, p. 18.

7. David Weissbrodt, "Human Rights Legislation and U.S. Foreign Policy," *Georgia Journal of International and Comparative Law* 7, supplement (Summer 1977):237–8.

8. Ibid., p. 237n.

9. *Department of State Bulletin* 75 (July 5, 1976):1.

10. *Department of State Bulletin* 75 (November 15, 1976):603. For an earlier statement about the potential costs of supporting human rights in the Soviet Union, see *Department of State Bulletin* 69 (October 29, 1973): 529.

11. *Washington Post*, September 25, 1977, p. C3.

12. In earlier speeches—to the Chicago Council on Foreign Relations on March 15, 1976, and particularly to the Foreign Policy Association of New York City on June 23, 1976—Mr. Carter emphasized the need to "restore the moral authority of this country in its conduct of foreign policy" by discarding "policies that strengthen dictators or create refugees, policies that prolong suffering or postpone racial justice." During the course of the New York speech, he advocated that the United States "take the lead in establishing and promoting basic global standards of human rights." The B'nai B'rith speech in September, then, was notable for its emphasis on human rights considerations, not for its uniqueness. Only after this speech did the media firmly make the issue of human rights in foreign policy a major feature of the Carter campaign.

13. *Department of State Bulletin* 66 (February 14, 1977):121–2.

14. "Foreign Policy Priorities for 1978" (Speech to the National Foreign Policy Conference on Human Rights, Washington, D.C., February 27, 1978).

15. Tom Quigley et al., *U.S. Policy on Human Rights in Latin America (Southern Cone): A Congressional Conference on Capitol Hill* (New York: Fund for New Priorities in America, 1978), p. 41.

16. U.S., Congress, Senate, Committee on Appropriations, Subcommittee on Foreign Assistance and Related Programs, *Foreign Assistance and Related Programs Appropriations: Fiscal Year 1978*, 95th Cong., 1st sess., 1977, pp. 161, 196.

17. *Department of State Bulletin* 79 (January 1979):1–2.

18. Cyrus Vance, "Human Rights and Foreign Policy," *Georgia Journal of International and Comparative Law* 7, supplement (Summer 1977): 223–4, 228.

19. *New York Times,* September 17, 1977, p. 6.

20. *Department of State Bulletin* 77 (July 18, 1978):70.

21. The instruction consisted of a four-hour discussion with Assistant Secretary of State for International Organization Affairs Charles W. Maynes, during which Tyson steadfastly resisted Maynes's demand that he resign. Maynes, incidentally, was the author of a 1976 study urging "U.S. support for defending human rights more vigorously," in Charles William Maynes et al., *U.S. Foreign Policy: Principles for Defining the National Interest* (New York: Public Agenda Foundation, September 1976), p. 15.

22. U.S., Congress, House, Committee on International Relations, Subcommittee on International Organizations, *Human Rights and United States Foreign Policy: A Review of the Administration's Record,* 95th Cong., 1st sess., October 25, 1977, pp. 30–1.

23. Terence A. Todman, "The Carter Administration's Latin American Policy: Purposes and Prospects" (Speech at the Center for Inter-American Relations, New York, February 14, 1978).

24. Arnold S. Kohen, "U.S. Diplomacy and Human Rights: The Cruel Case of Indonesia," *Nation* 225 (November 26, 1977):556; U.S., Congress, House, Committee on Banking, Finance, and Urban Affairs, Subcommittee on International Development Institutions and Finance, *International Development Institutions—1977,* 95th Cong., 1st sess., March 22, 23, and 24, 1977, p. 84.

25. U.S., Congress, Senate, Committee on the Judiciary, Subcommittee to Investigate Problems Connected with Refugees and Escapees, *Refugee and Humanitarian Problems in Chile,* 93d Cong., 1st sess., September 28, 1973, p. 41.

26. As for the charge of right-wing sympathies, it is worth noting that the proportion of liberals in the Department of State exceeds by far that of the U.S. population as a whole. Bernard Mennis, *American Foreign Policy Officials: Who They Are and What They Believe Regarding International Politics* (Columbus, Ohio: Ohio State University Press, 1971), pp. 117, 170.

27. Interview with William D. Rogers, November 6, 1975, Washington, D.C.

28. *United States Policies and Programs in Brazil,* pp. 281–2.

29. U.S., Congress, House, Committee on International Relations, Subcommittee on International Organizations, *Religious Persecution in El Salvador,* 95th Cong., 1st sess., July 21 and 29, 1977, p. 34.

30. I. M. Destler, *Presidents, Bureaucrats, and Foreign Policy: The*

Politics of Organizational Reform (Princeton: Princeton University Press, 1974), p. 248. That such a mentality is not peculiar to ARA is demonstrated, for example, in the testimony of the personnel of the Bureau of East Asian and Pacific Affairs on the issue of repression in Indonesia. U.S., Congress, House, Committee on International Relations, Subcommittee on International Organizations, *Human Rights in Indonesia and the Philippines*, 94th Cong., 1st and 2d sess., December 18, 1975, and May 3, 1976, pp. 105–7; U.S., Congress, House, Committee on International Relations, Subcommittee on International Organizations, *Human Rights in Indonesia: A Review of the Situation with Respect to the Long-Term Political Detainees*, 95th Cong., 1st sess., October 18, 1977, p. 23.

31. In fact, throughout the 1969–1975 period the Nixon-Ford State Department opposed the formal creation of a bureau for humanitarian affairs, voicing its doubts that "inserting an additional bureau into the picture would increase the effectiveness of the Department's work in this sphere." *International Protection of Human Rights*, pp. 321, 506. The State Department could not oppose the administration's 1971 recommendation that a bureau be created, of course, but it made no effort to promote the idea.

32. House Report 93-664, p. 54.

33. *International Protection of Human Rights*, pp. 506–7; John Salzberg and Donald D. Young, "The Parliamentary Role in Implementing International Human Rights: A U.S. Example," *Texas International Law Journal* 12 (Spring–Summer 1977):274.

34. As a further indication of the limited importance given the regional human rights activity, the 1975 State Department telephone directory did not list the human rights officers. Beginning in 1977, ARA's human rights officer was listed immediately after the assistant secretary of state, with the title of special assistant and human rights officer. Similar examples are plentiful: The term "human rights" does not appear in a September 1976 publication that describes in some detail the duties and organization of the Department of State, but by 1978 the State Department was publishing separate booklets on the subject of human rights and U.S. foreign policy. U.S., Department of State, Bureau of Public Affairs, Office of Media Services, *Foreign Policy and the Department of State*, Department of State publication 8869, September 1976; U.S, Department of State, Bureau of Public Affairs, Office of Public Communication, *Human Rights and U.S. Foreign Policy*, Department of State publication 8959, December 1978.

35. Salzberg and Young, "The Parliamentary Role in Implementing International Human Rights," pp. 274–6. The State Department informed Representative Fraser of its intentions in August 1974. The first coordina-

tor actually started work in June 1975.

36. International League for Human Rights, *Report of the Conference on Implementing a Human Rights Commitment in United States Foreign Policy* (New York: International League for Human Rights, March 4, 1977), p. 15.

37. U.S., Congress, Senate, Committee on Foreign Relations, *Foreign Assistance Authorization: Arms Sales Issues,* 94th Cong., 1st sess., June, November, and December, 1975, pp. 465–6.

38. Interview with James M. Wilson, December 15, 1978, Washington, D.C.; *Foreign Assistance Authorization: Arms Sales Issues,* p. 467. Wilson was never confirmed by the Senate, and his only scheduled appearance before Congress was cancelled due to lack of time and perhaps interest on the part of the senators involved. As a reward for a job that they considered poorly done, Carter administration officials exiled Wilson, an FSO-1, to the Education and Relocation Staff. Wilson is remembered by several ARA officials as the person who helped to block the issuance of a visa to Peruvian political activist Hugo Blanco.

39. Derian was criticized by human rights activists for conceding on some issues. In 1978, for example, she defended the Carter administration's aid request for the very repressive Marcos government in the Philippines because, as she told Congress, "the Philippine bases are of vital importance to the security of the United States." U.S., Congress, House, Committee on Appropriations, Subcommittee on Foreign Operations, *Foreign Assistance and Related Agencies Appropriations for 1979,* 95th Cong., 2d sess., 1978, pt. 2:444.

40. "Foreign Policy and Human Rights" (Speech to the National Foreign Policy Conference on Human Rights, Washington, D.C., February 27, 1978).

41. Quigley, *U.S. Policy on Human Rights in Latin America (Southern Cone),* pp. 53–4.

42. Louis Henkin, "The United States and the Crisis in Human Rights," *Virginia Journal of International Law* 14 (Summer 1974):666.

43. U.S., Congress, House, Committee on Foreign Affairs, Subcommittee on International Organizations and Movements, *Review of the U.N. Commission on Human Rights,* 93d Cong., 2d sess., 1974, p. 42; *International Protection of Human Rights,* p. 189.

44. Thus, for example, in 1972 the United States, with the United Kingdom, South Africa, and Portugal opposed seven of the eight General Assembly resolutions on southern Africa and colonialism, and it abstained on the eighth. *International Protection of Human Rights,* p. 168. The Nixon-Ford protectionist policy continued to the end, as demonstrated by the December 1976 vote against a resolution to investigate the annexa-

tion of East Timor by Indonesia. U.S., Congress, House, Committee on International Relations, Subcommittee on International Organizations and Subcommittee on Asian and Pacific Affairs, *Human Rights in East Timor and the Question of the Use of U.S. Equipment by the Indonesian Armed Forces,* 95th Cong., 1st sess., March 23, 1977, p. 17.

45. U.S., Congress, House of Representatives, Committee on International Relations, *Report of Secretary of State Kissinger on His Trip to Latin America,* 94th Cong., 2d sess., March 4, 1976, p. 20.

46. *Review of the U.N. Commission on Human Rights,* pp. 42, 92; U.S., Congress, House, Committee on Foreign Affairs, Subcommittee on Inter-American Affairs and Subcommittee on International Organizations and Movements, *Human Rights in Chile,* 93d Cong., 2d sess., December 1973 and May, June 1974, p. 130; Salzberg and Young, "The Parliamentary Role in Implementing International Human Rights," pp. 258–9.

47. Representative Donald Fraser called the U.S. abstention "a loud and clear statement of support for the Chilean regime and its brutal suppression of human rights." *Washington Post,* October 23, 1974; *New York Times,* October 23, 1974, p. 15.

48. *New York Times,* November 7, 1974, p. 6; Salzberg and Young, "The Parliamentary Role in Implementing International Human Rights," pp. 260–1; U.S., Congress, Senate, Committee on the Judiciary, Subcommittee to Investigate Problems Connected with Refugees and Escapees, *Refugee and Humanitarian Problems in Chile, Part III,* 94th Cong., 1st sess., October 2, 1975, pp. 106–8.

49. *Department of State Bulletin* 75 (July 5, 1976):4.

50. *Department of State Bulletin* 76 (April 11, 1977):332.

51. *International Protection of Human Rights,* pp. 214, 492.

52. *Department of State Bulletin* 76 (May 9, 1977):454.

53. The resolution passed by a vote of fourteen to none, with eight abstentions (Argentina, Brazil, Colombia, Chile, El Salvador, Guatemala, Paraguay, Uruguay) and three absences (Bolivia, Honduras, Nicaragua).

54. Richard Barnet, *Roots of War* (New York: Atheneum, 1972), p. 116; Earl E. T. Smith, *The Fourth Floor: An Account of the Castro Communist Revolution* (New York: Random House, 1962), p. 227; Quigley, *U.S. Policy on Human Rights in Latin America (Southern Cone),* p. 74.

55. Arthur M. Schlesinger, Jr., *A Thousand Days: John F. Kennedy in the White House* (Boston: Houghton Mifflin, 1965), p. 414.

56. Smith, *The Fourth Floor,* p. 23.

57. Schlesinger, *A Thousand Days,* p. 769.

8
The Impact of U.S. Human Rights Policy: Argentina

Joseph S. Tulchin

The administration of President Jimmy Carter, in deliberate and marked contrast to its predecessor, chose to emphasize the moral virtues of democracy in its relations with other nations. This Wilsonian approach to foreign policy questions soon became identified as a defense of human rights. Relations with several countries were complicated by the U.S. insistence upon certain minimum legal guarantees to individuals against the state. On more than one occasion, the defense of human rights around the world conflicted with strategic considerations, as in South Korea, and there is some evidence that the U.S. posture on human rights contributed to the movement that overthrew the Shah of Iran.

But U.S. foreign relations have nowhere been strained more by the issue of human rights than in the case of Argentina. The Argentines deeply resent having been pressured by the U.S. government. It appears to have touched the very nerve centers of Argentine nationalism and to have set off internal debates that threaten the present regime. Comments by minor officials in the Department of State or by members of private organizations, such as Amnesty International, have prompted angry responses from the highest levels of the Argentine government as well as full-dress campaigns in the public media explaining and justifying Argentine comportment while denouncing the nation's critics and impugning their motives. The result has been a high level of tension in the relations between the two nations.

Part of this tension certainly can be attributed to objective differences on the human rights question and on other issues. Normal, friendly relations do not preclude serious differences. But the tension in our relations with Argentina goes far beyond normal levels, and to understand why, we must explore the historical pattern of relations between the two countries. This is not the first time that seemingly minor issues have estranged the two nations while reshaping or threatening to reshape the configuration of political forces in Argentina.

Most studies of Argentine foreign policy in this country have characterized Argentine behavior as individualistic or isolationist. With reference to Argentine participation in hemispheric affairs, the terms are often more perjorative: idiosyncratic or obstructionist. A number of authors have implied that Argentine governments deliberately and perversely block all efforts at hemispheric cooperation because of their jealous competition with the United States for leadership in Latin America or for some more generalized xenophobia.[1] The shortcomings of this view, however plausible it might appear at first, are that it does not allow for the existence or expression of Argentine national interests independent of U.S. desires or objectives and that it is anachronistic—it ignores the possibility that basic principles of Argentine foreign policy are founded upon national experiences in the nineteenth century when the United States was but a minor factor in Argentine international relations. We need, therefore, a broader perspective on Argentine foreign policy so that we can understand better the history of our relations with that country, evaluate more intelligently current questions at issue between our two countries, and project with greater precision likely Argentine responses to conflictual encounters.

The most logical point at which to begin a historical survey of a nation's foreign relations is the moment of its independence. Even so, we must take into account the central assumptions about the world that the leaders of the new nation brought with them out of their colonial experience. How did the struggle for independence shape the definition of the new nation and determine its posture in international affairs?

The first significant episode in the creation of the Argentine nation was the British attempt in 1806 to wrest control of the

River Plate from Spain. The creole militia played a crucial role in halting the invading forces. This "Reconquista," as it came to be known, was a source of local pride and a symbol of resistance to foreign domination.[2] It was the first definition of Argentine patriotism, and it flowed naturally from the colonial experience, in which foreign domination had been a central feature. Creoles in the River Plate became increasingly restless under Spanish rule and sought to expand the area of decisions over which they had direct control. Until the Bourbon reforms at the end of the eighteenth century, creoles in the River Plate considered the restrictions imposed on economic activity to be arbitrary and prejudicial to their interests. Convinced that Spain's formal control was not matched by the ability to satisfy the needs of subordinate units, the creoles wanted to bring the power to decide their fate closer to them. The Reconquista was proof of their ability to defend their own interests. Other lessons that Argentines learned from their colonial experience were that strong nations pick on weaker nations, that diplomacy can be used to protect the interests of weaker nations, and that treaties respecting political or legal rights are rarely kept.

The struggle for independence from Spain shaped the Argentine nation in the most literal sense—it defined the nation's boundaries. Those who were instrumental in the movement had assumed from the very beginning that the new nation would encompass the territory of the viceroyalty of the Rio de la Plata. The Spanish military presence in the Altiplano of Peru (Bolivia) challenged those aspirations, and then Paraguay and Uruguay established their regional autonomy. Bolivia ultimately did the same. Argentine leaders nevertheless continued to harbor the belief that they ought to exercise control over all the territories that had comprised the viceroyalty. The case of Uruguay was especially sensitive as it involved a direct confrontation with the Portuguese empire and, later, with Brazil. As soon as their economic and military situation permitted, the Argentines under unitarist leadership attempted to impose their will in Uruguay. They failed, and the circumstances of their failure had important consequences for the development of the nation's foreign policy. First, it brought foreign affairs directly into domestic politics and fixed the rhetorical lines between nationalist and internationalist for the next 150 years. The federalists did not recapture Uruguay, but they did establish a xenophobic model for future assertions of Argentine nationalism and sovereignty. However, the xenophobia used as a political weapon against the unitarists must be understood in the context of the federalists' continuing interest in international trade and special privileges for foreigners. Whenever the model is invoked in Argentine foreign policy or in domestic politics, this context remains prevalent. Xenophobia did not necessarily mean, nor has it since meant, an aversion to international contact or a retreat to autarchy.

The second important consequence of the Uruguayan campaign was the success of Great Britain in forcing both Argentina and Brazil to accept a buffer state between them and in establishing a regional balance of power on the east coast of South America guaranteed by British power. The British intervention, based upon commercial and manufacturing capacity as much as on naval power, symbolized the replacement of Spain by Great Britain as the predominant external factor in Argentine development.

By the time the federalists consolidated their control under Juan Manuel de Rosas, foreign relations had been devoted almost exclusively to the definition of Argentina's boundaries. If we consider foreign policy as the expression of a nation's objectives in its relations with other nations, we might well conclude that the new nation's policy had been remarkably unsuccessful. Under Rosas, nationalism was, quite literally, national defense. By adopting foreign models for Argentine growth and invoking foreign support in its campaign to oust Rosas, the liberal opposition lent further credence to the dichotomy between super patriot/illiberal (later, authoritarian) on the one hand and cosmopolitan/liberal (later, democratic) on the other. This simplistic dichotomy has colored Argentine politics ever since and still affects foreign policy.

Rosas ultimately was ousted with the aid of an international coalition. For nearly ten years thereafter, the nation teetered on the edge of disintegration as regional forces rendered ineffectual all efforts at central government. Finally, it was an external threat that held the nation together and put an end to the divisive regionalism. The liberal cosmopolites, centered in the city and province of Buenos Aires, exerted their will over the different provinces in time to plunge the nation into a five-year war against Paraguay. The vulnerability of Uruguay created by internecine conflicts and the territorial losses suffered by Paraguay were important lessons for the Argentine leadership, underlining the importance of national cohesion. During this period of insecurity, President Bartolomé Mitre refused an invitation to attend a conference in Lima to coordinate Latin American efforts in response to a threat from Spain. Given the fragility of Argentine nationality, Mitre shunned foreign adventures not directly tied to national survival.

The liberal triumph over Rosas marked the deliberate or conscious introduction into Argentina of a positivist growth model. Argentina's entrance into the international market economy would enable the country to emulate the United States and certain European nations and to attain their levels of civilization. Argentina was to be remade in a foreign image defined by the European idea of progress—European immigrants would populate the pampas and improve the creole race, and European capital would pay for the infrastructure necessary to transfer the agricultural products from the fertile pampas to the consumers of Europe. The norms under which the Argentine economy was to function were those of liberal free trade; the political norms by which society would be held together were those of Anglo-American democratic constitutionalism.

The growth model worked and Argentina experienced an economic boom of unprecedented proportions. As more and more land was brought into production, Argentina became increasingly dependent upon European markets for the sale of its surplus staples and upon European capital to finance that trade. Great Britain was the paramount foreign power in Argentine affairs and, year by year, more and more of the Argentine national product was devoted to satisfying the needs of British investors and consumers. Increasingly, the Argentine economy was molded to the needs of the British economy, and decisions concerning the distribution of resources in Argentina were made in Great Britain or by those who had British rather than Argentine interests foremost in their minds. Thus a dependency pattern formed that had some parallels to the colonial subjugation to Spain. British-owned railroads carried the products of the pampas to ports where British-owned ships carried them overseas. For all intents and purposes, Argentina was part of what has been called the British informal empire.[3]

It might be an exaggeration to say that Argentine foreign policy formulators during this period of growth sought to create the conditions of structural dependence upon Great Britain; yet it is correct to say that the principal objective of the government was to facilitate the expansion of the nation's exports. The belief at the time was that the market mechanism was to determine the pattern of relations among nations. Argentina would be friendly toward all, independent politically of all, and follow the links established by the international market. The Argentine leadership after 1880 believed that the nation's interest required maximizing the export of its agricultural staples at the most advantageous price. All efforts in international relations were to be exerted to achieve that end. Limitations on the nation's freedom of action that might inhibit trade with Europe were to be avoided. In practice, this came to mean avoidance of formal international commitments.

Seen in this light, Argentina's caution in the first few Pan-American meetings was both logical and reasonable. Anything that turned Argentine energies away from Europe was wasteful or harmful. Then, too, the Argentines viewed the obvious dominance of the United States in the Pan-American movement as inimicable. For them, the rate of Argentine economic growth meant that their nation soon would approximate and undoubtedly surpass the extraordinary levels of material accomplishment the United States had achieved, while preserving the higher values of European civilization.[4]

There were other reasons for Argentine recalcitrance in Pan-American councils. If the central function of their foreign policy was the resolution or diminution of political friction among states to allow maximum freedom of commercial interchange, then institutionalized relationships such as those proposed for the Pan American Union could only prove mischievous. The exertion of economic influence by one nation over another was considered unexceptional. However, the exertion of political influence by one state over another was considered anathema. The Argentine concept of sovereignty had evolved from concrete experiences in which portions of the nation's territory had been despoiled by foreign powers. Sovereignty could not be compromised by cooperation in a hemispheric organization, particularly one dominated by a rival power.

Argentines were not the only Latin Americans to express suspicion of or disdain for what they considered the crass materialism of the United States. This syndrome, known as the Ariel complex, took its name from a famous essay by the Uruguayan, José Enrique Rodó, in which Latin Americans were described as Ariel to the Caliban of the United States.

Despite its reluctance to make commitments to the Pan-American movement, Argentina assumed a more assertive position in the international relations among hemispheric nations as it realized its dream of development. Most notable in this period were efforts to settle the War of the Pacific fought among Chile, Bolivia, and Peru and to fix the Argentine boundary with Chile, which was finally accomplished in 1902. The Argentine government expressed its solidarity with Venezuelan efforts to settle the latter's boundary dispute with Great Britain, although there was considerable debate among policymakers as to the proper attitude toward U.S. intervention in that episode. The majority was unwilling to recognize the validity or applicability of the Monroe Doctrine asserted by Secretary of State William Olney in his famous note to British Foreign Minister Salisbury.

The continental scope of the international rivalry was emphasized when Argentina, Brazil, and Chile entered into the arms race as the new century began. Latin American nations seeking to emulate European models viewed professionalization of the military and increased stores of modern armaments as facets of civilization. Strategic planning was introduced when military missions from one European power or another were invited to Argentina—and to other Latin American nations—to ensure that armies would be ready to defend the national territory. Just as Alfred Thayer Mahan had exerted tremendous influence over policy formulators in the United States, so, too, in Argentina, men like Estanislao Zeballos enjoyed a considerable following for their notions—similar to those of Theodore Roosevelt—of geopolitics and preparedness. Zeballos, thrice foreign minister, nearly precipitated an armed confrontation with Brazil over naval competition. At the last minute President José Figueroa Alcorta decided peace was more important and removed his foreign minister from the cabinet.[5]

The aggressive stance Zeballos typified was a minority position in Argentine foreign policy. The more common approach was characterized by extreme caution, dedication to the letter and spirit of international law, moralism, and a firm conviction that the nation's destiny was linked more closely to affairs in Europe than in America. Given this traditional, Eurocentric approach, an individual president or foreign minister might well bring a strong current of idealism—some called it romanticism— to the conduct of Argentine foreign affairs. Thus José Luis Murature, foreign minister in the administration of Victorino de la Plaza (1914–1916), willingly joined Brazil and Chile in an attempt (1915) to mediate the differences between Mexico and the United States that had tied the Wilson administration in knots. He then joined in a series of treaties among the ABC (Argentina, Brazil, Chile) powers designed to assure peace on the continent. He felt that this and other efforts would give Argentina a chance for leadership in the Southern Hemisphere, without embarassing the nation's economic ties to Europe.

The outbreak of war in Europe was a shock to the Argentine economic system. The Argentines learned to their dismay that in moments of crisis, their relationship to Great Britain was fundamentally different from that of formal members of the empire. The British treated Argentina like any other foreign country; they stopped exporting coal and capital, limited the movements of all shipping tonnage, and imposed severe restrictions on all imports. In the S.S. *Mitre* case, which involved registered Argentine coastal shipping suspected of German ownership, the Argentines learned that they could expect no special considerations in the interpretation of neutrality regulations. Argentina declared its neutrality in 1914 despite official and unofficial sympathy for the Allied cause. There was no reason to do anything else. All the nations of the hemisphere declared their neutrality.[6]

The same conditions held in October 1916 when Hipólito Yrigoyen succeeded Victorino de la Plaza. However, they changed dramatically when the United States entered the war in March 1917 and called upon the nations of the hemisphere to join in the campaign to save the world for democracy. From the U.S. point of view, all the nations should have jumped in. From the Argentine perspective, a declaration of war would have had to come from adequate justification. After the initial disruption of the international market in August 1914, the British had re-established the trade links with Argentina and the flow of goods was resumed at favorable prices. The interruption in the flow of capital and heavy machinery was considered an inconvenience; however, it did not threaten the national interest in the way a cessation of exports would have. Aside from the trade in food-stuffs, which the British were likely to continue under any circumstances, the Argentine government had as many grievances against the Allies as against the Central Powers. German sub-marines sank two Argentine vessels in 1917. In each case, the Argentine chancellery fired off strong notes that verged on ultimatums, and there is evidence in the Argentine archives that the government was prepared to declare war if the Germans did not satisfy their demands. The Germans met the Argentine con-ditions both times and apologized for insulting the Argentine flag. On the other hand, once the United States entered the war, conflicts with the Allies were exacerbated. The United States enforced more rigidly such controls as the blacklist, the disposi-tion of shipping tonnage and fuel supplies, and the prices of products required for the war effort. These measures underlined the dependent relationship between Argentina and the Allies, most particularly Great Britain. Worse, the British and the Americans seemed unsympathetic to Argentine defense of its sovereignty. There were at least two occasions prior to the armistice in which Argentina came within a hair of severing rela-tions with the Allies, not the Central Powers. The confrontations developed out of Argentine perceptions of violations of its sovereignty and its obdurate insistence upon the letter of inter-national law in the settlement of international disputes.

The United States, with its attention focused on events in Europe, considered Argentina and Latin America generally as strategically subordinate and expected the Latin American states to fall in line. Some did. Argentina could not see why it should subordinate its national interests to the achievement of U.S. or Allied objectives, no matter how glowingly those objectives were described. Yrigoyen adopted an idiosyncratic approach to international relations. He paid little attention to protocol or to the traditional niceties of diplomacy. When he felt right was on his side, he was not inhibited in his actions or his language. He ordered an Argentine naval vessel to salute the Dominican flag in Santo Domingo during the U.S. occupation of that republic. He proposed a league of Latin American neutrals in 1917 and, in 1918, put forward a proposal for a Latin American trade treaty. The United States construed these acts, together with Argentine neutrality, as hostile or mischievous. From the Argentine perspective, however, they were innocent enough. For Yrigoyen, there was not adequate reason to declare war on the Central Powers. He accepted and carried forward the traditional central commitment to the export of agricultural staples. Wartime trade with the Allies was favorable. Other issues simply were much less important, and seemingly capricious actions concerned only matters of form that did not touch the substance of national interest. In dealing with minor issues, Yrigoyen felt, like leaders before and after him, that he could afford to behave in a manner that was morally correct. Not incidentally, he also called attention to himself through behavior others might have considered uncompromising or unpragmatic.

Yrigoyen's conduct of foreign affairs might be said to represent the tradition of Wilsonianism in Argentine foreign policy, even though he often opposed Wilson. On occasion, as in the Argentine response to the League of Nations, it might be interpreted as Wilsonianism run amok. Offended that it had not been consulted on the formation of the league, at the first meeting of the league assembly the Argentine government called publicly for drastic reforms that would eliminate the distinction between victors and vanquished, between small states and large, and would convert the organization into a truly democratic organ of world government. Naturally enough, the proposals were tabled and the Argentine delegation withdrew from the assembly in a huff, stating that their nation could not, in good conscience, participate in an organization of victors. At the same time, Yrigoyen withheld recognition from a de facto government in Bolivia on the Wilsonian grounds that the new government was unconstitutional and did not represent the will of the people.

Since contemporary relations between the United States and Argentina appear to hinge on issues of morality, especially the sanctity of human rights, it is instructive to highlight Argentine conceptions of moral behavior by nation-states at the time of World War I. There was little or no discrepancy between the codes of conduct for the U.S. and Argentine governments. If they applied the codes differently it was because their perceptions of the world were not the same and their national interests often did not coincide.

A later example of idealistic and idiosyncratic behavior in an international forum, which is often taken as mischievous Argentine anti-Americanism, is the public criticism of intervention during the debates at the Havana Pan-American conference in 1928. Again, the central point to bear in mind is that Pan-American meetings were not considered vital to the Argentine national interest. As a consequence, Honorio Pueyrredón, the special representative to the Havana conference, felt at liberty to use his participation for purposes of domestic politics in Argentina. He tried to embarrass President Marcelo T. De Alvear, who had set himself against Yrigoyen's policies in an election year. Moreover, Pueyrredón was venting his frustration—and his government's—with the disturbing pattern of U.S. exclusion of Argentine products. In a lengthening series of conflicts, one Argentine product after another was excluded from the U.S. market because of sanitary problems or simply exclusionist tariffs. The economic damage to Argentina, while not insignificant, paled in importance compared to the nation's damaged pride. The U.S. government barred Argentine beef on the grounds that it was unclean, that it was infected with hoof-and-mouth disease. If the exclusion were to be made general or if the British were to imitate it, the consequences for the Argentine economy could have been disastrous. So long as the United States maintained that Argentine beef was unclean, relations between the two countries remained strained. Pueyrredón tried to call the attention of the U.S. government to this fact.

The Great Depression, which threatened the very basis of Argentine economic well-being, brought foreign policy into the spotlight of domestic politics. The nation's overseas markets were in peril after 1929, and this was an issue that involved all sectors of the society. Throughout the decade, adjustment to the depression was debated in the press and specific decisions were the product of intense intergroup negotiations and compromise. Argentina did not get all that it wanted from its international relations, but it probably did as well as could have been expected under the adverse circumstances.

The principal lesson from studying Argentine foreign policy during the depression, as I have written elsewhere, is that there was only one important issue that caught the attention of the Argentine public—the preservation of their export markets. Other issues could become personal playthings of the foreign minister or of a particular sectoral elite.[7] The overweaning ambition of Foreign Minister Carlos Saavedra Lamas is absolutely inexplicable unless this is borne in mind; he dallied with other nations to suit his fancy and to further his campaign for the Nobel Peace Prize. Seen in this light, Argentina's neutrality in World War II, like its behavior during the depression and its neutrality during World War I, was based upon its national interest in protecting export markets and upon the conviction that neutrality, rather than involvement on one side or the other, was most conducive to the achievement of national objectives. This is not to say that there were no groups or people in Argentina who rooted for the Axis; there were. Rather, I would argue that the pro-Axis forces within Argentina did not dictate the policy of neutrality. The policy was the result of a fairly broad consensus within the society, including numerous groups that were pro-Allies in their sentiments.

In the years just prior to the outbreak of hostilities in Europe, the international environment became unpleasant for Argentina. The informal imperial link with Great Britain no longer provided the support Argentina needed, and the United States was persistently unwilling or unable to step in and fill the role Great

Britain had played for so long. In addition, the ability to secure military matériel was being jeopardized by the suppliers' reluctance to sell anything to any but the most vital potential allies— and Argentina was not likely to fit that category as much for its geographic isolation as for its political attitudes, whereas Brazil was having a signal success in winning promises for armaments and heavy machinery from both the Axis and the Allies. As a clincher, the harvests of 1938 and 1939 were either very poor or unsold, producing excruciating financial pressures on the federal government.

The administration of President Roberto Ortiz tried to reverse the adverse flow of events by maneuvering Argentina into a position crucial to the Allies. In April 1940 the government proposed that all American nations join in declaring their non-belligerency in the European war. Ortiz and his foreign minister, José Maria Cantilo, hoped to link Argentine interests with the United States so as to guarantee both defense supplies and markets for agricultural commodities and, by so doing, undermine the antidemocratic forces in their own country. The United States spurned the proposal and continued to drag its feet in meeting Argentine demands for matériel and for trade guarantees. Ortiz became ill and withdrew in favor of his vice-president, Ramón S. Castillo. Foreign Minister Cantilo fell and, after a brief interlude, was replaced by Enrique Ruiz Guiñazú, a man noted for his admiration of "virile fascism." Given the configuration of domestic political forces in Argentina and of international forces, military and economic, there really was no viable alternative to neutrality for Argentina after 1940.[8]

As the pressure on Argentina to join the Allies mounted, its resistance to the pressure earned—justifiably or not—the label of nationalism; and nationalism together with a drive for economic self-sufficiency became linked with antiliberalism, just as it had a century earlier during the regime of Juan Manuel de Rosas. The military who ousted Castillo in 1943 were concerned that Argentina was falling further and further behind Brazil in strategic capability and believed that in order to make Argentina independent of threats to its sovereignty, it would be necessary to impose upon the country a program of industrialization that would enable Argentina to satisfy its own needs for strategic materials in times of international crisis. The military view of the national interest included concern for Argentina's geopolitical position in the hemisphere, which had the effect of reasserting the importance of competition with Brazil along the lines indicated by Zeballos at the beginning of the century.

After 1943, Argentina and the United States entered a period in which their relations were hardly cordial. Not only had Argentina assumed a posture of neutrality in a war in which the United States saw neutrality as a cover for supporting the Axis enemies, but it had now abandoned all pretenses of democratic government as well and was ruled by military men who were suspected of harboring sympathies for German or Italian forms of fascist social organization. The U.S. government persistently pressured the Argentine government first to cooperate more enthusiastically in the war effort and, after 1945, to conform more closely to the accepted norms of democratic behavior. Repeatedly, this pressure had the unintended effect of undermining the political faction most sympathetic to the United States and strengthening the faction that was more nationalistic, more antiliberal, and less friendly to the United States. In other words, U.S. interference in Argentine domestic affairs then had the effect, and has had the effect over and over again, of pushing the government further to the right or further toward xenophobic nationalism and away from reasonable interaction with the United States.

The so-called Storni affair is a case that illustrates the general principles to which I have referred. The Junta that ousted Castillo gave early indications that it would be more cooperative toward the Allies than its predecessor. In fact, a majority of the military leaders, in spite of the German sympathies of a certain sector, had serious reasons for complaint against the Castillo regime—its weaknesses, corruption, and, above all, its incapacity to obtain arms from the United States when it had allowed Brazil to forge ahead of Argentina in this respect. General Arturo Rawson was quickly substituted by General Pedro Ramírez and cabinet shuffle replaced several members with Axis sympathies with others who were notoriously pro-Allies, most notably Admiral Segundo N. Storni as foreign minister. Upon assuming his new office, Storni declared: "Bit by bit, the actions of the Argentine government will continue the policy of American solidarity. . . . Argentina will arrive where it must be in international relations. The foreign policy of Argentina will imply a meticulous fulfillment of her obligations with the American countries."

Secretary of State Cordell Hull continued to pressure the Argentine government. He wanted a quick decision to break relations with the Axis, no strings attached. Such a clear-cut decision was politically impossible in Argentina. The question of foreign policy had become the central issue in the struggle for power within the military. Ramírez tried to place himself between the two extreme groups that were fighting among themselves, but just as the nationalists within the military were increasing their power, he was gradually losing control of the situation. The initial commitment to break with the Axis was becoming more and more difficult to carry out. Finally, at Hull's insistence, Storni agreed to put in writing the Argentine commitment to rupture relations with the Axis. In the text of the letter, which caused considerable debate within the government, Storni tried to explain why Argentina could not break relations at that time without cause. He denied that the Argentine regime sympathized with the Axis. He insisted that his government would spare no efforts to comply with obligations assumed. However, to terminate relations without a cause would provide arguments for those who might think that the Argentine government was operating under pressure or threat from foreign agents. And this would be tolerated neither by the people nor by the armed forces of the country. He concluded,

> I can affirm to you . . . that the Axis countries have nothing to hope for from our government and that public opinion is daily more unfavorable to them. But this evolution would be more rapid and effective for the American cause if President Roosevelt should make a gesture of genuine friendship toward our people; such a gesture might be the urgent provision of airplanes, spare parts and machinery to restore Argentina to the position of equilibrium to which it is entitled with respect to other South American countries.

Storni's letter closed with a plea for understanding and friendship on the part of the United States toward the Ramírez government during its difficult initial period.

Hull answered Storni's note in a most scathing manner. He went on at great length excoriating the Argentine government for its failure to carry out its obligations. He expressed surprise that fulfillment of contracted obligations could provide evidence of Argentine submission to foreign agency pressure, when the obligations had all been freely subscribed to by the U.S. republics and had been fulfilled by all except Argentina. He specifically rejected the appeal for arms and termed the questions of a South American equilibrium inconsistent with the inter-American doctrine of a peaceful solution for international disputes, to which doctrine Argentine statesmen had made so many contributions.

The publication of the Hull letter in the Argentine newspapers inflamed nationalist sentiments. Leaflets against Storni were scattered throughout the city—leaflets written and printed by the conspiratorial military group Grupo de Oficiales Unidos (GOU). *Noticias Gráficas,* which had dared to publish an editorial condemning the neutralist attitude of the government, was ordered closed and the edition was confiscated. The position of Storni became untenable, and he had to resign the following day. Since the situation of the chief of state himself was compromised, Storni sent him a letter assuming full responsibility for the document. On the same day, the president declared that the "historical tradition of a nation . . . cannot be weakened by the confidential expressions of a functionary." Ironically, when Ramírez finally ruptured relations with the Axis a few months later, Hull, instead of supporting the move, pushed for further concessions and precipitated the fall of the Ramírez government, paving the way for Edelmiro Farrell and Juan Perón to take power.

The means by which Perón ultimately consolidated his power are not a subject for this paper. Suffice it to say that he built a coalition of the military and organized labor and skillfully recalled the nationalistic lineage going back to Yrigoyen and Rosas, linking the liberal oligarchy both to social injustice and to subservience to imperialistic powers. When Perón tried to legitimize his authority through popular elections in 1946, the United States made known its disapproval through publication, fifteen days before the election, of the famous "blue book," detailing the links between the Argentine government and the Axis and singling out Perón as the principal collaborator. The result of this overt interference redounded to the benefit of Perón. To present Perón as the champion of Argentine sovereignty was the sole objective of his strategy in the last of the electoral campaign. According to such propaganda, the Argentines would have to choose on election day between Spruille Braden or Perón. On February 24, 1946, they chose the candidate the United States pointedly disliked.

By way of contrast, it might be useful to mention one episode in which vigorous defense of the national interest by the relatively pro-U.S. elements within the Argentine government served to enhance its power. In 1937, Franklin D. Roosevelt offered seven old destroyers to Brazil to improve relations with the nation in South America that U.S. military planners considered of greatest potential strategic significance. The Argentine foreign minister, Carlos Saavedra Lamas, complained bitterly of a gratuitous insult to Argentina and of the perilous risk to South American balance of power in the proposed transfer of armaments. Hull reconsidered and ultimately withdrew the offer, suffering a momentary embarrassment in relations with Brazil in order to prevent any deterioration in relations with Argentina. The success of the Saavedra Lamas defense of the national interest had the effect of enhancing the strength of the democratic and pro-Allies faction, favored by incoming president Roberto Ortiz. Ultimately Foreign Minister Cantilo led the effort to tie Argentina more closely to the United States by means of the Non-Belligerency Pact.

After Perón was deposed in 1955, the first democratically elected president, Arturo Frondizi (1958–1962), tried to stimulate economic growth by massive investments in infrastructure, much of it with foreign capital. His foreign policy gave emphasis to hemispheric affairs in a manner that seemed a throwback to Ortiz and Cantilo prior to World War II. He cultivated the friendship of the United States; he was one of the strongest supporters of the Alliance for Progress; he made shrewd use of the personal ties between his foreign minister, Miguel Angel Cárcano, and the family of John F. Kennedy. At the same time, he tried to make a mark in hemispheric affairs by maintaining relations with Castro's Cuba. This displeased the United States and upset the military, whose ideological propensities were hostile to doctrines of change.

Here, perhaps, is the opportunity to introduce another example of how U.S. pressure embarrassed the Argentine government, strengthened the hands of extreme nationalists who called for the rejection of U.S. intervention in Argentine affairs, and weakened the political position of those in the government who were, relatively speaking within the Argentine political context of the moment, friendly toward the United States. Frondizi's domestic economic policy, known as Developmentalism, was devised to control the foreign investment entering the country in order to free Argentina from its dependence upon foreign capital. This policy called for mild doses of nationalistic rhetoric. Frondizi was a moderate, however, in comparison to some of his nationalistic critics who opposed all foreign investment and who were skeptical of the virtues of democratic government. In April 1961, Frondizi signed a treaty of friendship and consultation with the president of Brazil, Jânio Quadros, in the border city of Uruguayana. This rapprochement with Brazil was part of Frondizi's efforts to build a block of underdeveloped countries and to use foreign policy to further his nation's economic development, as was explained by the undersecretary of foreign relations in March of the same year:

> Argentina is a Latin American country, that is to say, it is made up of a geographical area belonging to the underdeveloped continents of the world, but she has conditions of negotiations that are very inferior to those of the other areas by virtue of her lesser strategic significance. . . . Our present solidarity with Latin America rises not only from the obvious traditional sympathy by reason of blood and language, but also from the conscience that only action can call attention to our necessities, as was demonstrated, though in limited measure, by the partial success achieved with Operation Pan-America.

The key to Frondizi's hemispheric policy was to be his attempt to arbitrate the growing differences between Cuba and the United States. In rebuffing the Argentine initiative and increasing the pressure on Frondizi to break relations with Cuba, the United States managed to coerce a rupture in relations. However, as in World War II, it achieved its narrow objective at the cost of playing into the hands of extreme nationalists, in this case the military, who were looking for an excuse to be rid of Frondizi. The parallels with earlier events are striking. Frondizi publicized his efforts to mediate between Cuba and the United States. The U.S. response was harshly critical. In September, the U.S. government brought to the attention of the Argentine government a batch of documents purloined from the Cuban embassy in Buenos Aires purporting to show the links between Cuban and Argentine officials. These documents were made public and created a stir in Argentina. Frondizi's government reacted strongly, characterizing the documents as forgeries, denouncing a Cuban exile group for their interference in Argentine affairs, and complaining to the U.S. government about unfriendly pressure to break relations with Cuba. The defense of Argentine sovereignty helped Frondizi for a little while, but it did not win him any permanent political allies. The combination of pressure from the United States and from his own military forced Frondizi to break relations with Cuba in February 1962 and led, in the space of little more than a month, to his ouster.

Politics in Argentina from 1955 to 1973 have been characterized as an "impossible game." Hard-liners kept Perónists from voting, which meant that any regime governed without the approval of that portion of the electorate. Once in office, minority governments tried to effect social and economic policies to stimulate the economy and realized that they needed the cooperation of the highly organized labor movement. To win labor support, they held out the carrot of political participation and promised to temper economic policies that might hurt labor. As the government and Perónists drew closer, the military grew more wary until they could stand by no longer and ousted the elected leaders, starting the process all over again. This process repeated itself even in situations of military rule, where factions of the military out of power constantly took more rigid positions than the faction in power. The economy went through a series of "stop-go cycles" characterized by high levels of inflation and vulnerability to fluctuating international prices for the export staples. Foreign policy during this period was without clear focus. Concern grew for geopolitical questions, and there were moments in which the government took a position in opposition to the United States. But on balance, Argentina remained firmly committed to the Western side in the Cold War.[9]

In 1972, General Alejandro Lanusse, then in charge of the ruling military junta, chose to break this Gordian knot by bringing back Perón. Perón's foreign policy in his second incarnation was pragmatic, though suffused with highly rhetorical appeals for Third World camaraderie and nationalism. His strongest allies were in the Confederación General de la Empresa (CGE), the association of entrepreneurs representing the domestic market. His most striking success was a highly publicized trade agreement with Cuba that included the export of cars. The irony built into this deal—and into the development strategy generally—was that the cars were produced by subsidiaries of U.S. corporations and many of the nontraditional products that Argentina expected to sell abroad were produced by multinationals. This pragmatic approach to problems, together with the leader's declining health, created schisms among his supporters. The left wing of Perón's movement declared its opposition to him and there was a resumption of the terrorist activities that had helped convince the military to turn back the reins of government to Perón in the first place.

This split widened after Perón's death in 1974. López Rega, the dominant force in Isabelita Perón's government, is said to have encouraged private death squads that carried out counterterrorist activities under the name of the Argentine Anti-Communist Alliance (AAA). Perhaps inspired by the AAA, each of the military forces employed its own secret service to combat "subversive elements," and the army intensified its campaign against armed bands of insurrectionists, especially in the province of Tucumán. The killing and disappearances increased on both sides through 1975 and 1976, eventually reaching the intensity of a civil war. The rule of law became a mockery; the economy was in turmoil. The military assumed control of the government again in March 1976, declaring that this time they would not relinquish power until they had accomplished a total restructuring of society to secure Argentina its rightful position in world affairs. This process would begin with the total extirpation of subversive elements from the body politic by whatever means necessary.

This was not to be a caretaker military government, then, content to rule until the civilian politicians had settled their differences sufficiently to allow for another round of elections in the impossible game. This was to be a regime that would define national goals, formulate policies to reach these goals, and employ the entire administrative capacity of the state to execute the policies. Unlike previous military regimes, this "bureaucratic authoritarian state," as Guillermo O'Donnell has dubbed it, has been inextricably linked to international capital, even while it professes nationalism and a geopolitical stance on international affairs, positions previously associated with support for economic independence and hostility toward economic liberalism. The Videla junta turned the economics ministry over to José Alfredo Martínez de Hoz, perhaps the country's most prominent proponent of international liberal capitalism. Martínez de Hoz set out to revive the economy by stimulating the traditional export sector and by encouraging a flow of foreign capital into the country. Developmentalist critics of the regime's policies were either shouted down in the muzzled and controlled press or hounded into silence and exile.

Parallel to these efforts, there was a tendency in 1976 and 1977 toward some form of cooperation among the military regimes in the hemisphere. The junta seems to have decided that any form of isolation was too costly for Argentina in its weakened condition. Until its national strength could be restored, Videla dampened Argentina's international aspirations and accepted, at least temporarily, a subordinate position to Brazil in South American power politics, played out in public in negotiations over two potentially competitive hydroelectric projects on the upper reaches of the River Plate basin, both involving Paraguay. In 1978, Videla handled the dispute with Chile over the Beagle Channel with great moderation, a position that cost him dearly among the younger officers—the air force particularly—and among the nationalists in the population at large who welcomed a chance in November to teach the Chileans a lesson, once and for all.[10]

Because his regime today is so closely identified with economic liberalism, historically associated with antinationalism, and because he has curbed the hawks and the geopoliticians on the Beagle and hydroelectric competition, Videla has stacked his nationalist chips on one issue, an issue on which he refuses to compromise, negotiate, or allow anyone to outflank him: the rejection of international criticism of human rights violations in Argentina. By 1979, the refutation and rejection of the international "campaign" against Argentina had become an obsessive issue in foreign policy and had spilled over into areas of political and economic policy.

The activities of the paramilitary death squads and the pattern of disappearances had become a foreign policy question even before the *golpe* in March 1976, as leaders of a number of Western nations indicated their displeasure with the way in which the rights of individual citizens were trampled in Argentina. On more than one occasion, loans or aid projects of different organs of the U.S. government were blocked by the State Department's Office of Human Rights or by the persistent probing of members of Congress. Organizations such as Amnesty International kept up a steady drumbeat of criticism of the military government's complicity in kidnapping, disappearances, torture, and the assassination of civilians. At first, the military government brushed aside such criticism by saying that if such atrocities occurred they were the unwarranted but inevitable excesses in a military campaign against an armed internal enemy who fought dirty. About a year later, the line began to change as it became increasingly important to show the world that stability and order had returned, particularly as the government set its sights on the World Cup in June 1978, which they hoped to turn into a showcase of Argentina's progress since the *golpe*. The official position on the human rights violations was that reports in the foreign press were grossly exaggerated or that such reports were the lamentable but understandable overzealous reaction of patriotic elements to the general malaise of subversion in the society and to the terrorism of revolutionary guerrillas who kidnap and kill civilians and military personnel.

The issue of human rights had assumed significant proportions by 1978. The accusation touched the very heart of the military's sense of its mission and threatened its long-term objectives. This brought the question of human rights violations into increasingly higher relief, until it seemed to block out or color all other questions. Argentines could not understand why Americans persisted in their attacks. They never perceived that the statements or attacks were coming from the office of the State Department, charged exclusively with the evaluation of human rights all over the world, rather than from the secretary of state or from the president. As had happened so many times in the past, the U.S. government had unthinkingly stumbled upon an issue that was peripheral to its concerns but absolutely vital to the Argentine government. A high-ranking official of the foreign relations ministry, who had done a tour of duty in the Washington embassy during the Carter administration, told me at the end of 1978 that he was sick and tired of the human rights issue. That was all he had worked on while he was in Washington. He wished the issue would go away so that the two countries could get down to more serious business.

Of course the issue will not go away as long as the climate of repression persists in Argentina. And the tension between the two nations will persist as long as each government continues to be blind to the other's perception of the issue. It is as if one party considers the question too important to negotiate, while the other considers it too unimportant for serious, high-level negotiation. Like Woodrow Wilson, Cordell Hull, or Spruille Braden before them, President Carter and the head of the State Department's human rights office, Patricia Derian, do not comprehend Argentine reluctance to comply with their requests or demands because to them the issue is so clear-cut—a case of black and white. They do not realize that their pressure has generated in Argentina stronger efforts to protect the independence of the government from outside interference. Videla's ability to withstand external interference on this issue has been made a measure of his legitimacy among his military colleagues. As has happened so many times in the past, U.S. pressure on the Argentine government is indirectly encouraging groups hostile to the government who represent positions even less friendly to the United States.

The Videla government's problem is compounded by the fact that, in one sense at least, the issue *is* black and white. Human rights are and have been systematically violated in Argentina. The problem is how to explain such violations in a country fighting to preserve Western, Christian values. Following upon the broadly based popular euphoria induced by the Argentine victory in the World Cup, there was a rising clamor in the local press to the effect that those who criticize Argentina do not know the real situation and intentionally distort reality for their own ends. One glossy news weekly ran a story on police brutality in the Philadelphia rent strike suggesting broadly that the United States had no right to criticize conditions in Argentina. A woman's weekly ran a page of cut-out postcards showing bucolic scenes of parents playing with children or of soccer stadiums crowded with orderly fans. The facing page ran the addresses of members of the U.S. government, officials in the United Nations and in Amnesty International, to whom the postcards were to be sent. In December 1978, the campaign entitled La Verdadera Argentina ("the Real Argentina") was repeated, by popular demand.

Although no one in the Videla government wants to defend violations of human rights per se, there are high-ranking members of the military and a few in second-echelon government positions who are quite willing to do so. These men care not one whit for the form or substance of political democracy. They are concerned with capturing once and for all the greatness that has eluded Argentina. Given such a premise, criticism of Argentina from abroad, however correct from a logical or a moral standpoint, is merely another obstacle to that broad goal.

Videla's dilemma is to drive for the national goal with all the energy of the hard-liners while maintaining as broad a coalition as possible of civilian elements without whose support his rule would be severely weakened. This dilemma has been reflected in the self-censored press, as the media has grasped for a new vocabulary or new set of categories with which to defend or explain the country and the military government at the same time it defends such timeless Western and Christian virtues as democracy and human rights. By the end of 1978, phrases such as "responsible democracy" and "organic democracy" had become clichés, shorthand allusions to "irresponsible" and "inorganic" forms that presumably characterized the polity during the chaos, inefficiency, and social tensions of the civilian regimes before the *golpe* in 1976.

As this is being written, the majority of the Argentine people is disposed to accept the present regime, with its horrible repression, as the best possible alternative. For this acquiescent majority, external pressure on the government prompts a hostile reaction and self-defense. In terms of the political forces at play, the internal situation is remarkably similar to the debate on neutrality in 1941.

The United States must do everything in its power to improve the protection of human rights in Argentina—because it is morally right and because it is in U.S. national interest to do so. But, learning from the historical experience of relations between the two countries, we must recognize that direct pressure on the Argentine government will most probably prove counterproductive. If the United States undermines the Videla government, it will be less, not more, likely that U.S. influence will be felt in Argentina in the future; and it will be less, not more, likely that Argentina will emerge soon from the dark shadow of dictatorship and repression that has characterized the nation in the 1970s.

Notes

1. A recent work by an Australian depicted Argentine foreign policy as a querulous, ineffectual reaction to Brazilian initiatives. See Glen Barclay, *Struggle for a Continent: The Diplomatic History of South America, 1917–1945* (New York: New York University Press, 1972).

2. It is interesting to note that Argentines tend to consider early Brazilian resistance to foreign penetration—the Dutch invasion and, later, British tutelage—as a critical, formative experience that explains Brazil's confident sense of its national identity. Somehow, the Reconquista rarely is credited with the same impact on Argentine self-confidence. See Carlos Pérez Llana, "¿Potencias intermedias o países mayores? La política ex-

terior de Argentina, Brazil y México?" *Estudios Internacionales* 8, no. 29 (1975):62–63, 80–87.

3. For a summary of this period, see H. S. Ferns, *Britain and Argentina in the Nineteenth Century* (London: Oxford University Press, 1960). The classic statement on informal empire is J. Gallagher and R. Robinson, "The Imperialism of Free Trade," *Economic History Review,* 2d ser. 6:1–15.

4. See, for example, Thomas F. McGann, *Argentina, the United States and the Inter-American System, 1880–1914* (Cambridge, Mass.: Harvard University Press, 1957).

5. On these matters, see the essays collected in Roberto Etchepareborda, *Historia de las relaciones internacionales argentinas* (Buenos Aires: Editorial Pleamar, 1978).

6. On the impact of the war on Argentina, see my "The Argentine Economy During World War I," *Review of the River Plate,* nos. 3750–52 (June–July 1970).

7. Joseph S. Tulchin, "Foreign Policy," in M. Falcoff and R. H. Dolkart, eds., *Prologue to Perón: Argentina in Depression and War, 1930–1943* (Berkeley: University of California Press, 1975), Chapter 4.

8. I have dealt with this episode in "The Argentine Proposal for Non-Belligerancy, April 1940," *The Journal of Inter-American Studies* 11, no. 4 (1969):571–604.

9. On this period, see, among many others, Gustavo Ferrari, "Constantes de la política exterior argentina," *Economic Survey,* Suplemento Especial, no. 1370 (February 27, 1973); Juan Carlos Puig, "La política exterior argentina y sus tendencias profundas," *Revista Argentina de Relaciones Internacionales* 1, no. 1 (1975); Roberto Etchepareborda, "Presencia nacional en el exterior. Elementos de la política de los estados," *Respuesta Argentina,* Suplemento (July 1974); and Dardo Cúneo, "Argentina's Foreign Policy," in Carlos A. Astiz, ed., *Latin American International Politics* (Albany: State University of New York Press, 1969). General surveys include Celso Lafer and Félix Peña, *Argentina y Brasil en el sistema de relaciones internacionales* (Buenos Aires: Nueva Visión, 1973); and Michael J. Francis, *The Limits of Hegemony: United States Relations with Argentina and Chile during World War II* (Notre Dame: University of Notre Dame Press, 1977).

10. On the importance of geopolitical thinking in Argentina, see the writings of Juan E. Guglialmelli in *Estrategia;* for example, "Itaipú-Corpus. Operar en el frente principa; y no confundirse con los frentes secundarios," no. 33 (1975); or "Argentina-Brasil, enfrentamiento o alianza para la liberación," no. 36 (1975). To appreciate the degree to which these basic geo-

political concepts have permeated the thinking and writing about Argentine relations with Brazil and the rest of the world, see *La Nación,* June 1, 1978, an article by Fernando de la Púa and Cesáreo T. Lachiondo; or the editorials on October 12, 1978, and November 16, 1978; *Somos,* Año 3, no. 112 (1978):11, 56; and *Carta Política,* no. 60 (1978):5.

9
Human Rights and Development: Lessons from Latin America

Richard L. Clinton
R. Kenneth Godwin

We treat the human rights issue as the greatest hurdle to [the Basic Human Needs Strategy of Economic Development]. I do not disagree with this assessment, but at the same time I also see the human rights issue as the one which has the greatest long-term potential for bridging much of the present perceptual gap and value gap between North and South.

—Roger D. Hansen[1]

In commemoration of the thirtieth anniversary of the proclamation by the United Nations of the Universal Declaration of Human Rights on December 10, 1948, President Carter reiterated that human rights would continue to be the "soul" of his administration's foreign policy.[2] The establishment of human rights as the cornerstone of U.S. foreign policy has been attacked from various quarters. Some observers deem it naive in a world of realpolitik. Some see it as hypocritical, given our own less-than-perfect record domestically and the frequency with which political, military, and economic considerations override our professed commitment to human rights in our international relations. Others view it as ethnocentric; in effect, a new form of cultural imperialism.

In the following pages we will attempt to show that at least for one important part of the world, a U.S. foreign policy grounded on and oriented toward the promotion of human rights, far from being naive, is the most realistic we could adopt. We acknowledge that in our relations with military allies, major trading partners, and our principal adversaries, it may be neither possible nor desirable to grant primacy to human rights criteria in formulating our policies. We will argue, however, that human rights provide the optimal guideline for our stance vis-à-vis Latin America and other late-modernizing states. In our view, no other philosophical underpinning supplies such a solid basis for our foreign policy toward countries whose present political and economic institutions have failed to accommodate to conditions of rapid population growth, capital and resource scarcity, and subhuman living conditions for great masses of their people.

In the argument we develop here, we are fully aware that we are advocating a double standard: human rights are to be our major guideposts to action vis-à-vis poor, "developing," or late-modernizing countries, but human rights are to be only one of a combination of criteria for determining our nation's posture toward rich, industrialized, modernized countries. We believe this approach, although superficially inconsistent, accurately reflects the complexities of political reality, an intractable tangle seldom containable within neat formulas. Where our national security or other legitimate interests are directly involved, it is quixotic to expect human rights considerations to be the most salient influence on our national policies. This is not to say, however, that our allegiance to human rights should ever be denied. We can and always should protest violations of human rights wherever they occur and do everything we can to prevent them, consistent with our government's primordial responsibility—the safety and well-being of our own people.

To concede these limitations on the use of human rights as a factor in the formulation of U.S. foreign policy does not, we contend, detract from their importance. As we hope to show below through an examination of the Latin American case, human rights afford a firm philosophical foundation for a positive approach to a group of nations containing more than three-quarters of the human race. Surely this is contribution enough for one set of principles. Moreover, to clarify where and why these criteria can best be applied—and where they must inevitably be subordinated to others—should lessen the tendency to challenge their validity and to decry their use as hypocritical.

To the charge that the U.S. conception of human rights is

ethnocentric, we plead guilty. If the UN Universal Declaration of Human Rights lacks the eloquence of Thomas Paine or Thomas Jefferson, it nevertheless echoes the essence of their thought. As Peter Berger has pointed out, "Contemporary notions of human rights are historically and intellectually derived from the Enlightenment, a specifically Western phenomenon."[3] Does this mean that these ideas lack validity for others with different cultural heritages? Although skeptical himself about the use of human rights as a basis for our foreign policy, Berger admits that "if the moral discoveries of the Western tradition—prominent among them the ideas of individual liberty and of the fundamental equality of all human beings—are valid for us, they are valid for all mankind."[4]

Paradoxically, in questioning the universality of U.S. conceptions of human rights, Berger provides compelling grounds for our attempting to make them the normative basis for our dealings with those foreign states only recently entering the modern world. It is worthwhile quoting his own formulations:

> Modernity originated in Europe. Its basic institutional embodiments are European inventions—science and technology, bureaucracy, the economic systems of both capitalism and socialism, political democracy as well as the nation-state. So are the basic ideologies that legitimate these institutions—including our contemporary notions of human rights. . . . Whether one likes it or not, the process of modernization has everywhere been, at least in part, a process of Westernization as well.[5]

However:

> The modern state (and not just the repressive or the totalitarian version of it) . . . exercises historically unprecedented power—with the implication that human rights are more than ever before at the mercy of unrestrained rulers. It was, indeed, precisely in order to impose restraints upon governmental power that modern democratic institutions arose in the West.[6]

We would argue that precisely because modernism is rushing across the globe so inexorably, engulfing cultures and sweeping away traditional forms of social control and societal cohesion, it is more urgent than ever that Western concepts of human rights also be disseminated as rapidly as possible. Because the West, and especially the United States, has unleashed this uncontainable force upon the world, it might even be said that we bear a special responsibility to ensure that concern for the protection of human rights is a concomitant of that corrosive process.

With some truth, U.S. predication of human rights and the institutionalizing of incentives and disincentives to promote them in other nations can be called a form of cultural imperialism. To do so, however, seems to confuse the issues. The diffusion of modernization is the signal cultural event of our time. This is, indeed, cultural imperialism on a massive scale. By comparison, the effort to spread the only known antidotes to this in many ways harmful process is but a misdemeanor, hardly meriting the ire it so often provokes.

Human Rights and the Concept of Development

A focus on Latin America is useful in demonstrating the linkage we wish to establish between human rights and U.S. foreign policy toward late-modernizing states. On a broad range of development criteria—from per capita GNP to more meaningful measures such as life expectancy and literacy—the Latin American nations, except for Haiti and Bolivia, enjoy a relatively favored position in comparison with most Asian or African states.[7] This relatively more favored position holds true as well in regard to population density, natural resources, and access to the sea, plus in terms of a greater cultural proximity to Western thought, language, and forms of socioeconomic and political organization. If the outlook for success of the currently accepted approach to development is not good even in Latin America, the case for seeking an alternative is therefore considerably strengthened. The alternative we feel most appropriate emphasizes a human rights–based approach to development.

In linking together human rights, development, and U.S. policy toward late-modernizing states, we base our argument on one definition and three basic propositions. Following James Kocher we define development as "(1) a general improvement in levels of living, together with (2) decreasing inequality of income distribution, and (3) the capacity to sustain continuous improvements over time."[8] Our three propositions are (1) Latin America as a whole does not have access to sufficient resources at low enough prices to achieve capital-intensive industrialization at a level similar to that of the United States, Western Europe, and Japan; (2) Latin America's current rates of population growth severely inhibit development, whether it is defined as an increase in GNP per capita or according to Kocher's criteria; and (3) the existing distribution of political power in Latin America prevents changes in present socioeconomic institutions that would make possible the pursuit of an approach to development oriented toward improvement of living conditions in rural areas and the creation and deployment of "appropriate technologies."

In the discussion below we will amplify the definition of development, provide empirical support for our three propositions, and indicate what a human rights orientation toward Latin America actually means in terms of concrete actions.

The Human Factor in Development

Kocher followed his definition of development with the sentence "The components of socioeconomic well-being are the substance of development." We would argue that these components include the reduction of malnutrition, disease, illiteracy, squalor, unemployment, and inequality.[9] Moreover, we agree with Ruth Dixon, who adds that increases in the regularity and amount of purchasing power, reduction in the hours of work required to meet subsistence needs, and control over one's earnings are also important components of development.[10] Finally, in our view, the complex concept of development must include the basic democratic freedoms of speech, assembly, and the opportunity to influence governmental decisions. In other words development requires not only that people be more healthy and less poor but also that they have greater security of continuing health and income and wider opportunities to utilize these improvements by having more control over their lives.

Such a conceptualization of development, although vastly

different from reliance on indicators such as per capita GNP or energy consumption, is certainly not new. In fact, every element of it can be found in the UN Declaration of Human Rights. Far earlier than the UN declaration, "life, liberty, and property" appeared in several state constitutions, exemplifying what Thomas Jefferson and James Madison, and before them John Locke, saw as the prerequisites of the good life. Property was included along with life and liberty because these thinkers believed that without security in their personal property individuals are unable to enjoy and protect life and liberty. For this same reason Dixon added security of income to her fundamental definition of development. It is important to recognize that property in these formulations does not refer so much to "real property" as to the means to pursue the liberties available in society. Thus, the right to an adequate diet is a meaningless liberty if one cannot find work and earn a living wage, and the right to read what anybody has written is an empty guarantee to the illiterate.

Rationales for a more inclusive conceptualization of development than commonly accepted indicators or the level of industrialization have been explicated elsewhere.[11] These arguments may be essentially humanistic, based on the premise that health, literacy, and control of one's life are essential to a fully human existence. They may be pragmatic, based on the premise that, in light of available resources and alternatives, human-capital investment, appropriate technologies, and rural development are more viable means of achieving long-term development—even development defined in terms of GNP—than an approach based on capital-intensive high technology. Or they may be ecological, based on the premise that humanity's future depends on more socially efficient[12] exploitation of natural resources and that the global ecosphere would be massively disrupted if Latin America, Asia, and Africa were to emulate the wastefulness and luxury of the currently industrialized countries. It is important and encouraging, we believe, that the pragmatic and ecological arguments coincide with the humanistic rationale. This alone indicates that a foreign policy based on human rights deserves serious consideration.

Resources and Development

In a recent review of Latin America's resource base, James Street documented the severe limitations on natural resources in Latin America. Street concluded that only Brazil was sufficiently well endowed to be able to overcome the high population growth, premature urban concentration, market exhaustion, slow agricultural innovation, and failure to develop entrepreneurial skills that characterize the economies and societies of Latin America.[13] Although Mexico with its apparently extensive oil reserves might also be included with Brazil in the most favored category, no country in Latin America is absolved of all the distortions that Street enumerates. Moreover, one author of this chapter has argued that Street overestimated the opportunities available in Latin America and, more seriously, underestimated the obstacles to effectively exploiting them.[14]

Latin America is already experiencing severe economic and social dislocations in large part attributable to its development strategy based on high rates of urbanization, concentration of investment in the industrial sector, and the corresponding failure to invest in people and in agricultural innovation. These dislocations have been exacerbated by the drastic leap in energy prices since 1973. We cannot overemphasize the importance of recognizing that the era of cheap energy has ended, at least for the foreseeable future, for its availability is the unspoken assumption underlying the development strategy currently being pursued in Latin America and throughout most of the late-modernizing countries. Except for nuclear holocaust or a worldwide financial collapse, nothing—neither Mexican oil nor technological breakthroughs—can alter the fact that the cost of energy will continue to rise, at least for the remainder of this century. Yet this is the crucial period during which, for demographic reasons, the challenge of development must be met if Malthusian outcomes are to be avoided. It does not seem to be widely enough understood that for the late-modernizing states cost, not depletion, is the key consideration regarding fossil-fuel energy sources during the next few decades. There can be little doubt that as the price of energy goes higher, the rich countries—"for which petroleum, in particular, is truly the life blood"—will outbid the poor countries for whatever is available.[15] Hence we feel the urgency to recast our ideas about development so as to emphasize improvement in the general well-being of the populace and greater local self-sufficiency through labor-intensive activities in agriculture, infrastructure construction, public health, and education.[16] Only thus can a viable basis be laid for continuing future improvement.

Industrialization and Income Distribution

What if new sources of cheap energy were secured either through new discoveries of fossil fuels or through technological "fixes" such as solar energy or nuclear fusion? Would this alter the thrust of our arguments? Although significant reductions in the cost of energy might again allow the Latin American countries to reach the 6 percent annual growth rate in GNP (2 percent in GNP per capita) that many achieved in the 1968–1974 period,[17] the point is that these rates of growth were accomplished without "development." The countries experiencing the greatest increases in GNP had increasing rather than decreasing degrees of income inequality, with practically all the gains in income going to the upper third of income recipients.[18] This tendency for income inequality to increase during periods of rapid growth is not confined to Latin America but is a worldwide phenomenon that is particularly acute in the late-modernizing countries.[19] The studies just cited conclusively debunk the great development myth of the "trickle-down" effects of economic growth as measured by GNP. Thus, although increased energy supplies at lower costs might allow Latin American countries to cope better with the short-term problems of huge balance-of-payment deficits, large external debts, and stagflation, cheap energy will not eliminate the long-term problems cited by Street, Clinton, and others. Paradoxically, a return to cheap energy might even exacerbate these problems.

It may appear that we have argued that expensive energy has created problems for Latin America and inexpensive energy might make these problems worse. Actually, we are arguing that the capital-intensive, modern-sector, and import-substitution development approach of the Latin American countries has created the problems; the energy crisis merely brought these problems into focus by provoking a short-term crisis. Import substitution and investment in the "modern" sector had already achieved most of their potential prior to 1960, and at the cost of creating serious long-term economic disequilibria.[20] Most significantly this strategy led to increased income inequality[21] and neglected the major economic resource of any region—its human capital.[22] If energy were again to become relatively inexpensive, the long-term problems would not go away, but because the short-term crisis might be alleviated, it is all too likely that efforts to find a more appropriate development strategy would be less strenuously pursued.

Human Capital and Economic Development

Perhaps the greatest shortcoming of the literature on economic development is its general failure to recognize that only a small portion of a nation's economic growth can be attributed to capital investments. With characteristic insight, Simon Kuznets has shown that the quantity of capital, labor, and land—and traditional economic inputs—account for only about 10 percent of the growth that has occurred in currently industrialized countries.[23] The remaining 90 percent he attributes to "improved quality of the inputs and improved organizational arrangements."[24] Of these improvements, the quality of the labor force appears to be the most significant.[25] To improve this factor input requires human-capital investment; i.e., the individuals in the society must have the necessary health and education to become effective producers.

Focusing on the contribution of human-capital investment to economic progress leads us directly back to the UN human rights declaration, which includes health, nutrition, and education among the basic human rights. We are also led to the issue of population growth.

Population and Development

The importance of the relationships between economic growth and demographic variables has become increasingly recognized in the last two decades. Although the causal linkages are complex and far from completely specified, both empirical research and positive theory indicate that economic growth and social development are related to reductions in fertility and mortality rates. This connection becomes apparent when we examine how demographic variables affect the process of improving human capital. Specifically, for instance, let us examine how decreases in fertility can improve health, intelligence, and education.

Recent empirical research in both industrialized and nonindustrialized societies indicates that family size and child spacing are critical to the health of both children and mothers. Children in large families with closely spaced births are more likely to be malnourished, to die before the age of five, to be smaller at birth, to be smaller at age five, and to have lower levels of intelligence than children from smaller families or families where birth intervals are greater.[26] Closely spaced births also pose significant threats to the health of the mother.[27] The negative correlation between family size and the intelligence of children appears to be related to the malnourishment of children, their small size at birth, and the amount of time parents spend with their children.[28]

Large family size also reduces educational attainment by children.[29] This problem is particularly acute among poorer families, which cannot afford to forgo the income from the children's labor. In addition, larger families have insufficient savings to educate all children. This typically means that female children especially will not receive the education that would make them more employable and less prone to have large families.

All of the above factors reduce the possibility of social development. The process is aptly summarized by Nancy Birdsall: "The loss of individual potential due to malnutrition or lack of educational opportunity can be translated into losses for a nation because of the lower aggregate levels of productivity and lower stocks of entrepreneurial ability and technological innovativeness."[30] Birdsall goes on to point out, as Daly demonstrated in 1971, that high fertility exacerbates the inequalities in the distribution of income in that it is the less-educated, lower-income parents who are more likely to have large families.

This further increases the inequalities of opportunity between the children of the different income classes in society and makes even more difficult the upward mobility that spurs innovation.

Other ways in which microeconomic arguments for reduced family sizes have important counterparts at the macrolevel can be mentioned. Rapid population growth has an obvious direct effect on the ability of a society to provide sufficient resources to the educational system. Under conditions of lower fertility, however, the same level of funds could provide each child with more, and presumably better, education, and the bottlenecks of teacher training and classroom construction would not be so severe. The same argument can be made for health services, where the differences in levels of services may be even greater given the interaction of large family size, health problems caused by malnutrition, and the high percentage of health services that are devoted to obstetric and pediatric needs, including the enormous number of abortion-related cases that are found in all Latin American hospitals.[31]

One of the problems long noted in the development literature on Latin America has been the high levels of unemployment and underemployment.[32] The failure of the capital-intensive, urban-oriented approach to absorb the ever-increasing labor force is manifest in every Latin American country. High fertility rates make this problem all the more intractable. Current fertility rates in Latin America, except for Argentina and Uruguay, mean that the labor force will triple in thirty years, even excluding increases in female labor activity that are needed to help reduce fertility.[33] This problem cannot be resolved by simply reverting to past labor-intensive techniques, for these are so inefficient that the capital-output ratio might be worse than the present rate and might not be competitive with imported goods.[34] Hence, along with the problems of distribution of income and political power, the task of developing appropriate technologies is one of the greatest challenges currently facing Latin America.

The rapid rates of population increase also have deleterious effects on the use of the limited resources of Latin America and on the ecological systems of the region. Street, in his sanguine appraisal of Latin America's opportunities, emphasizes the

potential of the region's "internal frontier."[35] He suggests that
land resources, hydroelectric capabilities, energy substitution,
agricultural innovations such as the green revolution, and the
creation of interior development zones offer the best possibilities. The realization of these alternatives depends, inter alia, on
the reduction of population growth, however. Population pressures are constantly pushing marginal areas into use without
adequate agricultural technology to prevent such severe over-
grazing and soil erosion that the land is destroyed. This problem
has already been extensively documented in Erick Eckholm's
Losing Ground: Environmental Stress and World Food Prospects
(1976). Such negative consequences of dams as river blindness,
schistosomiasis, and other water-borne diseases as well as the
more familiar problems of sedimentation and silting further
limit the realizable potential of the internal frontier as Street
envisions it.[36]

The above discussion certainly places us among the "new
Malthusians" and will surely evoke the objection from some
quarters that emphasizing the dangers of rapid population
growth bespeaks imperialist fears of threatened hegemony and
that population programs are merely a cheap substitute for
development assistance. Unquestionably the poor countries
have ample cause to believe that the United States and other
rich countries are looking for such a cheap substitute. The ill-
phrased statement by President Lyndon Johnson that one dollar
for birth control is more effective than five dollars for development assistance helped to fuel this suspicion as do the grudging
remarks in the U.S. Congress each year as the foreign aid budget
is debated. There can be no doubt, moreover, that the rich
countries could easily share a great deal more of their wealth
with the poor nations, and we would emphasize that the success
of the human rights approach prescribed here in fact depends
on the availability of much larger amounts of foreign assistance.
Having forsworn direct intervention, the United States can best
hope to influence foreign regimes' development policies and
treatment of their people by making them offers of assistance in
their development efforts that are too attractive to refuse. This
would mean, however, that we must not only begin living up to
our past pledges regarding the amounts of development assis-

tance we will provide—we are presently committed to 0.7 percent of our GNP but are providing only around 0.23 percent—but we must substantially increase these pledges as well.[37]

The argument against the neo-Malthusians is that reducing population growth rates does not necessarily cause development, but development will result in slower population growth, a claim we would not dispute. In fact, in our own writings we have frequently stressed the need to recognize that the causal relationships between population decline and development flow in both directions.[38] Again, however, the crucial consideration is what is meant by development—aggregate economic growth or improved well-being for all.

During the period between 1968 and 1978 the United States Agency for International Development (USAID) was increasingly called upon to redirect its population assistance away from an emphasis on contraceptive supply toward an emphasis on creating effective contraceptive demand. These appeals reached a crescendo at the World Population Conference in Bucharest in 1974. At Bucharest, the low-income countries insisted that higher levels of development were necessary to achieve any sustained fertility decline, for only as their life chances and living conditions improve would the desire of couples to limit their fertility grow and contraceptive demand increase.

The low-income countries based their proposals on the proposition that development brings about both mortality and fertility declines. Citing the experience of the more-industrialized nations and the theory of the "demographic transition," the "development-first" proposals suggest that development reduces fertility rates by first lowering mortality through better sanitation and nutrition, improved knowledge of disease, and more advanced medical technology. Development also reduces the demand for children by making them more expensive, less necessary for prestige and economic security, and less useful as a source of inexpensive rural labor. As the low-income countries accurately point out, fertility rates in Europe and North America dropped prior to the development of the IUD and the pill or even to the mass manufacturing of condoms. There is a lag between the drop in mortality and the drop in fertility, they admit, but if development proceeds rapidly enough this disequilibrium can be overcome. Latin American nations were especially vociferous in arguing this position, adding that they had too few people to fill their large unsettled regions and that population pressures would facilitate innovation and create larger markets, thus aiding rather than hindering the growth of their economies.

In the period since the close of the Bucharest conference, major international assistance and loan agencies such as the World Bank have attempted to achieve some consensus on this issue, recognizing that the causal relationships between development and population flow in both directions.[39] This search for consensus has led to valuable research concerning those factors in the process of social change most closely linked to fertility declines. This research again points toward the UN Declaration of Human Rights as a useful guide to development policy, for perhaps the most important finding in these studies is that a more equitable distribution of income in a society is at least as important a contributor to lower fertility as increasing the average income per capita. In a cross-national study for the World Bank, Timothy King and his colleagues found that for each additional percentage point of the total income received by the poorest 40 percent of the population the fertility index dropped by 2.9 points.[40] Other critical factors associated with fertility reduction include decreases in infant mortality, reduction of the rate of illiteracy, female labor force participation, female education, median number of years in school, and increases in life expectancy.[41] We do not claim that these attributes are necessarily the causes of the growing desire for smaller families, but they certainly seem to be concomitants of this tendency. It is our position that these factors derive from an underlying pattern of social change reflecting development and not merely increases in industrial outputs or overall GNP per capita.

Unfortunately, none of the Latin American countries that urged a "development first" orientation at Bucharest has made any attempt to pursue a development strategy that would actually reduce fertility, i.e., one oriented toward improving the living conditions and opportunities of the lowest 40 percent of its people.

Political Power and Development

The thrust of our argument thus far has been that the essence of development is greater equality and that the concepts of development and of human rights as defined in the UN declaration are complementary. At odds with these concepts, however, are the past and current economic modernization strategies pursued by most Latin American regimes. The "economic miracle," Brazil, best demonstrates this assertion.

Brazil's current regime and its predecessors since the 1964 military takeover have violated almost every basic political and social right. The torture and terror that followed the overthrow of civilian authority are well documented. The continued limitations on free speech, press, and assembly have brought the Brazilian regime and the current U.S. administration into direct confrontation, with the Brazilian president openly critical of Carter's human rights policy. At the same time, however, we would do well to remember that President Johnson sent a congratulatory telegram to the leaders of the 1964 coup, and since that time many millions of dollars of public assistance and private investment have flowed from the United States to Brazil. Brazil has continued its strategy of industrialization, import substitution, high rates of urbanization, and encouraging foreign investment that represent the traditional approach to economic modernization. Meanwhile, however, its foreign debt increased from $276 million in 1972 to $29 billion in 1976—the highest of the Third World countries.[42] Nearly 40 percent of its foreign exchange earnings each year must go to service its foreign borrowings, and the annual rate of inflation approximates 30 percent.[43]

In view of these sorts of figures, why does Brazil (and almost every other Latin American and late-modernizing country) continue such an economic strategy? First, it is not easy for a country to reorient its economy from a capital-intensive, high-technology, and urban-oriented approach to one based on human-capital investment, "appropriate" technologies, and rural development. Second, relatively little work has been done either in Latin America or elsewhere to develop appropriate technologies, i.e., small-scale, affordable techniques that take advantage of local resources and respond to local needs.[44] Third, any development strategy, once in place, acquires a momentum that is difficult to reverse. This is particularly true of capital-intensive development accompanied by huge external debt as in Brazil. Fourth, many of the steps required, such as greater independence and economic opportunities for women, run counter to deep cultural values. Finally, and most importantly, present allocations of political power and economic resources are built on and maintained by the current approach to economic change. When all is said and done, the type of development we are prescribing requires a substantial redistribution of economic wealth and political influence. The change would threaten not only Latin American elites but also powerful economic interests in the United States and, to a lesser extent, in Europe.

We are not suggesting the existence of either a national or international conspiracy to obstruct development of alternative technologies or a redistribution of wealth and opportunities; it would be both foolish and unnecessary to do so. We are simply saying that for those who have the power to make the decisions necessary to reorient Latin American countries toward development strategies based on human rights, the cultural, economic, and political incentives are arrayed in the opposite way. To expect Latin American elites to disregard these incentives is to expect too much.

What Can Be Done?

We began this chapter with the suggestion that human rights can provide a viable basis for U.S. foreign policy, at least toward a sizable set of countries. In the above discussion we have attempted to demonstrate that human rights, as defined in the UN declaration, and development, as defined by Kocher and others, are fully compatible. We have argued, however, that the dominant approach to economic modernization in Latin America and, by extension, other late-modernizing states, is incompatible with effective strategies for fulfilling the human rights guaranteed by the UN declaration. The dominant approach has also led to short-term crises and long-term structural problems. Unless this approach is changed, Latin America and similar areas will never achieve development as we have defined it.[45] This pessimistic conclusion is based on their relatively poor resource base, their high rates of population growth, the inevitability of higher prices for energy during coming decades, and the structural disequilibria already produced by past adherence to mistaken models of development. One of the most important of these structural disequilibria is the incentive structure of present economic and political elites, which prevents their abandoning these mistaken approaches. If these political and economic elites cannot be expected to change directions, is the only alternative revolution?

Our estimation is that, while revolution may be one way, it is not the only way. Chile elected a government that was willing to make many of the changes suggested above. Unfortunately, the United States at that time was more committed to blind anti-Communism than to development and human rights. Despite the lip service paid by the United States to greater equality and development, our government has actively opposed the few regimes that have followed words with action concerning any redistribution of wealth. Guatemala in 1954, Cuba in 1961, and Chile in 1973 have each been the target of overt and/or covert intervention. In each case the leftist governments were responsible for far less bloodshed and repression than has been occasioned by right-wing oppression with U.S. support in Brazil, Chile, and Nicaragua. The events in Guatemala, Cuba, and Chile prove that the emergence of local leadership committed to a more equitable distribution of opportunities is not an impossibility. In fact, it is quite possible that if the United States had merely remained neutral rather than giving arms and counterinsurgency training to right-wing authoritarian governments, several countries in Latin America might today be governed in a manner that would facilitate genuine development.

If we were to go two steps further and direct our assistance toward the types of programs conducive to development and refuse to support projects that will heighten inequalities and are oriented toward inappropriate technologies, we might find that Latin Americans know better than we do the structural difficulties inherent in their current approach. Noted Latin American economists such as Raúl Prebisch and Celso Furtado have long since demonstrated their insight into these matters.

To a degree, some of the necessary changes in the process of development assistance have already begun. The World Bank has stated that it will orient its assistance toward rural development,[46] and the United States Agency for International Development has signaled that it, too, will follow a rural and community development strategy focused on the poorest of the poor.[47] Whether the bankers and bureaucrats are flexible enough and willing to follow through on these pledges remains a crucial question. But certainly the prospects would be brighter if our foreign policy were explicitly anchored in a clear and consistent commitment to the global advance of human rights.[48]

There is one further step the United States could take to secure the broader enjoyment of human rights in the late-modernizing countries. We could utilize our economic leverage to facilitate the downfall of repressive regimes such as those in Nicaragua, Haiti, Chile, and Brazil. The authors confess to ambivalence concerning this option. Earlier U.S. efforts to determine another country's government have resulted in extensive deaths and repression in Haiti, the Dominican Republic, Guatemala, Nicaragua, Chile, Brazil, Bolivia, and Uruguay—to confine ourselves to Latin America. Successful installation of revolutionary regimes might well lead to similar loss of life and violation of human rights.

Human Rights Violations by Development-oriented Regimes

In trying to improve the circumstances of the poorest sectors of society, it may be unavoidable that a development-oriented regime will violate the rights of the better-off. History and almost everything we know about human behavior tell us that the more advantaged in society will be resourceful in their opposition to measures to achieve a more equitable distribution of goods and opportunities—particularly in a situation of relative scarcity. It is only human to wish to protect one's possessions and perquisites. Yet possessions and perquisites are political resources, translatable into political power. Given this universal tendency, any regime that attempts to redistribute wealth and opportunities under conditions of scarcity would be remiss if it did not seek to deprive those with a disproportionate share of wealth, prestige, and privilege of these sources of power. Not to do so would be to invite frustration of its efforts and very possibly its own demise. The resulting necessity for what may be injustice to certain individuals when their cases are viewed individually is an inherent tragedy of social reconstruction.

This problem brings us to the final question of vital importance to the perspective of this essay: What should the United States do when regimes that are attempting to achieve the redistribution of income and opportunities necessary for development violate the rights stipulated in the UN declaration? Certainly China and Cuba transgressed the rights of free speech, press, and assembly, among others, in their drive to provide a better life for the masses, justifying their actions as necessary to prevent the traditional elites from blocking the redistributive efforts essential to their programs.

We are painfully aware of the moral quandary this question raises. In seeking its resolution we are guided by the following propositions:

1. The threat posed by rapid population growth to the ecological carrying capacities of many areas in the low-income countries as well as to these countries' development prospects is so immense and relatively immediate that only desperate measures can be expected to improve the situation.

2. To deny development-oriented regimes the use of repressive measures against their opponents ignores the appalling levels of structural violence that would continue in the absence of radical change (e.g., infant and child mortality from malnutrition, contaminated water, and lack of medical attention; female deaths related to induced abortions; deaths from mild ailments because of lowered resistance resulting from malnourishment or undernourishment; and the incalculable amount of psychological damage caused by the ignorance, unemployment, in-

security, and squalor that are the daily lot of hundreds
of millions on this tortured planet). Some degree of repression is often the only viable way of overcoming the resistance of vested interests to the redistributions that are
the sine qua non of development as we have defined it.

3. Creativity and innovation are indispensable to the development of appropriate technologies, and freedom from
   oppressive orthodoxies is essential to creativity and innovativeness.

4. General recognition of the desperateness of the situation
   in which most late-modernizing states find themselves is
   more likely and the support of the people for effective
   development programs more probable under conditions
   of free expression.

5. Life—security in one's person—is surely the most basic
   human right.

6. If human rights criteria for receipt of U.S. development assistance were clearly understood and consistently
   observed, we should be in a position to influence the
   behavior of late-modernizing states toward their citizens,
   moderating any repression that might occur.

It is tempting to suggest that the Ariadne's thread that would
lead us out of this maze of conflicting propositions is to priori-
tize the components of development adumbrated at the outset
of this chapter, recognizing that a development-oriented regime
may be unable to avoid violation of the "higher" needs of some
groups and individuals in order to meet the "lower" or more
basic needs of larger groups. Christian Bay, in his book *The
Structure of Freedom*,[49] took this approach, arguing for a
hierarchy of needs similar to that postulated by Abraham
Maslow.[50] In such a system, fundamental physical needs such as
adequate nutrition, housing, and health care are logically prior
to such higher needs or rights as education and greater control
over both personal life and governmental decisions. Although
theoretically appealing, this approach suffers in practice from
one critical flaw: it overlooks that the new governmental decision makers will inevitably be concerned about meeting their
own higher needs, hence the temptation to form a new privileged

class in postrevolutionary societies is pervasive if not universal. For the same reason that the old vested interests can be expected to use their resources to protect their perquisites, possessions, and privileges, it is equally probable that the equally human agents of new regimes will do likewise, and the net result may be worse than before the new regime came to power.

Our suggested solution to this dilemma is for the United States to give priority to only two fundamental human rights: the security of one's person and freedom of expression. The security of person is necessary to prevent the terror and torture that a victorious revolutionary regime might be tempted to employ against those who oppose its efforts to create new political, social, and economic institutions conducive to development. Freedom of expression would help to guarantee that the security of person is not being violated and also provides an invaluable feedback mechanism to the regime concerning how its policies are perceived by the people most affected by them.

Beyond these two rights, the United States must allow regimes to develop their own hierarchy that will hopefully be best suited to achieve comprehensive development in the particular circumstances at hand. U.S. policies and assistance would still reflect U.S. priorities in that active support would only be given to those programs that encourage improvements in the general levels of living, that decrease inequalities, and that utilize appropriate technologies so that continuous improvements would be possible. The level of assistance would also reflect a dialogue with the countries in which they can argue their plans and present their needs as they see them. It is our contention that this could be accomplished by explicitly stating and rigorously observing standards of conduct for governments vis-à-vis their citizens and making these standards the minimal criteria for the receipt of U.S. development assistance and, if possible, that from international sources as well. The success of this approach requires, of course, that the levels of potential development assistance be vastly greater than the meager amounts available today. Thus, regimes of all political persuasions would recognize that if they are to qualify for potentially very useful development assistance, they must not only reorient their development efforts toward the lower 40 percent of their population but also deal as humanely as possible with those opposed to their policies. The Velasco regime in Peru from 1968 to 1975 provides a beginning example of such a process (even in the absence of the "carrot" of massive foreign aid). Although many of the regime's more prominent opponents were harrassed and, in some cases, imprisoned or exiled, and some blood was shed on occasion in confrontations with demonstrators or striking miners, none of the kidnapping, torture, and murder common to the Brazilian, Uruguayan, and Chilean experience occurred in Peru.

Unquestionably, the sort of foreign policy we are urging is an interventionist one. We do not believe a nation as powerful as the United States can avoid affecting, hence interfering in, the internal affairs of smaller nations in this new era of global interdependence. We do believe, however, that our intervention can be in a mild rather than a harsh form and salutary rather than pernicious in its consequences.

Perhaps just as importantly, a foreign policy solidly grounded in the principles of human rights carries forward a fundamental tenet of American society. Consistency with the Enlightenment ideas of freedom and humanitarianism expresses our unique heritage as a nation,[51] connects us with what is best in the long tradition of Western civilization, and helps to fulfill the promise we have symbolized for so many as "the Mother Country of Liberty."[52] It might also help to restore our sense of purpose as a nation and give us an ennobling project through which our youth might find meaning in their lives.

Summary and Conclusion

We began this chapter with the assertion that a foreign policy based on human rights is not as naive as is generally supposed and, on the contrary, offers the best option available in our relations with Latin America and other late-modernizing states. Human rights cannot, however, be thought of solely in terms of political liberties; the concept must also include the economic well-being and equality of opportunity that make such liberties meaningful. To achieve these goals, an orientation to development different from that currently in vogue is necessary. This orientation would stress greater self-sufficiency and more equitable distribution of opportunities through rural development, appropriate technologies, human-capital investment, and reduction of population growth rates. Such a shift of priorities is as drastic as it is improbable because current elites in late-modernizing states have no incentives to support it. Only a new attitude on the part of the industrialized nations and much larger amounts of foreign assistance can be expected to encourage the needed changes, and a foreign policy designed to promote human rights appears uniquely well suited to this historic task.

Notes

1. We discovered the article from which this excerpt was drawn after the present chapter was completed. Its thesis so substantially coincides with our own and its marshalling of evidence and argument is so magisterial, we can only urge interested readers to seek it out. Roger D. Hansen, "Major U.S. Options on North-South Relations: A Letter to President Carter," in John W. Sewell et al., *The United States and World Development. Agenda 1977* (New York and London: Praeger Publishers for the Overseas Development Council, 1977), pp. 160–69.

2. *New York Times,* December 11, 1978, p. A9.

3. Peter L. Berger, "Are Human Rights Universal?" *Commentary* 64 (September 1977):61.

4. Ibid., p. 63.

5. Ibid., p. 61.

6. Ibid., p. 63.

7. Sewell, *The United States and World Development.*

8. James E. Kocher, *Rural Development, Income Distribution, and Fertility Decline* (New York: Population Council, 1973), p. 4.

9. Mahbub ul Haq, quoted in William Rich, *Smaller Families Through Social and Economic Progress* (Washington, D.C.: Overseas Development Council, 1973), p. 23.

10. Ruth B. Dixon, *Rural Women at Work: Strategies for Development in South Asia* (Baltimore: Johns Hopkins University Press for Resources for the Future, 1978), p. 5.

11. Denis Goulet, *The Cruel Choice: A New Concept in the Theory of Development* (New York: Atheneum, 1973); Robert L. Ayers, "Develop-

ment Policy and the Possibility of a 'Livable' Future for Latin America,"
American Political Science Review 69 (June 1975):507–25; Herman E.
Daly, "Developing Economies and the Steady State," *The Developing
Economies* (Tokyo) 13 (September 1975):231–42; Richard L. Clinton,
"Ecodevelopment," *World Affairs* 140 (Fall 1977):111–26.

12. By socially efficient we mean that externalities are included in
the efficiency calculation.

13. James H. Street, "The Internal Frontier and Technological Progress
in Latin America," *Latin American Research Review* 12 (1977):43.

14. Richard L. Clinton, "Wishful Thinking as an Obstacle to Development in Latin America: A Critique of Street's Internal Frontier," *Latin
American Research Review* 13 (1978):175–79.

15. Richard L. Clinton, "The Never-to-be-developed Countries of Latin
America," *Bulletin of the Atomic Scientists* 33 (October 1977):24.

16. Clinton, "Ecodevelopment."

17. Inter-American Development Bank, *Annual Report* (Washington,
D.C., 1975), p. 10.

18. R. Kenneth Godwin, "Mexican Population Policy: Limitations on
Decisionmaking by Consensus," in *The Future of Mexico,* ed. Lawrence
Koslow (Tempe, Arizona: Arizona University Press, 1977).

19. Irma Adelman and Cynthia Morris, *Economic Growth and Social
Equality in Developing Countries* (Stanford: Stanford University Press,
1973); Robert Repetto, "The Relation of the Size Distribution of Income
to Fertility" and "The Implications for Development Policy," in *Popula-
tion Policies and Economic Development: A World Bank Report,* ed.
Timothy King (Baltimore: Johns Hopkins University Press, 1974); Barry R.
Chiswick and June A. O'Neill, *Human Resources and Income Distribution:
Issues and Policies* (New York: W. W. Norton, 1978).

20. David Felix, "Latin American Power: Take Off or Plus C'est la
Même Chose?" (Paper presented at the annual meeting of the International
Studies Association, Toronto, Canada, February 1976); Street, "The Inter-
nal Frontier."

21. Adelman and Morris, *Economic Growth and Social Equality in
Developing Countries.*

22. Frederick H. Harbison, *Human Resources and the Wealth of Na-
tions* (New York: Oxford University Press, 1973); Theodore W. Schultz,
Investment in Human Capital: The Role of Education and Research (New
York: Free Press, 1971); Simon Kuznets, *Modern Economic Growth* (New
Haven: Yale University Press, 1966); Ayers, "Development Policy."

23. Kuznets, *Modern Economic Growth.*

24. Nancy Birdsall, "Analytical Approaches to the Relationship of
Population Growth to Development," *Population and Development*

Review 3 (March–June 1977):63–102.

25. Edward F. Denison, *Why Growth Rates Differ* (Washington, D.C.: Brookings Institute, 1972); Schultz, *Investment in Human Capital*; Harbison, *Human Resources.*

26. Joe D. Wray, "Population Pressures on Families: Family Size and Child Spacing," *Rapid Population Growth,* vol. 2 (Baltimore: Johns Hopkins University Press, 1971); Kenneth W. Terhune, *A Review of the Actual and Expected Consequences of Family Size,* Calspan Report no. DP-5333-G-1. Publication no. 75-779 (Washington: National Institutes of Health, 1974); R. B. Zajonc, "Family Configuration and Intelligence," *Science* 192 (April 1976):227–36.

27. Frank W. Oechsli and Dudley Kirk, "Modernization and the Demographic Transition in Latin America and the Caribbean," *Economic Development and Cultural Change* 23, no. 3 (April 1975):391–419.

28. Robert Buchanan, *Effects of Childbearing on Maternal Health,* Population Reports, Series J, no. 8 (George Washington University Medical Center, November 1975); Zajonc, "Family Configuration."

29. Ansley J. Coale and Edgar M. Hoover, *Population Growth and Economic Development in Low Income Countries* (Princeton: Princeton University Press, 1958); Research Triangle Institute, *Social and Economic Correlates of Family Fertility: A Survey of the Evidence* (Research Triangle Park: Research Triangle Institute, 1971); Theodore K. Ruprecht and Frank I. Jewett, *The Micro-Economics of Demographic Change: Family Planning and Economic Well-Being* (New York: Praeger, 1975).

30. Birdsall, "Analytical Approaches," p. 76.

31. J. L. Pérez De Salazar et al., "Aborto provocado en México y problemas de población," *Ginecología y Obstetricia de México* 23 (1968): 639–47; Rolando Armijo and Tegualdo Monreal, "The Problem of Induced Abortion in Chile," *The Milbank Memorial Fund Quarterly* 43, pt. 2 (October 1965):263–80; Mariano Requeña, "The Problem of Induced Abortion in Latin America," *Demography* 5, no. 2 (1968):785–99.

32. Lauchlin Currie, *The Basis of a Development Program for Colombia* (Baltimore: Johns Hopkins University Press for the World Bank, 1950); Albert O. Hirschman, *The Strategy of Economic Development* (New Haven: Yale University Press, 1958).

33. Increases in female participation in the labor force are desirable, of course, for many other reasons as well, e.g., to utilize their productive potential and to enhance their status and individual autonomy in society. Bruce Herrick and Ricardo Morán, *Declining Birth Rates in Chile: Their Effects on Output, Education, Health and Housing* (Santa Barbara, Cal.: General Electric–Tempo, 1972).

34. Amartya Sen, *Employment, Technology, and Development* (Oxford: Clarendon Press, 1975).

35, Street, "The Internal Frontier."

36. Peter Freeman, "The Environment and Large Scale Water Resources Projects" (Paper prepared for United Nations Water Conference, March 1977); Birdsall, "Analytical Approaches."

37. Greater generosity on this front can only occur, however, if the disproportionate share of our wealth now consumed by the defense budget is significantly reduced. We cannot address these issues here, but we do wish to make explicit the linkage between disarmament, reduced defense spending, greater levels of development assistance, and the prospects for success of a human rights–based foreign policy toward late-modernizing states.

38. Richard L. Clinton and R. Kenneth Godwin, "Introduction: The Study of Population by Political Scientists," in *Research in the Politics of Population,* eds. R. L. Clinton and R. K. Godwin (Lexington, Mass.: D. C. Heath, 1972); Richard Lee Clinton, "Population, Politics, and Political Science," in *Population and Politics: New Directions in Political Science Research,* ed. R. L. Clinton (Lexington, Mass.: D. C. Heath, 1973); R. Kenneth Godwin, "Introduction," in *Comparative Policy Analysis: The Study of Population Policy in Developing Countries,* ed. R. K. Godwin (Lexington, Mass.: D. C. Heath, 1975).

39. See, for example, Michael S. Teitlebaum, "Population and Development: Is Consensus Possible?" *Foreign Affairs* 52 (July 1974):742–60; Robert S. McNamara, *One Hundred Countries, Two Billion People: The Dimensions of Development* (New York: Praeger, 1973); idem, "The Population Problem" (Address given at the Massachusetts Institute of Technology, Cambridge, Mass., April 1977); Marshall Green, "New Directions in U.S. Foreign Assistance for Population Programs," *Population and Development Review* 3 (September 1977):319–22.

40. Timothy King, *Population Policies and Economic Development* (Baltimore: Johns Hopkins University Press, 1974), pp. 147–48.

41. Ibid.; Steven E. Beaver, *Demographic Transition Theory Reinterpreted: An Application of Recent Natality Trends in Latin America* (Lexington, Mass.: D. C. Heath, 1975); K. S. Srikaten, *The Family Planning Program in the Socio-economic Context* (New York: Population Council, 1977); Dixon, *Rural Women at Work*; William P. McGreevey, "Socioeconomic Change and Family Planning: Their Impact on Fertility," Batelle Population and Development Policy Program, Working Paper no. 1 (Washington, D.C., 1978); Parker W. Mauldin and Bernard Berelson, "Conditions of Fertility Decline in Developing Countries 1965–75," *Studies in Family Planning* 9 (May 1978):89–147.

42. Gary W. Wynia, *The Politics of Latin American Development* (Cambridge, Eng.: Cambridge University Press, 1978), p. 234.

43. Street, "The Internal Frontier," pp. 28–32.

44. For a discussion of appropriate technology see Rutherford M. Poats, *Technology for Developing Nations: New Directions for U.S. Technical Assistance* (Washington, D.C.: Brookings Institution, 1972); Nicholas Jéquier, ed., *Appropriate Technology: Problems and Promises* (Paris: Development Center of the Organization for Economic Cooperation and Development, 1976); Richard S. Eckaus, *Appropriate Technologies for Developing Countries* (Washington, D.C.: National Academy of Sciences, 1977).

45. Clinton, "The Never-to-be-developed Countries of Latin America."

46. McNamara, *One Hundred Countries.*

47. Green, "New Directions in U.S. Foreign Assistance."

48. The recent decision by the World Bank to spend $7.5 billion for financing the expansion of petroleum and coal production in low-income countries may indicate that this most important of development-assistance agencies still finds it easier to support large, capital-intensive, high-technology projects than smaller, more numerous, appropriate-technology approaches. For the details of this program see World Bank, "A Program to Accelerate Petroleum Production in the Developing Countries," mimeographed (January 1979).

49. Christian Bay, *The Structure of Freedom* (New York: Atheneum Press, 1965).

50. Abraham Maslow, "A Theory of Human Motivation," in *Twentieth Century Philosophy,* ed. P. L. Harriman (New York: Philosophical Library, 1946).

51. Henry Steele Commager, *The Empire of Reason* (Garden City, N.Y.: Anchor Press/Doubleday, 1978), p. xii.

52. Ibid., p. 12.

Index